Where the Animals Go

Where the Animals Go

**Tracking wildlife with technology
in 50 maps and graphics**

James Cheshire
Oliver Uberti

W. W. Norton & Company
Independent Publishers Since 1923
New York • London

Copyright © 2016 by James Cheshire and Oliver Uberti
First American Edition 2017

First published in Great Britain in 2016 by Particular Books, an imprint of Penguin Books

For information about permission to reproduce selections from this book, write to
Permissions, W. W. Norton & Company, Inc., 500 Fifth Avenue, New York, NY 10110

For information about special discounts for bulk purchases, please contact
W. W. Norton Special Sales at specialsales@wwnorton.com or 800-233-4830

ISBN 978-0-393-63402-0

W. W. Norton & Company Inc.,
500 Fifth Avenue, New York, NY 10110
www.wwnorton.com

W. W. Norton & Company Ltd.,
15 Carlisle Street, London W1D 3BS

1 2 3 4 5 6 7 8 9 0

JAMES
for Isla

OLIVER
for Gavin, Kalie, and Alina

This, O my Best Beloved, is a story—
a new and a wonderful story—a story
quite different from the other stories.

—RUDYARD KIPLING

[CONTENTS]

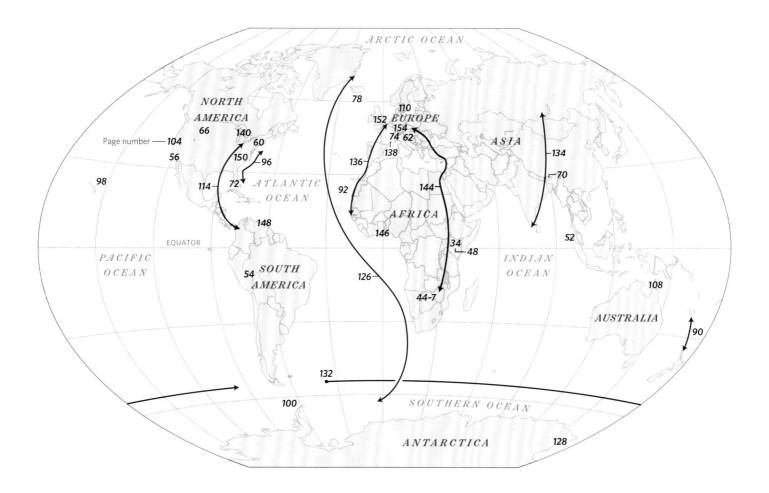

[ACKNOWLEDGMENTS]

AS MUCH AS THIS BOOK is about animals, it is also about the people who study them. We are extremely grateful to those who have supported this project. Their data and insight have given individual animals a voice that we hope we have been able to amplify through our maps and graphics.

A few researchers have been particularly instrumental in their willingness to share data, offer advice, and connect us with other scientists. Special thanks to: fellow giraffe enthusiast David O'Connor for discussing his own research with us and for connecting us with (1) Save The Elephants (2) colleagues at San Diego Zoo Global, and (3) Julian Fennessy, who gave us whatever data we needed on giraffe; Damien Farine for his songbird and baboon data, for giving James a lift from Konstanz, and for his continued enthusiasm for the book; Martin Wikelski for sharing his vision and for directing us toward so many brilliant people at the Max Planck Institute for Ornithology; and Lucy Hawkes for the torrent of data and energy that kept us going. We are enormously indebted to Iain Douglas-Hamilton, Frank Pope, and their entire team at Save The Elephants for hosting Oliver and for the incredible conversations and access they provided; and to Filipa Samarra for inviting James along to the Westman Islands and for being so hospitable during his time spent with the team. Thanks also to Volker Deecke for being such good company adrift in the North Atlantic.

ONE
Thanks to: Robin Naidoo and Hattie Bartlam-Brooks for sharing their zebra tracks; Gabriele Cozzi for his hyenas; and to Serge Wich for his pioneering work with drones. Thanks to Mathias Tobler for squeezing in calls and emails about jaguars between trips to the Amazon. We must thank Martin Gamache for introducing us to Winston Vickers, a true hero for wildlife. When not trying to protect mountain lions from extirpation, the man rescues marine life from oil spills. Thanks to Hubert Potočnik for sharing Slavc's journey with

James on a wet autumn day in Ljubljana and to Scott LaPoint for sharing his studies on fishers. Arthur Middleton is a busy guy and would rather be tracking elk than answering email, but he always got back to us with fine suggestions. We probably never would've caught his ear without an introduction from Jenny Nichols, who also tipped us off to Naidoo's record-breaking zebras. Thanks also to Shannon Pittman for her pythons and to Danielle Mersch for her ants. And though we shifted his story to the introduction, this seems like the spot to thank Michael Noonan for explaining how magnetic fields can track badgers underground—even if it did give James a nosebleed.

TWO

Huge thanks to Mark Johnson and René Swift for introducing us to their amazing tech and for taking the time to explain an echogram. Thanks too to Patrick Miller for sharing his whale sonar data with us. We are grateful to Claire Garrigue for her humpback whale research and to Matthew Witt and Nuria Varo for their turtles. Graeme Hays was so kind as to share data for both turtles and jellyfish. Thank you to Neil Hammerschlag for sharing his "Landscape of Fear" and to Kim Holland for regaling Oliver with shark tales. Clint Blight was exceptionally generous with his time and introduced James to so many other great researchers at St Andrews. Mike Fedak deserves a slice of cake for discussing Rudolf's journey with us on his birthday. We are indebted to Tim Tinker, Michelle Staedler, and Sarah Espinosa for their help and advice with Monterey Bay's otters and to Jenny Keller and Cecelia Azhderian for

connecting us with them in the first place. We thank Craig Franklin and Ross Dwyer, who were always game to discuss crocodiles and data sharing, and Mikael Ekvall, who provided the tracks of quantum-dotted plankton.

THREE

A brightly-feathered thanks to Steve Kelling, Chris Wood, and the team at eBird for welcoming us to Sapsucker Woods. Ian Davies was especially generous to take us birding on a frigid April morning. Thanks to Bart Kranstauber for talking James through "bird highways," and to Yossi Leshem for talking Oliver through bird radar. Many thanks to Carsten Egevang and Ruben Fijn for sharing their tern data and to Richard Phillips for sharing his albatrosses. Peter Fretwell hosted James twice in Cambridge to chat about penguins and albatrosses, while Rory Wilson gave up an afternoon to discuss the book in Swansea. Thanks to his team members, Emily Shepard and Hannah Williams, for helping us understand a vulture's spiral. We are grateful to Peter Desmet for his gulls and advocacy for open data; to Dina Dechmann for her fruit bats; and to Andrea Flack for her storks. Henry Streby was kind enough to invite us into his home on a snowy evening to discuss warblers. And special thanks to Dave Brinker and Scott Weidensaul, who run Project SNOWstorm at a world-class level *in their spare time* and who offered some of that time to help us observe a snowy owl in Ontario.

Thanks to Dirk Steinke for a tour of the Biodiversity Institute of Ontario and to its founder Paul

Hebert and data-wrangler Sujeevan Ratnasingham for sharing the secrets of animal DNA. Final thanks to Brian Brown, Urska Demsar, Robin Freeman, David Jacoby, Melinda Holland, Ryan Kastner, Josh Kuhn, Jed Long, Megan Owen, Stesha Pasachnik, Kamran Safi, James Sheppard, and Jeff Tracey for their advice in the early stages of the book.

Many other experts helped us with the non-animal elements of this book. Jerome Cookson, a good friend and great cartographer, somehow vetted all these maps in a ten-week blitz. Case in point: did *you* know that a ferry (not a road) crosses the Niger River at Timbuktu? Did you know that Timbuktu should actually be spelled *Tombouctou*? For this and so many keen queries and edits, we thank him.

The Geography Department at University College London is full of invaluable talent. Huge thanks to: Alistair Leak for his detective work, sourcing, and compiling data for the basemaps; Oliver O'Brien for helping us label faraway places; Alyson Lloyd for her Twitter catchments; Tom Knight for setting up the servers that crunched the numbers; and Mirco Musolesi for introducing us to the Sea Mammal Research Unit at St Andrews. Thank you to all at the Consumer Data Research Centre for their support.

FROM JAMES: Creating this book required a degree of selfishness that could have left me very lonely were it not for the patience and generosity of those closest to me. Each time I came up for air, friends and family were there to spur me on. My heartfelt thanks to all of them. Thanks in particular to Moira for helping with the proofreading and for being such a great housemate. My final and greatest thanks to Isla for being so passionate about this book and for all she has done to help see it to completion. I could not have done it without her.

FROM OLIVER: Those who have known me awhile were not the least surprised to hear I wanted to attempt a book that combined art and animals. I can't thank Phil, Erin, Mike, and Glenn enough for encouraging me to pursue this idea from the start. Belated thanks to Bill McNulty for introducing me to Annie, and to Mike Fay, Michael Nichols, and the rest of the team at *National Geographic* who helped make her story so unforgettable. Thanks to Marisa Fulper for being such a great assistant. As always, my mother was just a phone call away to remind me that the answers would be there in the morning—and they always were. Finally, my love and deepest gratitude belongs with Sophie for believing I could pull this off when I did not.

This book would not have been possible without the support of our agent, Luigi Bonomi, and the team at Particular Books. We are especially grateful to Cecilia Stein for her sound edits and her unwavering faith in this project from proposal to press. Thanks also to Jim Stoddart for encouraging us to shoo the whale—with a "determined look on its face (as whales do)"—away from the giraffe's bum and to the color production team, who made these pages sing. We cannot overstate how lucky we feel to work with a publisher that believes books can and should be beautiful.

Annie *by Oliver Uberti*

In 2006, I was working as a designer for *National Geographic,* when our maps director invited me to paint a map for a story about elephants in central Africa, where poaching had cut their numbers from 300,000 in 1970 to 10,000 in 2005. The magazine sent ecologist Mike Fay and photographer Michael Nichols to southeastern Chad to document those remaining in one of the region's last strongholds: Zakouma National Park. They knew herds left the park in the

rainy season. What they didn't know was where the elephants went and how vulnerable they were to poaching outside the park. With the help of GPS tracking collars, they hoped to find out.

On May 23, 2006, the team collared a female with a calf near the park's northern border. They named her Annie. Some scientists still bristle at the thought of naming animals and encourage the use of ID numbers instead. Iain Douglas-Hamilton, the founder of Save The Elephants, finds such objections absurd. "It's much, much easier to

remember names," he says. "You might call it Zeus or Apollo or Clint Eastwood, but it stops having that meaning as soon as you put the name on the elephant."

By June, Annie and her calf had gone 50 miles in ten days. "I couldn't believe they had gone so far, so fast," Fay wrote in the magazine. For the rest of that summer, he and Nichols watched Annie's choices. They watched her go straight to the best vegetation. They watched her wait until night to cross roads—they presumed, in order to minimize her encounters with humans. In the previous twelve months, poachers had killed nearly 900 elephants in and around Zakouma. "If you can put yourself in their place," Nichols said in a video accompanying the article, "you think of all these babies we've seen frolicking at the waterhole with their mothers and then the terror that they're going to go through. And how many miles will they run before they fall from the bullet holes?"

Annie's journey continued for twelve weeks and 1,015 miles. On August 15, Fay noticed her collar wasn't moving. Then the signal went dead. Fay couldn't get back to Chad until September. By the time he reached Annie's last known position, all that was left was bones and skin and the tattered bodies of eight of her companions. There was no doubt that they had been poached.

Her story was the first time a map had ever engaged me in the life of an individual animal, and the shift in consciousness it provoked was irreversible.

IT'S BEEN TEN YEARS since I painted that map of Annie's steps, and still, every time I look at that trail of red dots, it reminds me of what Douglas-Hamilton said about an elephant's name. I don't just see dots. I don't just see some animal. I see Annie. Her story was the first time a map had ever engaged me in the life of an individual animal, and the shift in consciousness it provoked was irreversible.

From where I sat then, on the eighth floor of

National Geographic's headquarters in Washington, D.C., I began to notice two trends. At the same time as our photographers and writers were bearing witness to illegal wildlife trade, overfishing, pollution, deforestation, dying reefs, melting ice, rising seas, and all manner of awfulness that humans are increasingly inflicting on our planet, I also began to see more stories like Annie's coming across my desk: radio tracking a wolverine in Glacier National Park, satellite tracking tuna across the Atlantic, the light logger data of albatrosses circling Antarctica. The growing means by which scientists could connect us to animals offered tremendous hope.

Years later, I teamed up with James to produce our first book, a collection of maps and graphics that visualized a variety of open data available in London. We considered a follow-up on data from other cities, but then I remembered those tracking stories from my days at *Geographic*. We asked our publisher, "What about animal tracking?"

At first, it might not seem like a logical fit. James and I are not biologists. He's a geographer; I'm a designer. But that's the beauty of the animal-tracking revolution. The convergence of ecology and technology invites more people from more disciplines into the conservation conversation, in part because scientists are now gathering more data than they could ever process alone. Some tracking devices sample many times a second. After a week-long study, you're already talking millions of data points. Longer studies leave scientists inundated. They need help. They need engineers, coders, statisticians, geographers, and designers.

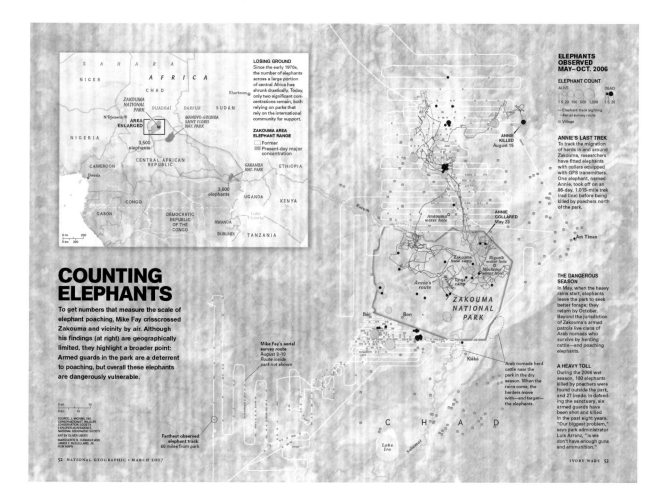

The red line shows Annie's 86-day trek in and out of Zakouma National Park in southeastern Chad. The white line shows an aerial survey route from which author Mike Fay counted 3,020 elephants (orange circles). During the 2006 wet season, poachers killed 127 (red circles).

In 2008, the Wildlife Conservation Society provided the park with a surveillance aircraft and poaching declined. Still, by 2012, nearly 90 percent of the population had been killed. Two kills in 2015—the first in three years—prove the fight for elephants is never over.

If you have dreams of working with animals or if you want to join a citizen science project, let this book be your compass. In the pages that follow, you will see the efforts of many pioneers who have assembled international and interdisciplinary teams to make the most of their animal data. They're always looking for new talent. If you are a scientist, we hope this offering will serve as a conduit to collaboration. Sharing ideas leads to faster breakthroughs. Sharing data saves animals.

Time and space no longer limit us. James lives in Europe; I live in North America. In much the same way that researchers write papers, we produced these stories and maps through cables across an ocean. We hope they will inspire discourse—and new graphics—about the geographic needs of animals. We hope a cetologist can learn a new technique from a chiropterologist and vice versa. But mostly, we hope these animals will inspire you the way Annie inspired me.

It seems that people are going off in all directions on the business of electronic tracking of animals.

—GEORGE SPRUGEL JR.

Head of the National Science Foundation's
Environmental Biology Program
1959

A New Kind of Footprint

From footprints to fallen feathers, nests to droppings, the history of where animals go has been a history of physical traces. This book is about a new era, one in which the traces we follow are imprinted not in the earth but in the silicon of computer chips. And while the maps and studies we feature rely heavily on data processing, the desire to study animal movements with new inventions long predates the Information Age. In 1803, John James Audubon was tying threads to the legs of

songbirds in order to prove that the same individuals returned to his farm each spring; a map from 1892 illustrates the month-by-month migration of seals in the North Pacific (see pp. 22–3); in 1907, a German apothecary equipped pigeons with automatic cameras in order to document their journeys; in 1962, three scientists from the University of Illinois taped a radio transmitter to a duck; and in 1997, two of the world's first GPS collars confirmed that elephants from Kenya sometimes cross the border into Tanzania.

Not every species needs to be tracked to be studied. For many, a pair of good binoculars and a camera will suffice. As Megan Owen at San Diego Zoo Global put it, "non-invasive observation is still the gold standard of zoology. You sit quietly and observe undetected." But for other species, such as the polar bears she studies in the Arctic, that kind of extended observation is not feasible. So wildlife researchers have started working with engineers to develop new ways of studying animals from afar. Satellites, radar, cellphone networks, camera traps, drones, apps, accelerometers, and DNA sequencing now allow us to see the natural world like never before. The field goes by many names: bio-logging, biotelemetry, movement ecology. For most of the stories in this book, we're talking about "tagging," wherein a scientist has attached a device to an animal. With the rise of mobile technology and the miniaturization of computing power, these devices—or "tags"—can gather gigabytes of behavioral, physiological, and environmental data on everything from the spirals of a soaring vulture (see pp. 138–9) to ocean temperatures off Antarctica (see pp. 100–103) to the flight of a bumblebee (see pp. 154–5).

TO UNDERSTAND just how quickly technology is accelerating our knowledge of animals and how we act to conserve them, consider the giraffe. According to David O'Connor, a conservation ecologist at San Diego Zoo Global, "Where we are with giraffe is where elephant researchers were about thirty years ago." Scientists have studied their physiology—how their small but strong hearts can pump blood all the way up their necks; how their oversized lungs keep them from passing out; how their prehensile tongues can strip leaves from thorny trees—but they still don't know much about how the species as a whole operates in the wild. "Giraffe are weird," says O'Connor. "They don't seem to have clear leaders, so we're just learning how they organize into herds. We don't know how they communicate. We don't know why they fight. We don't know well the limits of their ranges." And scientists only recently discovered that there is not one but four giraffe species, each

This hand-plotted map from 1892 shows the month-by-month densities of fur seals in the North Pacific Ocean. Black dots represent females; red ones are young seals of both sexes under two years of age. Starting in February, adult females migrate north to meet males at breeding colonies. There, they give birth and raise pups until late October, when the herds thin out and females head south to feed.

Mapping such movements may have contributed to the knowledge that led the US, Great Britain, Japan, and Russia to ban open-sea seal hunting two decades later. The Fur Seal Treaty of 1911 was the first international agreement for the conservation of wildlife.

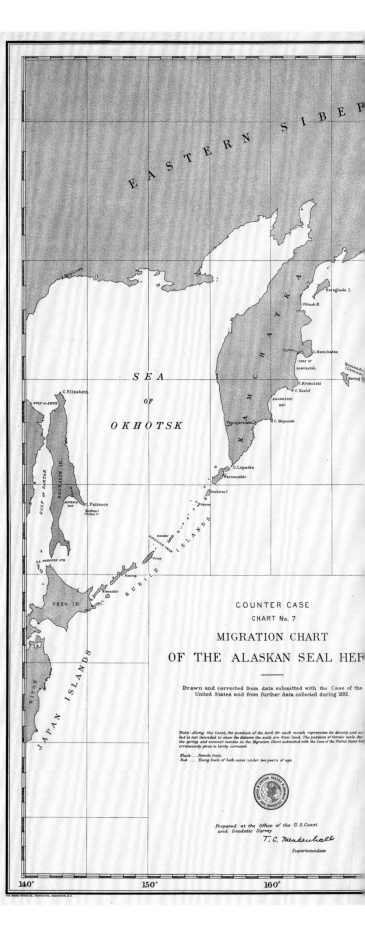

COUNTER CASE
CHART No. 7

MIGRATION CHART
OF THE ALASKAN SEAL HER

Drawn and corrected from data submitted with the Case of the United States and from further data collected during 1892.

Note: Along the Coast, the position of the herd for each month represents its density and is but is not intended to show the distance the seals are from land. The position of female seals dus the spring and summer months in the Migration Chart submitted with the Case of the United States be erroneously given is hereby corrected.

Black——Female Seals.
Red——Young Seals of both sexes under two years of age.

Prepared at the Office of the U.S. Coast and Geodetic Survey
T. C. Mendenhall
Superintendent

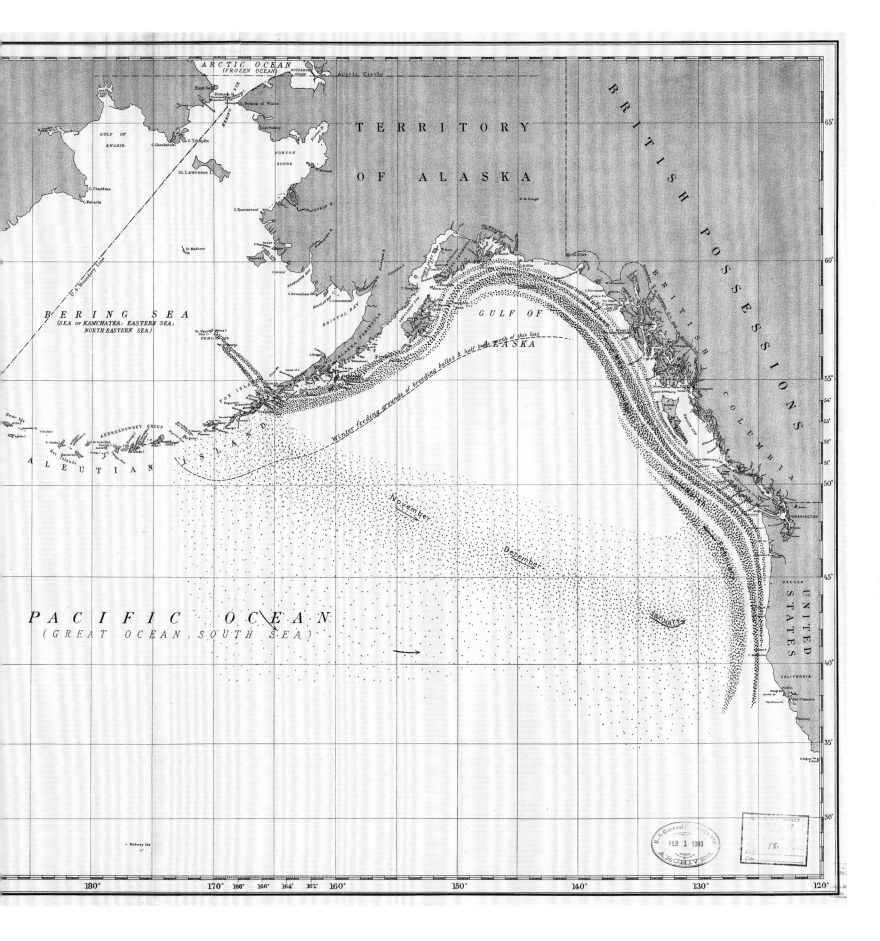

with unique genetics and spot patterns ranging from orange polygons to black blotches. If it weren't for Julian Fennessy, we'd know even less.

Fennessy is the world's leading authority on giraffe and co-director of the Giraffe Conservation Foundation. He calls giraffe "Africa's forgotten megafauna." We asked him why he thinks they're overlooked. "People assume giraffe are every-where," he said. "No one ever thought there was an issue with them. Only in the last five to ten years, when we've started to look into their numbers and threats, have we seen that, like many animals, they're declining." The main culprits are the usual suspects: habitat loss and the bushmeat trade. Rumors that giraffe brains and bone marrow can cure HIV/AIDS have driven up the price. We rarely hear about giraffe being endangered, but that doesn't mean they aren't. Across Africa, there's a "silent extinction" occurring. Giraffe numbers have fallen from 153,000 to 100,000 since 1986, and they've disappeared in seven countries—a quarter of their former range. Fennessy is using GPS technology to gather as much data as he can about where giraffe go before it's too late.

The first giraffe ever equipped with GPS was one named Chopper. Fennessy collared him in Namibia back in 2000 in order to see how giraffe survive in arid areas. Today, Fennessy is pioneering other uses for animal-tracking technologies. In the Democratic Republic of the Congo, the tags are a form of policing. Fewer than 40 giraffe remain in the whole country, so the government brought Fennessy in for advice. Working with African Parks Network (APN), they collared ten giraffe and organized community-based tracking teams to protect them from poachers, thereby creating jobs and local investment. In Namibia, he advised the government on moving giraffe from national parks to smaller community conservancies and used tags to watch how the animals adjusted to their new homes (see right). And in Ethiopia, his efforts have helped APN vet the boundaries of a proposed national park. "The government knew there were species in that area that needed protection," he said, "and they just drew a big line around it." Their heart was in the right place. Unfortunately, the giraffe weren't. Once Fennessy and his team had tagged three giraffe, they saw that the animals were mostly living outside the designated area. Giraffe feed primarily in acacia savanna, but that type of vegetation wasn't present within the pro-posed boundary. The GPS tracks were undeniable. The park boundaries had to move.

Fennessy saw Chopper, his first tagged giraffe, again in August 2015. He was still running around the desert. Chopper was at least four years of age when Fennessy collared him, so he knew he must be around twenty now. "That's the first long-term knowledge of an individual giraffe and how long it has lived," Fennessy said. "Which is sad, actually. For the tallest animal in the world, we have so little information. If that's for giraffe, what do we have on the other critters out there?"

IN THIS BOOK, we hope to help answer that question. We've spoken to scientists from around the globe and combed through periodicals and online data stores to show you some of the most cutting-edge studies on land, sea, and sky. Take, for instance, Michael Noonan's PhD research on

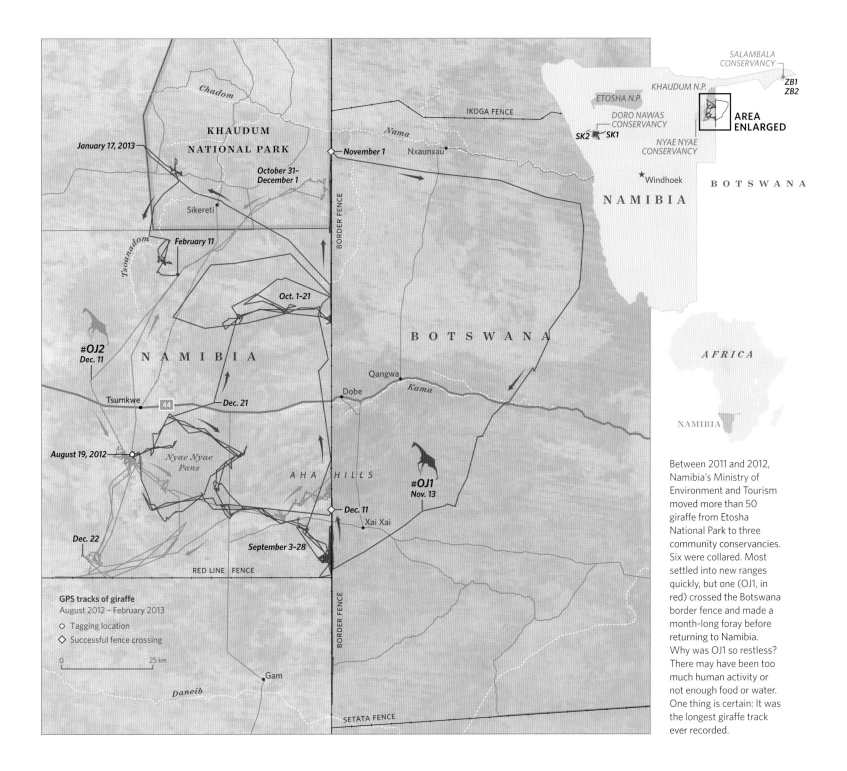

SALAMBALA
CONSERVANCY

ZB1
ZB2

KHAUDUM N.P.

AREA
ENLARGED

ETOSHA N.P.

DORO NAWAS
CONSERVANCY

SK2 SK1

NYAE NYAE
CONSERVANCY

★ Windhoek

N A M I B I A

B O T S W A N A

AFRICA

NAMIBIA

KHAUDUM
NATIONAL PARK

January 17, 2013

October 31–
December 1

Chadom

IKOGA FENCE

Nama

November 1

Nxaunxau

Sikereti

February 11

Tsoanadom

Oct. 1–21

BORDER FENCE

B O T S W A N A

#OJ2
Dec. 11

N A M I B I A

Qangwa

Dobe

Kama

Tsumkwe

44

Dec. 21

*Nyae Nyae
Pans*

August 19, 2012

A H A   H I L L S

#OJ1
Nov. 13

Dec. 22

Dec. 11

Xai Xai

September 3–28

RED LINE FENCE

GPS tracks of giraffe
August 2012 – February 2013

○ Tagging location
◇ Successful fence crossing

0 ———————— 25 km

Gam

Daneib

BORDER FENCE

SETATA FENCE

Between 2011 and 2012,
Namibia's Ministry of
Environment and Tourism
moved more than 50
giraffe from Etosha
National Park to three
community conservancies.
Six were collared. Most
settled into new ranges
quickly, but one (OJ1, in
red) crossed the Botswana
border fence and made a
month-long foray before
returning to Namibia.
Why was OJ1 so restless?
There may have been too
much human activity or
not enough food or water.
One thing is certain: It was
the longest giraffe track
ever recorded.

SOURCES: JULIAN FENNESSY, GIRAFFE CONSERVATION FOUNDATION; GADM; WDPA

badgers. To track their movements underground, he couldn't use GPS. Instead, he tried something that could penetrate the earth with high precision: a magnetic field. He equipped each badger with a collar and set up a grid of energized wires above their burrow. As the badgers moved from chamber to chamber underground, the collars recorded changes in the magnetic field strength above them. From this work, Noonan could see that badgers are far more active in their burrows than previously thought. Although he set the collars to record a location every three seconds, that wasn't fast enough to capture the network of tunnels between chambers (see right). Considering that 60 percent of land mammals use burrows, Noonan's method offers a way to discover a lot more about life underground.

For life underwater, we visited bio-logging pioneer Rory Wilson at the University of Swansea. In the early 1980s, he was completing his PhD research on the behavior of African penguins when he realized that the sensors he needed didn't exist. So he made some himself out of cork, piano wire, and syringes. Those early tags returned the first measurements of a penguin's swimming speed and the distance it traveled while feeding. Eventually his analog sensors became digital ones, but they were still primitive by today's standards. "There was no memory," Wilson says, "so we were recording penguin dive depth every 15 seconds, thinking it was bloody cool. Now we record 40 times a second at depth alone." Wilson is still inventing because off-the-shelf hardware has never quite kept pace with his ambition. At the moment, he's working on improvements to his "beakometer,"

which records how much a penguin eats on a given day by how often and how widely it opens its mouth. Like so many bio-logging pioneers, Wilson's greatest technology is his imagination.

PAUL HEBERT'S IMAGINATION encapsulates everything from whales to water fleas. In fact, it encapsulates species that we haven't even discovered yet. Of the 10 million species estimated to live on Earth, fewer than a fifth have been formally named. Hebert wants to record them all but not in the way you might think.

The gaps in our knowledge were clear to him as far back as the 1970s, when he was a young researcher studying moth diversity in Papua New Guinea. One warm, rainy night, he hiked to a mountain pass and hung a white sheet in front of an ultraviolet light. Three hours later, the sheet was black with flying insects. "We had three or four thousand specimens," he says. "I went back to the Natural History Museum in London to identify them and realized that in that one night in New Guinea, I had collected probably a thousand new species. The rest of my life could have been describing those species. So I gave them away. I said, 'I have to go somewhere where there's a few less species, so I might be able to understand what the hell's going on!'" Hebert spent the next 25 years in the Canadian Arctic looking at the origins of biodiversity, as opposed to trying to measure it directly. But he could never quite shake the urge to somehow catalog the true range of life on Earth.

By the 1990s, advances in technology were making DNA easier to study. Hebert, who has a PhD in genetics, started playing around with a segment

How Much Data to Collect?

Think of all the places you go in a day. What if someone only knew where you were each day at 11 a.m.? That's where animal tracking was just a few years ago. Battery life was so short and memory was so limited that researchers could only sample locations once a day, if that. Now with the ability to sample more frequently or to change the sampling rate remotely, we can observe an animal's activity at all hours of the day.

As Michael Noonan's work with badgers shows, the more often you sample, the more interesting animal movements become. Here, circles represent chambers in a badger den; lines indicate how a single badger moved between them.

of an animal's DNA sequence called "CO1." "Pretty soon, I started to say, 'Gee, everything's got a different sequence and they are really easy to compare.'" What if these "barcodes"—as he called the CO1 sequences—could distinguish one species from another?

In the summer of 2000, he went out into his backyard in southern Ontario to test the idea. He turned on a moth light just as he'd done in Papua New Guinea years before. This time, none of the species he collected were new, but that was the point. In order to prove that DNA barcoding could accurately identify species, he needed to already know the names of what was there. He gathered about 200 moths and found that he could barcode them all. "If I could tell 200 species of moths apart in Ontario, I thought I should be able to tell apart all the species of animals on our planet."

What started in that backyard sixteen years ago is now the Biodiversity Institute of Ontario, a multi-million-dollar research facility at the University of Guelph. They receive specimens to

Underground movements of a European badger at three sampling rates
January – February 2011

Chamber

Daily
The badger appears to split its time between Chambers 3 and 5 only.

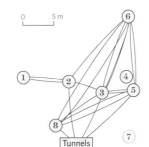

0   5 m

Hourly
Checking each hour reveals that the badger is actually moving between all chambers.

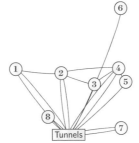

Every 3 seconds
The corners the badger seemed to cut in the hourly sample are now filled in. To see the tunnels between chambers, Noonan plans to sample ten times per second.

SOURCE: MICHAEL NOONAN AND ANDREW MARKHAM, UNIVERSITY OF OXFORD

sequence from researchers across the globe while their online presence—the Barcode of Life Data System (BOLD)—now contains barcodes from more than 5 million specimens, representing 500,000 species. (To see the barcodes for many species in this book, turn to page 174.)

Initially rejected by taxonomists, evolutionary biologists, and research journals, Hebert's first paper on DNA barcoding is now informing all kinds of animal research. In the past decade, researchers have pinpointed elephant poaching hotspots by connecting the DNA of seized ivory to the DNA of elephant dung; by analyzing the dung of two zebra species on the Serengeti, they've learned that each eats different plants in order to share the same ecosystem; and they've detected elusive animals from their DNA in the leeches, ticks, and mosquitoes that have bitten them. One day, DNA-identification may even reach your dinner table. Imagine being able to scan your food to confirm whether it's actually what you think it is.

The list of possible uses for the BOLD database is long, but it may never reach its full potential. Due to human impacts on the environment, many species that they've barcoded—and many more that they haven't—may go extinct in the coming decades. In the face of such a catastrophe, it should be easy for biologists to secure the funding they need. It isn't. In our discussions with researchers, the same analogy was used time and again. Hebert said it best:

"If astronomers realized that a sixth of the luminescent objects in our universe were going to go dark within the next 50 years, I can't imagine how much money they could mobilize in order to study

ENLARGED
ABOVE

See the DNA barcode for this painted lichen moth on p. 174.

2000
199 species

Backyard Biodiversity

Biodiversity scientists estimate that there are at least 10 million multicellular species on Earth, of which 1.7 million have been described. In 2000, Paul Hebert, a biologist at the University of Guelph, began to wonder how many of those might live in his backyard. He set up an insect trap and used DNA analysis to identify everything he caught (above). Over the next decade, Hebert ran the experiment a few more times with help from his team at the Biodiversity Institute of Ontario. "I now know I share my backyard with 5,000 species," he says. "And what I'm seeing is, my God, this is only the beginning. We could have the planet done in 20 years."

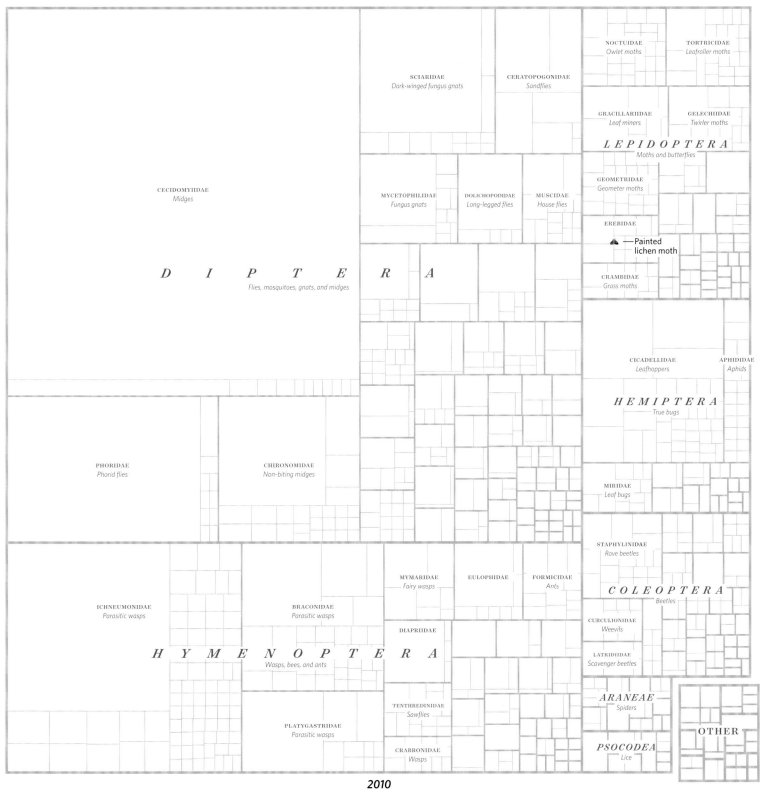

NOCTUIDAE
Owlet moths

TORTRICIDAE
Leafroller moths

SCIARIDAE
Dark-winged fungus gnats

CERATOPOGONIDAE
Sandflies

GRACILLARIIDAE
Leaf miners

GELECHIIDAE
Twirler moths

L E P I D O P T E R A
Moths and butterflies

CECIDOMYIIDAE
Midges

MYCETOPHILIDAE
Fungus gnats

DOLICHOPODIDAE
Long-legged flies

MUSCIDAE
House flies

GEOMETRIDAE
Geometer moths

EREBIDAE

— Painted
lichen moth

D   I   P   T   E   R   A
Flies, mosquitoes, gnats, and midges

CRAMBIDAE
Grass moths

CICADELLIDAE
Leafhoppers

APHIDIDAE
Aphids

H E M I P T E R A
— *True bugs*

PHORIDAE
Phorid flies

CHIRONOMIDAE
Non-biting midges

MIRIDAE
Leaf bugs

STAPHYLINIDAE
Rove beetles

MYMARIDAE
Fairy wasps

EULOPHIDAE

FORMICIDAE
Ants

C O L E O P T E R A
Beetles

ICHNEUMONIDAE
Parasitic wasps

BRACONIDAE
Parasitic wasps

CURCULIONIDAE
Weevils

DIAPRIIDAE

LATRIDIIDAE
Scavenger beetles

H Y M E N O P T E R A
Wasps, bees, and ants

A R A N E A E
— *Spiders*

OTHER

TENTHREDINIDAE
Sawflies

PLATYGASTRIDAE
Parasitic wasps

P S O C O D E A
Lice

CRABRONIDAE
Wasps

2010
3,704 species

Relative abundance
in Paul Hebert's backyard

O R D E R

FAMILY

SOURCE: PAUL HEBERT, UNIVERSITY OF GUELPH

those things before they went dark. And here we are as biodiversity scientists living on this planet, where we're very certain we're going to lose a lot of species in this century."

WITH SUCH HIGH STAKES, many researchers are now sharing their hard-earned data online. This trend for "open data" has become a force for good in many areas of science and government. Craig Franklin, the director of research for the Steve Irwin Wildlife Reserve, sees few downsides. "We all use data differently. Your perspective will be different from mine. As long as there is some acknowledgment of where the data came from, and publications are cited, that's all that's required." To Franklin, the real value is in the opportunities open data provides for the next generation of researchers like Ross Dwyer. Dwyer, who helps Franklin tag crocodiles (see pp. 108–9), shares his data on *zoaTrack*, a web platform for tracking data. He's eager to explore datasets from "old-school" researchers. "They're sitting on thousands of tracks that they've collected over the years, and they're all retiring and taking their data with them."

To some researchers, data sharing is not just about science, it's a moral issue. "As soon as we tag an animal, we become the executer of that animal's will," says Mark Johnson of the Sea Mammal Research Unit at the University of St Andrews. "It's our responsibility to do the right thing." If one whale has been tagged, sharing its data reduces the need to tag others for the same purpose. As Rory Wilson is keen to point out, "The simple act of catching an animal is about the most horrible thing that can occur to it. I mean, restraint for a

wild animal is terrifying. Even if you don't put a tag on, if you catch it and then let it go again, it'll have the heebie-jeebies for weeks."

We asked Iain Douglas-Hamilton, the founder of Save The Elephants, what he says to those outside of the bio-logging community who believe tagging is cruel and unusual. He said, "Of course, collaring is a stress for animals. If it's done professionally with professional vets that stress can be minimized. There's still residual risk that remains to the animal, but, in our judgment, that risk is outweighed by the enhancement of their survival chances that comes from what we learn through the tracking."

A FEW YEARS AGO, Martin Wikelski, director of the Max Planck Institute for Ornithology in Germany, and his longtime collaborator Roland Kays (North Carolina Museum of Natural Sciences) realized they could link movement and behavioral characteristics together into a census of the animal world. In 2007, they started a website called *Movebank*, where zoologists could upload their data, make maps, and share them with others. Online data stores already exist for city data, but this was one of the first designed exclusively for animal data. It seems to have filled a need. Users upload a few million data points each day. As of August 2016, the site held tracks from more than 550 species from 2,400 studies.

Movebank requires contributors to follow a set of rules that make it easier for others to download and use their data. "It's curated so you can start analyzing stuff right away," says Wikelski. What's more, Movebank can receive data from tags in

Which Tag to Use?

Modern animal tags are packed full of complex electronics that make it hard for researchers to develop their own. Instead most prefer to buy tags from vendors. Melinda Holland, CEO of Wildlife Computers, regularly fields requests for "as much data as possible, with as small a tag as possible, that lasts as long as possible, that is as cheap as possible." Even with today's technology, researchers can't have it all. She and her team talk scientists through an iterative process to determine what they need most to achieve their research objectives. On the right, we list the technologies featured in this book.

real-time. That made it the platform of choice for Wikelski's biggest project to date: attaching a bio-logging receiver to the International Space Station.

The project, known as ICARUS (International Cooperation for Animal Research Using Space), is taking animal tracking into orbit. When it launches in a few years, participating researchers will be able to deploy tiny, solar-powered tags on their animals that can beam data to the space station. From there, data will bounce down to Movebank's database and on to collaborators, all in real-time. At the moment, the only existing real-time, remote-sensing systems cover relatively small areas and a small number of animals. In Wikelski's grand vision, ICARUS will become a dashboard for all of Earth's wildlife. There will be plenty of pragmatic applications such as monitoring the spread of animal-borne diseases and evaluating risks to the pollinating insects on which our crops depend. But there's a less tangible aspect too. At a glance, we will be able to see ourselves and the animals— walking, swimming, flying—intertwined in one great beautiful tangle of tracks.

TAG TYPES FEATURED IN THIS BOOK

Acoustic tracking
These tags emit a "ping" that can be detected by receivers on shorelines, river-banks, and ocean buoys. The receivers record whenever a tagged animal passes by but cannot determine where it has been or where it's going. Because sound travels well underwater, acoustic tags are popular in aquatic research.

Argos (satellite tracking)
A satellite tag continuously sends out messages in short pulses. When one of the world's six Argos satellites passes overhead, it detects the tag's transmissions. The satellite can then locate the tag to within a few hundred meters— using the Doppler effect plus its own speed and position—and beam that data back to Earth for processing.

GPS tracking
Unlike Argos tags, GPS tags do not transmit. They record and store locations, to the meter, from the signals of at least three of the 30 "Global Positioning System" satellites. Data must then be retrieved manually. GPS also consumes more battery power than Argos, so tags may not last as long. For many research-ers, those are worthwhile trade-offs for the detail GPS provides.

Light loggers
Also known as geolocators, these tags are popular with ornithologists since they are small enough for many species of bird to carry. They record light levels to determine when the sun rises and sets. From this data, researchers can calculate approximate latitude from day length and longitude from the "solar noon" between dawn and dusk. What light loggers lack in precision, they make up for in longevity.

Radio tracking
In this technique, widely used since the 1960s, the animal wears a transmitter that emits radio waves. Researchers can detect these with an antenna/receiver and then locate or follow the animal based on the strength of its signal.

Other sensors
In addition to location sensors, researchers may also pack tags with thermometers to measure temperature; barometers to gauge altitude/depth; accelerometers to detect behaviors such as feeding or resting; and magneto-meters to determine an animal's precise orientation.

DATA RECOVERY METHODS

Manual retrieval
This "low-tech" solution requires the scientist to go back into the field to find the tag and download its data. They may need to recapture the animal or the tag itself could have an automatic release mechanism. For example, some marine tags release, float to the surface, and then emit a radio signal to help researchers locate them. Sometimes researchers will offer a reward to fishermen for retrieving any floating tags they find.

Transmissions
Tags that transmit data via satellite or cellphone networks allow researchers to receive data in near real-time. However these systems don't work underwater or out of range, so data are stored on-board until the tag can make a connection. In situations where bandwidth is an issue, researchers may opt for a dual approach. They'll take what they can from a tag's transmissions and then retrieve the tag to download the full dataset.

[ONE]

*You can hear them before
they've come and after they've gone,
rumbling like rivers,
ticking like clocks.*

—ANNIE DILLARD

The Elephant Who Texted for Help

by Oliver Uberti

OVER THE PAST FIFTY YEARS, Iain Douglas-Hamilton has tracked hundreds of elephants. Every one of them tells a story. There's Bahati, a female from Mali, who, after being rescued from a mud hole, walked 83 kilometers in 36 hours to find water. There's Eleanor, a matriarch from Samburu, whose death was mourned for a week by other elephants, even ones outside her family. There's also Monsoon, the practical joker, who climbed a steep hill two weeks to the day after Douglas-Hamilton published a paper stating that elephants avoid steep hills.

When I sat down with Douglas-Hamilton at his home in Nairobi to learn how he went from deploying the first radio collars on elephants in 1968 to deploying the first GPS collars on them in 1995, he told me about an elephant named Parsitau. "Parsitau was a wonderful bull from Amboseli [National Park]," he said. "We put a prototype on him and it lasted for all of ten days, and we thought this was absolutely the cat's whiskers."

Recording four locations per day, those 40 GPS points were the first ever recorded on an animal in Africa. "It was so incredible," Douglas-Hamilton recalled. "Here was a collar that would go across international borders, work by day, by night, inside forest, outside forest, up hills, down hills." Plus, GPS was far more precise than radio or traditional Argos satellite tracking.

"With radio tracking," he explained, "we'd have to physically go near the elephant, fly over it, and locate it with the antennae on either side of our airplane until we caught sight of it. Then, by sight, we'd estimate where we were on a map and mark a little cross there. That's just the way it was." Parsitau's tracks suggested that maybe it wouldn't have to stay that way.

Emboldened by this proof of concept, Douglas-Hamilton got in touch with scientists in Canada who were testing GPS technology on moose. He bought some of their collars and added longer straps to accommodate an elephant's neck. Packed into those early models were predecessors to many of today's advanced features: sensors for motion and temperature, a backup radio beacon, a chip with enough memory to sample hourly for five months, and a VHF modem for transmitting data.

In December 1996, Douglas-Hamilton deployed the new prototypes on two more bulls in Amboseli National Park. This time, he was hoping the technology would settle a controversy. Cynthia Moss, who'd been studying elephants in Amboseli since the 1970s, claimed that Kenyan elephants were crossing into Tanzania and getting shot by sport hunters there. The hunters, however, insisted that they were shooting only animals from Tanzania. When Douglas-Hamilton reviewed his tracking data months later, sure enough, one bull named Mr. Nick had crossed the border into the very area where other Kenyan elephants had been killed. The data supported a decision by the Tanzanian government to ban elephant hunting in the area. Hunters tried to object, but they no longer had an argument. Mr. Nick's track was undeniable.

When Douglas-Hamilton wrote up his findings, he concluded the paper with a prediction: *GPS animal-tracking systems are set to establish a*

From their offices in Nairobi, Save The Elephants can fly north, east, west, or south to reach elephants they're currently tracking in Kenya.

SOURCES: SAVE THE ELEPHANTS; SRTM; NE; OSM; WDPA

Tracking site
🐘 Current
🐘 Past

new standard for studies of daily movement patterns and ranges of large mammals over the next five to ten years. By the time the paper came out in 1998, Douglas-Hamilton—and his research and conservation organization, Save The Elephants (STE)—had already deployed GPS collars on elephants at five other sites in Kenya and Tanzania.

TWO DECADES LATER, I found myself thinking about those Amboseli bulls as I flew in an STE aircraft much like the one used to track them. I was returning to Nairobi with STE's Chief Operations Officer, Frank Pope, after an elephant-collaring operation in Tsavo National Park (see right). On the horizon, Kilimanjaro rose through the clouds. The wide plains of Amboseli lay somewhere below.

Murka
Mar. 15, 9:30 a.m.

Apr. 13

April 13

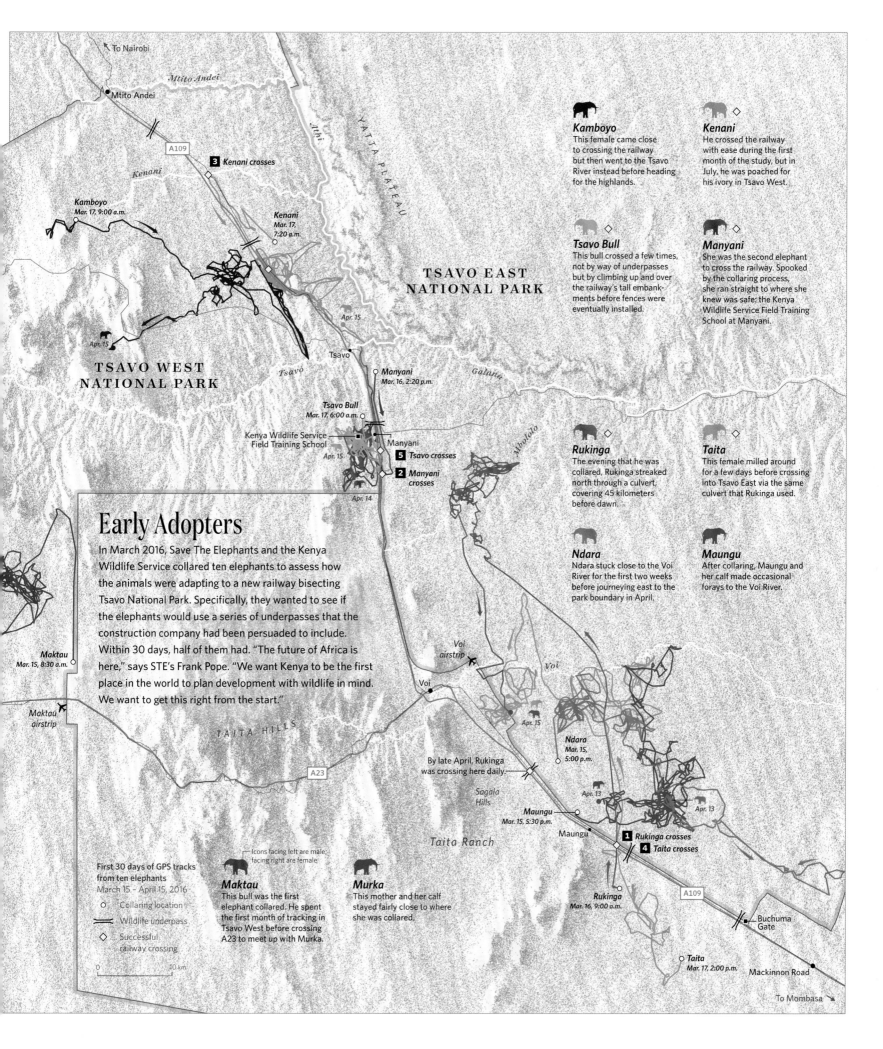

↖ To Nairobi

Mtito Andei

Mtito Andei

A109

3 Kenani crosses

Kenani

Kamboyo
Mar. 17, 9:00 a.m.

Kenani
Mar. 17,
7:20 a.m.

YATTA PLATEAU

Athi

TSAVO WEST
NATIONAL PARK

TSAVO EAST
NATIONAL PARK

Tsavo

Apr. 15

Tsavo

Galana

Manyani
Mar. 16, 2:20 p.m.

Tsavo Bull
Mar. 17, 6:00 a.m.

Kenya Wildlife Service
Field Training School

Apr. 15

Manyani

5 *Tsavo crosses*

2 *Manyani crosses*

Apr. 14

Mbololo

Kamboyo
This female came close
to crossing the railway
but then went to the Tsavo
River instead before heading
for the highlands.

Kenani
He crossed the railway
with ease during the first
month of the study, but in
July, he was poached for
his ivory in Tsavo West.

Tsavo Bull
This bull crossed a few times,
not by way of underpasses
but by climbing up and over
the railway's tall embank-
ments before fences were
eventually installed.

Manyani
She was the second elephant
to cross the railway. Spooked
by the collaring process,
she ran straight to where she
knew was safe: the Kenya
Wildlife Service Field Training
School at Manyani.

Rukinga
The evening that he was
collared, Rukinga streaked
north through a culvert,
covering 45 kilometers
before dawn.

Taita
This female milled around
for a few days before crossing
into Tsavo East via the same
culvert that Rukinga used.

Ndara
Ndara stuck close to the Voi
River for the first two weeks
before journeying east to the
park boundary in April.

Maungu
After collaring, Maungu and
her calf made occasional
forays to the Voi River.

Early Adopters

In March 2016, Save The Elephants and the Kenya
Wildlife Service collared ten elephants to assess how
the animals were adapting to a new railway bisecting
Tsavo National Park. Specifically, they wanted to see if
the elephants would use a series of underpasses that the
construction company had been persuaded to include.
Within 30 days, half of them had. "The future of Africa is
here," says STE's Frank Pope. "We want Kenya to be the first
place in the world to plan development with wildlife in mind.
We want to get this right from the start."

Maktau
Mar. 15, 8:30 a.m.

*Maktau
airstrip*

TAITA HILLS

A23

Voi
airstrip

Voi

Voi

By late April, Rukinga
was crossing here daily.

*Sagala
Hills*

Maungu
Mar. 15, 5:30 p.m.

Maungu

Taita Ranch

Apr. 15

Ndara
Mar. 15,
5:00 p.m.

Apr. 13

Apr. 13

1 *Rukinga crosses*
4 *Taita crosses*

Icons facing left are male;
facing right are female

First 30 days of GPS tracks
from ten elephants
March 15 – April 15, 2016

○ Collaring location

— Wildlife underpass

◇ Successful
railway crossing

0   10 km

Maktau
This bull was the first
elephant collared. He spent
the first month of tracking in
Tsavo West before crossing
A23 to meet up with Murka.

Murka
This mother and her calf
stayed fairly close to where
she was collared.

Rukinga
Mar. 16, 9:00 a.m.

A109

Buchuma
Gate

Taita
Mar. 17, 2:00 p.m.

Mackinnon Road

To Mombasa ↘

Though radio antennae remain on the plane's wing struts, Pope said they rarely use them anymore. In addition to the VHF modem, all of STE's collars are now equipped with onboard GSM transmitters that send data via cellphone networks, so STE seldom needs to follow the animals physically.

The breakthroughs keep coming. Just a few years ago, STE partnered with Google to develop a way for GPS locations to feed directly into Google Earth. And they have since created their own real-time tracking app for phones and tablets in partnership with Microsoft co-founder Paul Allen and his company, Vulcan. (For the security of both the elephants and their protectors, neither technology is available to the public.)

Pope had his phone mounted to the cockpit's instrument panel. "It's revolutionary," he said, as he panned and zoomed on the app. "Even with Google Earth, you had to print or transcribe the elephant positions onto a piece a paper before you got into the air. And you couldn't update it. Now when I'm flying, I've got their real-time positions. I can be in the wilderness and look at the app and go, *well, he should be here* and then look out the window and, *oh right, there he is*."

It's impossible to overstate the impact Douglas-Hamilton has had on the field of bio-logging. His 1998 paper revealed the potential of GPS to reduce conflict between people and wildlife. To this day, two of STE's main uses of the technology are for 1) identifying elephant movement routes and 2) keeping them safe from humans.

In addition to recording location, some of the collars contain an accelerometer that measures the animal's speed and direction. If its rate of movement suddenly speeds up—or drops below a threshold—the collar sends out an alert via email or text message. Pope's phone had been receiving alerts throughout the flight. Many were false alarms. As we were passing over the Chyulu Hills, his screen lit up again:

Low Speed Alert: Kulling has been moving slowly since 14-Mar 11:58

"Who's Kulling?" I asked. He said she was one of the elder females from a family in Samburu National Reserve that they'd been studying for almost two decades.

"We're sending a team to investigate today," he said. "We think she might have a gunshot wound."

LATER THAT NIGHT, I met Pope for dinner at Douglas-Hamilton's house in Nairobi. When I walked in, Pope was on a call in another room. Douglas-Hamilton was reviewing the latest collar data from Tsavo on his laptop.

"We haven't had these collars on for three days," he said, "and two of the elephants have already crossed the railway. I nearly died when I saw this! There's Manyani. She was collared up there, streaked down, crossed, and fled to safety. And guess where safety was?" Douglas-Hamilton pointed to a building beside the road. "This is the main Kenya Wildlife Service ranger training station. Look, she's within 500 meters of it. She's found the human beings she likes. That's hot stuff from the horse's mouth."

STE currently has more than 160 active collars

across ten African countries. New stories appear in the tracks every day. That evening, Douglas-Hamilton was still trying to wrap his head around the movements of an elephant named Morgan.

A month earlier, they'd collared him near the Kenyan port of Lamu. To their surprise, Morgan crossed into Somalia—a dangerous place for an elephant to be. In the 1970s, there were 20,000 elephants near the border. By 1978, poaching had dropped the population to 8,000. Today, the region is an al-Shabab stronghold, rife with poachers. Douglas-Hamilton said we'd be lucky if there were more than 300 left.

STE estimates elephant populations by conducting aerial censuses. But Morgan's tracks were tempting Douglas-Hamilton to question that approach. "From our intensive GPS tracking, we're now realizing that his behavior would make it very difficult for anybody from an airplane to ever see him. He barely moves by day. And at night, he will depart from thick cover, go out into the open, and move from one place to another. So now I think wider across Africa. We've had a lot of devastating losses of elephants where there have formerly been many. Given Morgan's behavior, it seems to me that other elephants may have adapted to an extremely nocturnal existence and to an extreme selection of dense cover during the daytime. If that is true, it means we could have more elephant survivors across Africa than we have been counting."

Pope entered the room.

"So, Iain," he said. "Kulling."

"What about her?"

"Covered in gunshots."

"Oh, God. Is she badly wounded?"

"She can hardly walk. Jerenimo spent the whole day with her. She's just south of Loijuk. There's a big lake there now, and the whole place is full of herders, thousands of cattle and about 150 elephants. Jerenimo said he heard at least 16 shots during the day because the herders are freaking out about all the elephants."

Douglas-Hamilton pulled up Kulling's tracks on screen. Incredibly, from his living room, we could clearly see the impact of her wounds (see inset, p. 42). All her GPS points from the past five days were clustered around the south side of the lake.

"I think, already, you're getting the picture," Douglas-Hamilton said to me. "While you've been here, there have been elephants who were shot at, and other elephants in Tsavo who were clearly terrified by their close shave with human beings. It would be great if you could get to Samburu and visit Kulling. She'll either be dead or wounded. If she's dead, then she's dead. As tragic as that would be, that's also important for you to see."

"Parsitau was a wonderful bull from Amboseli. We put a prototype on him and it lasted for all of ten days, and we thought this was absolutely the cat's whiskers."

JERENIMO LEPEREI met me at Oryx Airstrip in Samburu National Reserve. As STE's Community Outreach Officer, he spends much of his time helping the local Samburu people see the link between the health of elephants and the health of their communities. Every year, the reserve shares some of its proceeds with the neighboring community conservancies. Their boards decide how best to allocate the funds, be it for schools, buses, or health clinics. Leperei's mission now, he said, was to organize a meeting with the herders who shot Kulling.

"How is she?" I asked.

"Not good," he said. "The gunshot wounds are swollen. The vets fear a bullet broke her leg. We are going to give her two days to see if she can recover."

"And then?"

He paused. "They will euthanize her."

IT WAS TOO LATE in the day for us to check on Kulling, 50 dirt-road kilometers to the north. The next morning, I got in a truck with STE Security Officer Chris Leadismo. We headed west out of the park and into Westgate Community Conservancy (WGCC). Even at 8:30 a.m., the sun was merciless. We kept the windows down, even as Kenya's ferrous earth billowed up around us. Quickly, a fine orange dust accumulated on the sweat-soaked pages of my notebook, much as it does on the skin of the elephants.

Around 10:30 a.m., we began to get glimpses of the lake on our right. "See those cattle over there?" Leadismo asked. There were thousands of them between us and the lake, plus hundreds of goats and dozens of camels. He said they belonged to nomads from the north who had rushed to Loijuk because the lake suddenly had water for the first time in ten years.

Leadismo pulled over to speak with some

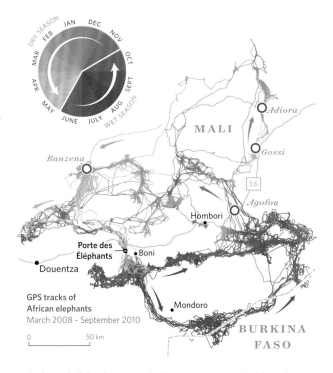

GPS tracks of
African elephants
March 2008 – September 2010

0   50 km

At the end of the dry season in May, temperatures in this region can exceed 50°C. Shallow lakes dry up. The herds cling to Lake Banzena until the June rains permit them to move on to forage farther south.

locals. They pointed us in the direction of a WGCC field camp. We turned off the road and wove through the acacias.

At the field camp, Leadismo spoke with two community scouts, friends from his days training with the Kenya Wildlife Service. "She's not very far from here," he told me. "These guys saw her this morning." The scouts hopped in the back of our truck and off we went.

At 11:06 a.m., we came upon a place with trampled grass and fresh dung. The scouts got out and surveyed the area. A few minutes later, they came back and led us to a circle of trees. Peering at us from within the branches was Kulling—alive.

   SOURCES: SAVE THE ELEPHANTS; SRTM; NE; OSM; WDPA

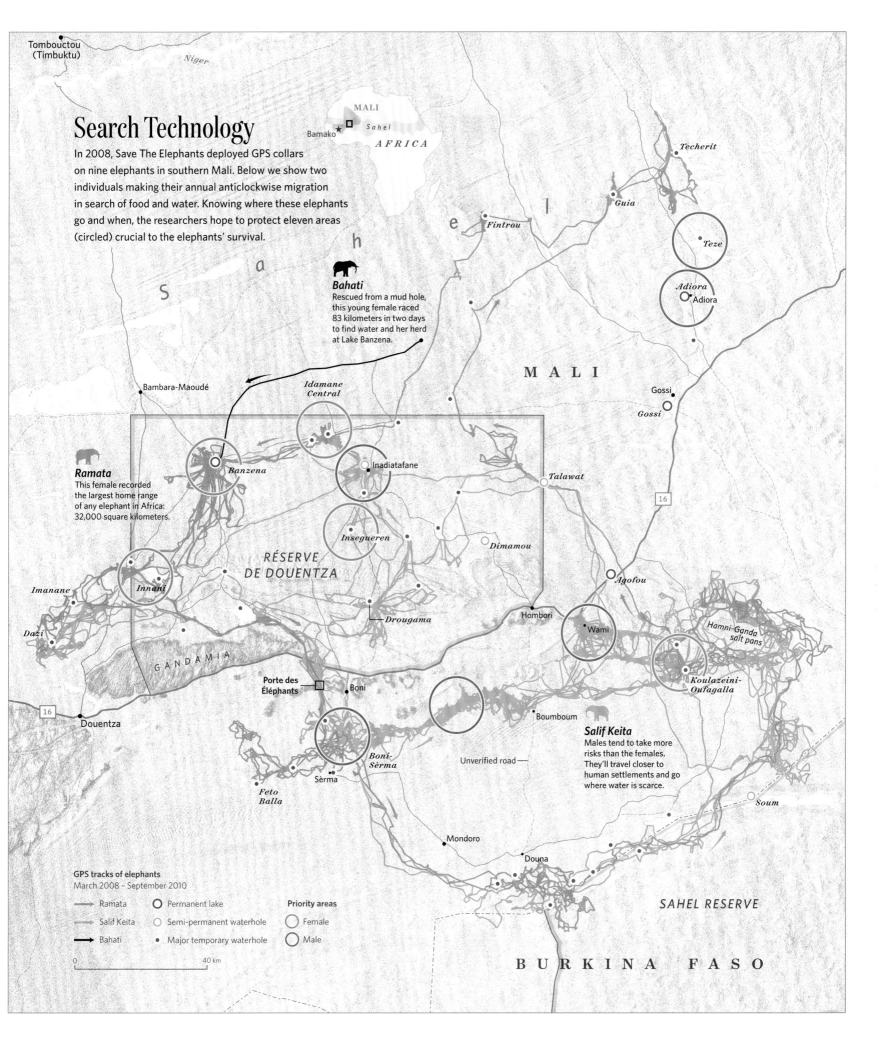

Search Technology

In 2008, Save The Elephants deployed GPS collars on nine elephants in southern Mali. Below we show two individuals making their annual anticlockwise migration in search of food and water. Knowing where these elephants go and when, the researchers hope to protect eleven areas (circled) crucial to the elephants' survival.

MALI
Sahel
AFRICA
Bamako

S a h e l

Tombouctou
(Timbuktu)

Niger

Techerit

Guia

Fintrou

Teze

Adiora
Adiora

Bambara-Maoudé

Bahati
Rescued from a mud hole, this young female raced 83 kilometers in two days to find water and her herd at Lake Banzena.

Idamane
Central

MALI

Gossi
Gossi

Ramata
This female recorded the largest home range of any elephant in Africa: 32,000 square kilometers.

Banzena

Inadiatafane

Talawat

16

Insegueren

Dimamou

RÉSERVE
DE DOUENTZA

Agofou

Imanane

Innani

Hombori

Wami

Hamni-Ganda
salt pans

Dazi

Drougama

Koulazeini-
Oufagalla

GANDAMIA

Porte des
Éléphants

Boni

16

Douentza

Boni-
Sèrma

Boumboum

Salif Keita
Males tend to take more risks than the females. They'll travel closer to human settlements and go where water is scarce.

Sèrma

Unverified road

Soum

Feto
Balla

Mondoro

Douna

SAHEL RESERVE

GPS tracks of elephants
March 2008 – September 2010

Ramata   Permanent lake   **Priority areas**
Salif Keita   Semi-permanent waterhole   Female
Bahati   Major temporary waterhole   Male

0   40 km

B U R K I N A   F A S O

"See the bullet holes?" Leadismo asked. I could see a splotch of caked blood in the middle of her left ear. He directed my eyes to a swollen wound on her trunk and another on her ear. She held her front left leg aloft like a person on crutches. Still, she was alive. "She's improving," Leadismo said. "They say she's been moving to the lake and taking water and coming back here."

Pope had asked me to document her condition, so I moved around the trees in search of a clear angle for a photo. Kulling followed me with her eyes. Her ears flapped. I found a spot behind a tree and crouched down. When I stepped forward into the open, Kulling reared up and attempted a short charge—a very good sign! As Leadismo told me, if she was moving well enough to charge me, her leg might not be broken after all.

I RETURNED TO THE US two days later but kept checking STE's Facebook page for updates. The following week, they posted one: *Sad news from the north of Kenya. Kulling has died. . . . [She] was treated by the Kenya Wildlife Service, but we always knew it would be hard for her to survive her wounds. She is survived by her three calves, who are all alive and well in Samburu Reserve.*

Many commenters wished to see the herders brought to justice. Jerenimo Leperei had assured me that such retribution would only make matters worse. The key to resolving human-animal conflict was education. In early April, he did end up meeting with herders and elders from the Loijuk community. About fifty men gathered, not far from where Kulling died, to share a meal and to recall the old ways of living in peace with elephants.

MEIBAE COMMUNITY CONSERVANCY

Lodungokwe

Dry season

Kulling migrated to wetlands in the Meibae Community Conservancy during the dry seasons.

Ewaso Ng'iro

Kulling's Last Days

The elephants of Samburu spend more than half the year outside the reserve boundaries. Here we show where Kulling spent the last three years of her life. Darker orange squares indicate her favorite areas, including Loijuk Swamp and various spots along the Ewaso Ng'iro River.

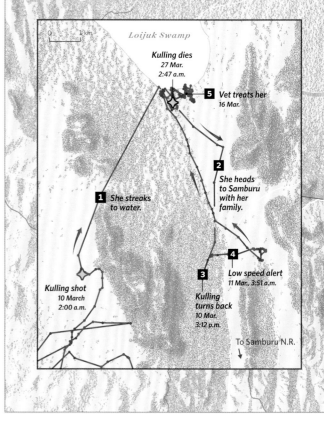

Loijuk Swamp

Kulling dies
27 Mar.
2:47 a.m.

5 Vet treats her
16 Mar.

2 She heads to Samburu with her family.

1 She streaks to water.

4 Low speed alert
11 Mar., 3:51 a.m.

3 Kulling turns back
10 Mar.
3:12 p.m.

Kulling shot
10 March
2:00 a.m.

To Samburu N.R.

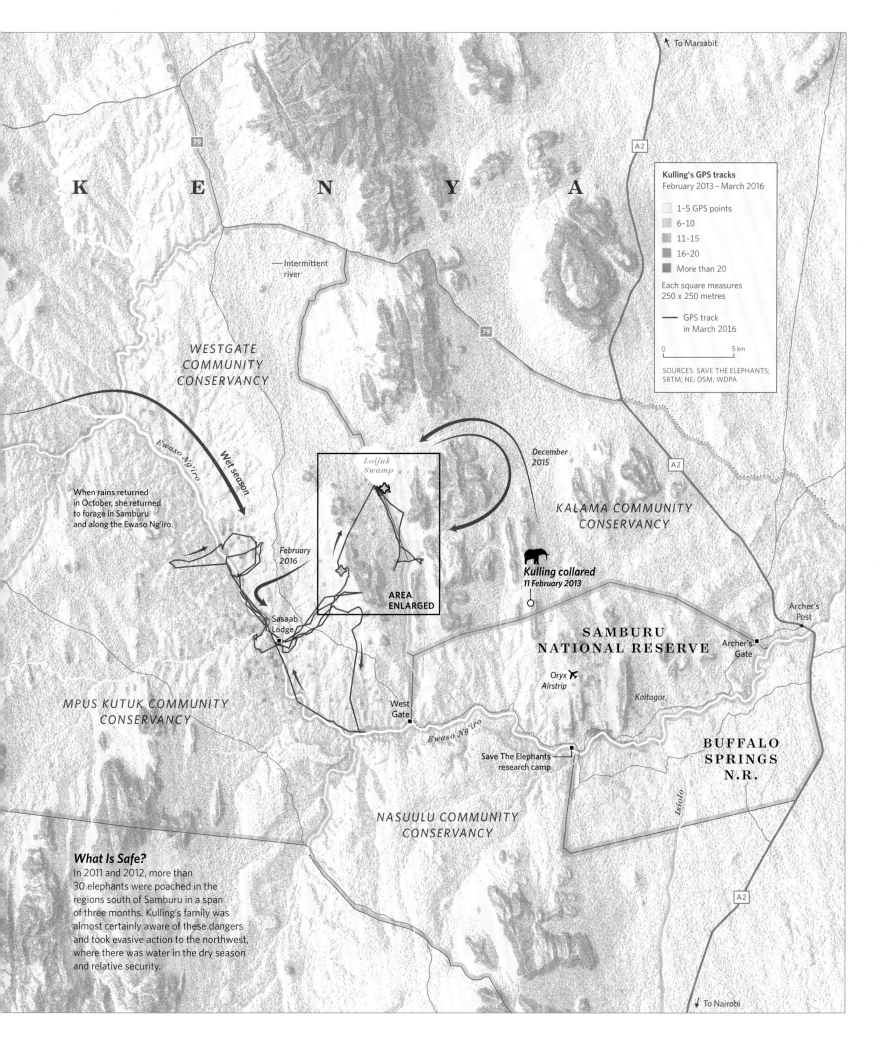

↑ To Marsabit

A2

K E N Y A

79

— Intermittent river

*WESTGATE
COMMUNITY
CONSERVANCY*

79

Ewaso Ng'iro

Wet season

December
2015

*Loijuk
Swamp*

When rains returned
in October, she returned
to forage in Samburu
and along the Ewaso Ng'iro.

A2

*KALAMA COMMUNITY
CONSERVANCY*

February
2016

**AREA
ENLARGED**

Kulling collared
11 February 2013

Archer's
Post

*Sasaab
Lodge*

*MPUS KUTUK COMMUNITY
CONSERVANCY*

West
Gate

**SAMBURU
NATIONAL RESERVE**

Oryx ✈
Airstrip

Archer's
Gate

Koitogor

Ewaso Ng'iro

Save The Elephants
research camp

**BUFFALO
SPRINGS
N.R.**

*NASUULU COMMUNITY
CONSERVANCY*

Isiolo

What Is Safe?
In 2011 and 2012, more than
30 elephants were poached in the
regions south of Samburu in a span
of three months. Kulling's family was
almost certainly aware of these dangers
and took evasive action to the northwest,
where there was water in the dry season
and relative security.

A2

↓ To Nairobi

The Zebras Migrating Once More

ZEBRAS NEED ROOM TO ROAM. We just never knew they needed so much. On this map, we show two of the longest land migrations on the planet. Both were discovered only a few years ago through the use of GPS collars.

In 2007, Hattie Bartlam-Brooks was conducting a survey of herbivore movements in the Okavango Delta when six of her tagged zebras took off for the Makgadikgadi Pans 290 kilometers away. "This was unexpected," she says, because for 36 years a wildlife control fence blocked that route. Although Botswana dismantled this fence in 2004, she figured the damage was done. Consider that the average zebra only lives fifteen years. "It's highly improbable that any of the zebra that made the migration historically were still alive in 2004," says Bartlam-Brooks. Yet somehow the knowledge persisted. Perhaps it was hardwired. Perhaps these zebras were simply exploring and stumbled upon the pans, thereby starting the migration anew. Either way, their resilience should be reason for hope.

Here's another: In 2011, Botswana and four neighboring nations signed a treaty to create a shared protected area the size of France (above left). In the twentieth century, governments were constructing fences to restrict animal movements. Now, they're forming partnerships to protect them.

AFRICA

KAZA Transfrontier Conservation Area

BOTSWANA

The Kavango-Zambezi Transfrontier Conservation Area (KAZA) includes more than 30 national parks, reserves, and wildlife management areas across Angola, Botswana, Namibia, Zambia, and Zimbabwe.

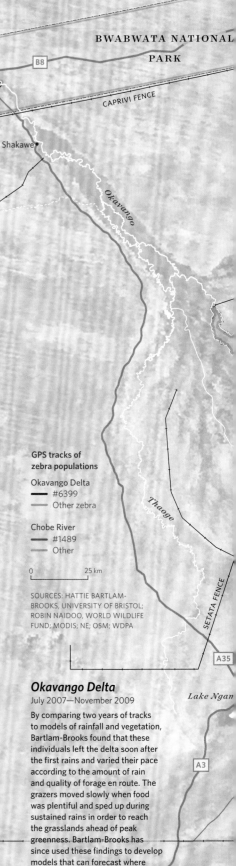

ANGOLA

BWABWATA NATIONAL PARK

B8

CAPRIVI FENCE

Shakawe

Okavango

GPS tracks of zebra populations

Okavango Delta
—— #6399
—— Other zebra

Chobe River
—— #1489
—— Other

0   25 km

SOURCES: HATTIE BARTLAM-BROOKS, UNIVERSITY OF BRISTOL; ROBIN NAIDOO, WORLD WILDLIFE FUND; MODIS; NE; OSM; WDPA

Thaoge

SETATA FENCE

A35

Okavango Delta

July 2007—November 2009

By comparing two years of tracks to models of rainfall and vegetation, Bartlam-Brooks found that these individuals left the delta soon after the first rains and varied their pace according to the amount of rain and quality of forage en route. The grazers moved slowly when food was plentiful and sped up during sustained rains in order to reach the grasslands ahead of peak greenness. Bartlam-Brooks has since used these findings to develop models that can forecast where zebra will be in near real-time.

Lake Ngan...

A3

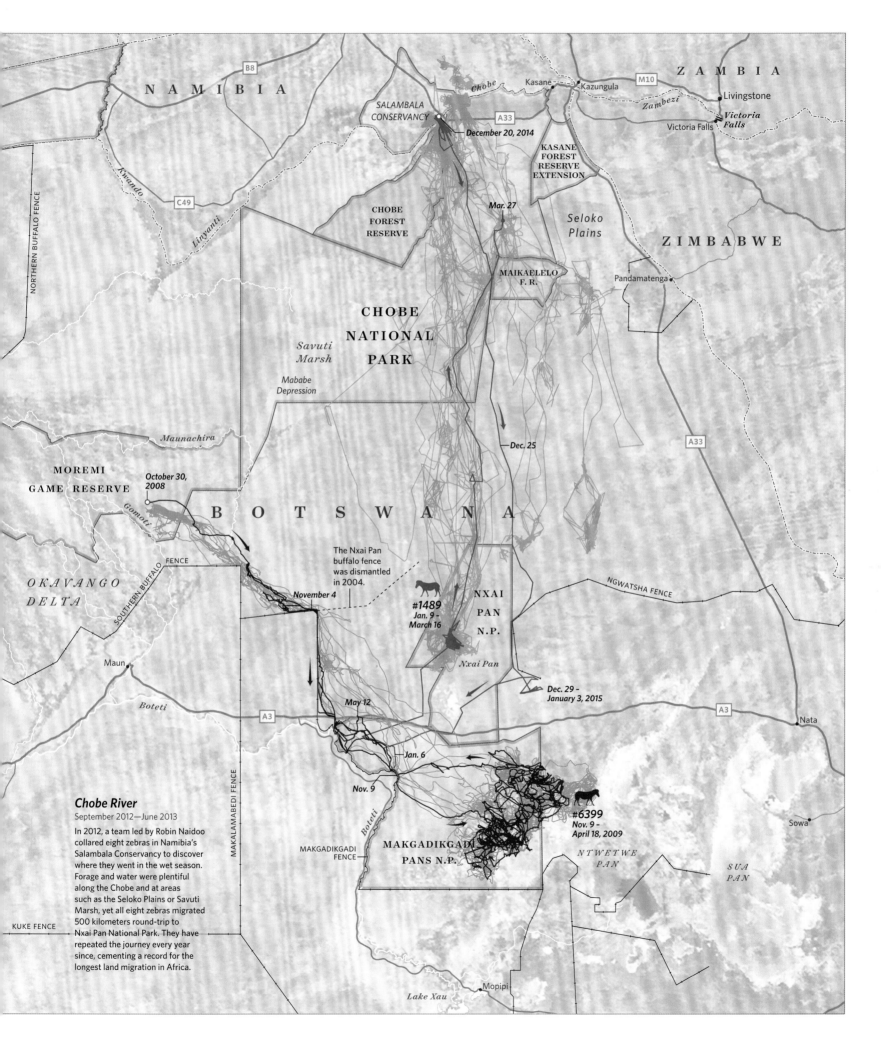

NAMIBIA

ZAMBIA

B8

Chobe Kasane Kazungula M10 • Livingstone

A33 *Zambezi*

**SALAMBALA
CONSERVANCY** ←— *December 20, 2014* Victoria Falls ***Victoria
Falls***

C49

Kwando **KASANE
FOREST
RESERVE
EXTENSION**

Linyanti **CHOBE
FOREST
RESERVE** *Mar. 27* *Seloko
Plains* ZIMBABWE

**MAIKAELELO
F. R.** Pandamatenga •

**CHOBE

NATIONAL

PARK**

NORTHERN BUFFALO FENCE

*Savuti
Marsh*

*Mababe
Depression*

Dec. 25

A33

Maunachira

**MOREMI
GAME RESERVE** *October 30,
2008*

Gomoti **B O T S W A N A**

The Nxai Pan
buffalo fence
was dismantled
in 2004.

#1489
*Jan. 9 –
March 16* **NXAI
PAN
N.P.** NGWATSHA FENCE

**OKAVANGO
DELTA** *November 4* *Nxai Pan*

SOUTHERN BUFFALO FENCE

*Dec. 29 –
January 3, 2015*

Maun • A3 *May 12* A3 • Nata

Boteti

Jan. 6

MAKALAMABEDI FENCE

Nov. 9

• Sowa

Chobe River

#6399
*Nov. 9 –
April 18, 2009*

September 2012—June 2013

Boteti *N T W E T W E
P A N* *S U A
P A N*

In 2012, a team led by Robin Naidoo
collared eight zebras in Namibia's
Salambala Conservancy to discover
where they went in the wet season.
Forage and water were plentiful
along the Chobe and at areas
such as the Seloko Plains or Savuti
Marsh, yet all eight zebras migrated
500 kilometers round-trip to
Nxai Pan National Park. They have
repeated the journey every year
since, cementing a record for the
longest land migration in Africa.

MAKGADIKGADI
FENCE **MAKGADIKGADI
PANS N.P.**

KUKE FENCE

Lake Xau • Mopipi

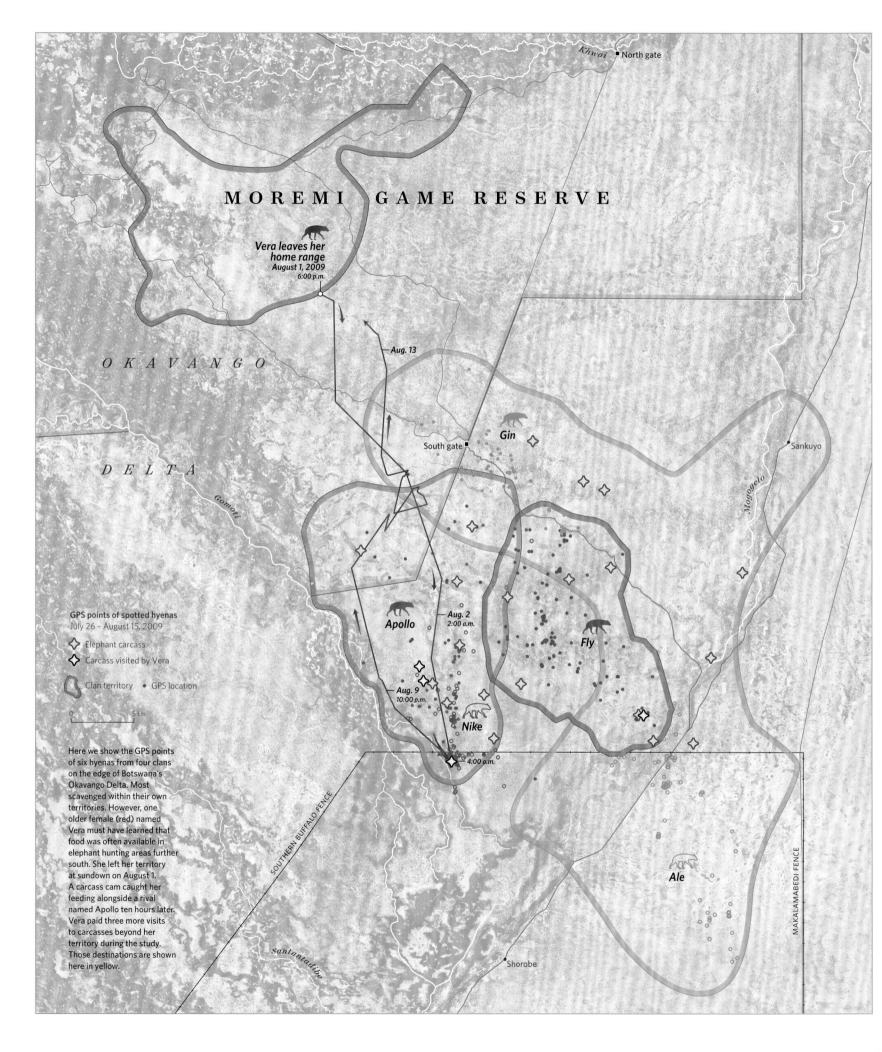

MOREMI GAME RESERVE

Vera leaves her home range
August 1, 2009
6:00 p.m.

O K A V A N G O

— Aug. 13

D E L T A

South gate ■

Gin

Sankuyo ●

Gomoti

Mogogelo

GPS points of spotted hyenas
July 26 – August 15, 2009

✦ Elephant carcass

✦ Carcass visited by Vera

Clan territory • GPS location

0   5 km

Apollo

— Aug. 2
2:00 a.m.

Fly

— Aug. 9
10:00 p.m.

Nike

— 4:00 a.m.

Here we show the GPS points of six hyenas from four clans on the edge of Botswana's Okavango Delta. Most scavenged within their own territories. However, one older female (red) named Vera must have learned that food was often available in elephant hunting areas further south. She left her territory at sundown on August 1. A carcass cam caught her feeding alongside a rival named Apollo ten hours later. Vera paid three more visits to carcasses beyond her territory during the study. Those destinations are shown here in yellow.

Santantadibe

Shorobe ●

Ale

SOUTHERN BUFFALO FENCE

MAKALAMABEDI FENCE

Khwai   ■ North gate

The Hyenas and the Trophy Kills

FROM A HYENA'S POINT OF VIEW, an elephant carcass is food, whether the elephant died from natural causes or the trigger of a trophy hunter. So what happens if you supply these carnivores with tons of them? Swiss researcher Gabriele Cozzi (University of Zurich) was convinced that extra carcasses in the Okavango Delta would change hyena behavior, but the question, he says, was for how long? In the first study of its kind, Cozzi and his team investigated to what extent trophy hunting distorts the lives of a species the hunter didn't pay to kill.

Using GPS collars, Cozzi tracked twelve spotted hyenas in and around Botswana's Moremi Game Reserve between 2008 and 2010. At that time, Botswana let professional hunters kill 14–17 elephants per year within designated hunting areas between the reserve and the southern buffalo fence. The hunters told Cozzi's team where to find their kills, which enabled the researchers to set up cameras in trees or shrubs near five carcasses.

From the footage, Cozzi saw hyenas (as well as jackals, lions and honey badgers) visiting carcasses consistently during the first 10–12 days after the elephants died (see below). Then the number of visitors and time spent at each carcass dropped off as the meat deteriorated. However, some hyenas continued to feed for as long as 50 days.

Over the course of the three-year study, trophy kills provided each of the resident groups—or clans—(shown in blue, yellow, and purple) with a month's worth of food each year on average. These findings suggest the effects of trophy hunting are more complex than they might seem. The government of Botswana simplified things: in 2013, they banned trophy hunting altogether.

AFRICA

BOTSWANA **☐ AREA ENLARGED**

Vera —

Nike —

Apollo —

August 1   *Aug. 5*   *Aug. 10*   *Aug. 15*

Feeding times
August 1-15, 2009

Vera feeds with rival clan

SOURCES: GABRIELE COZZI, UNIVERSITY OF ZURICH; LANDSAT; NE; OSM; WDPA

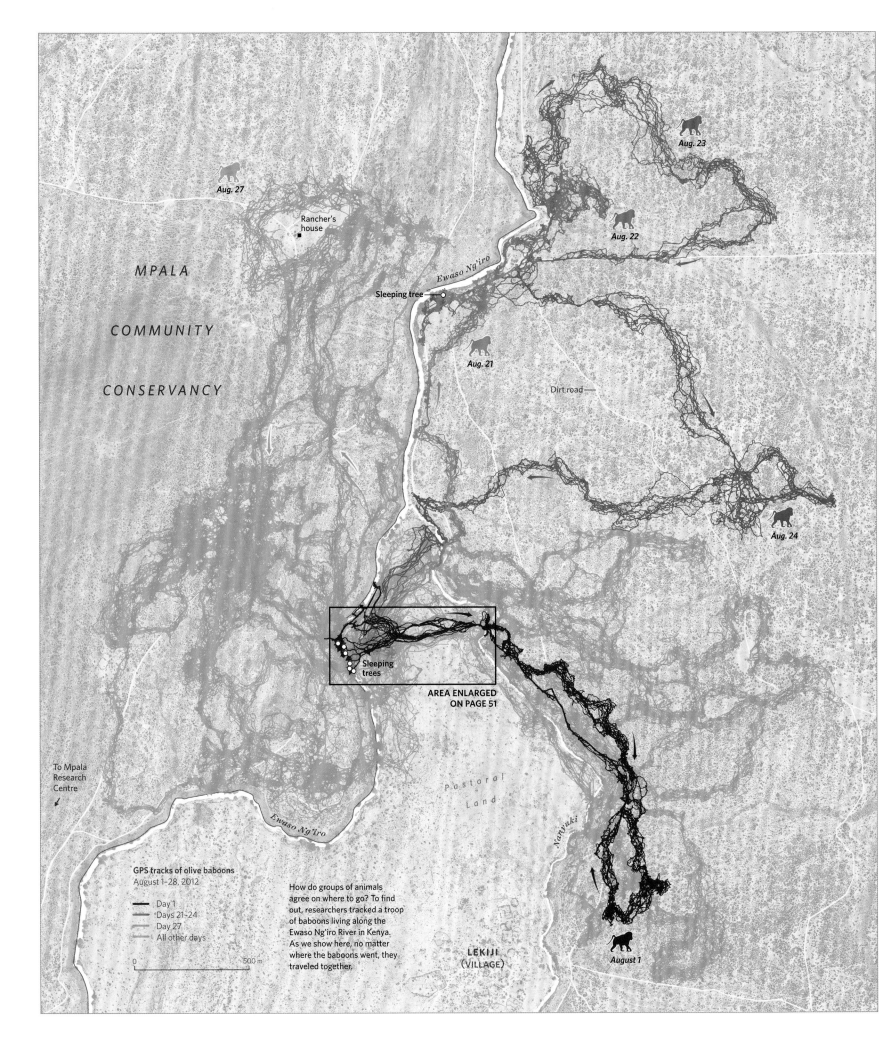

LEKIJI
(VILLAGE)

MPALA

COMMUNITY

CONSERVANCY

Rancher's
house

Ewaso Ng'iro

Sleeping tree

Aug. 27

Aug. 23

Aug. 22

Aug. 21

Dirt road

Aug. 24

Sleeping
trees

AREA ENLARGED
ON PAGE 51

To Mpala
Research
Centre

Pastoral
Land

Ewaso Ng'iro

Nanyuki

August 1

GPS tracks of olive baboons
August 1–28, 2012

Day 1
Days 21–24
Day 27
All other days

0   500 m

How do groups of animals
agree on where to go? To find
out, researchers tracked a troop
of baboons living along the
Ewaso Ng'iro River in Kenya.
As we show here, no matter
where the baboons went, they
traveled together.

How Baboons Move as One

WE'VE ALL BEEN THERE. You leave a restaurant with a group of friends in search of the night's next activity. Drinks? Dessert? Dancing? How do you decide where to go while two friends look for an ATM, another takes a call and three more are still in the restaurant? Baboons face similar problems every day, only in much larger groups.

Collective animal behavior has long vexed scientists, mainly because they had no means to track it in the wild. Then in 2012, anthropologist Margaret Crofoot found a way.

She and an international team of researchers collared 25 olive baboons from a troop of 46 near the Mpala Research Centre in Kenya. What distinguishes her data from other tracking studies is its scale. The slightest movement by one baboon could trigger others throughout the troop, so Crofoot set all 25 advanced GPS collars to record one position every second. Picture the high frame rate of a slow-motion camera. To make sense of the action, she needed to watch every frame. After collecting data for a few weeks,

Crofoot had more than 20 million data points.

The entire dataset shows the troop's decisions over a four-week period. From these meandering loops, we can see where they foraged. We can see the wide berth they gave villagers. We can see where they slept and how they found a new group of "sleeping trees" for a few nights while a leopard was on the prowl (August 21–24). These tracks provide context, but they don't answer the big question: How do baboons agree on where to go as a group? To do that, Crofoot needed to look point-by-point through the entire dataset. Fortunately, she had help.

Damien Farine of the Max Planck Institute for Ornithology and Ariana Strandburg-Peshkin from Princeton University wrote software that could identify a baboon's change in direction and compare it to movements of his or her neighbors. This analysis led to the identification of 57,000 baboon decisions, each with its own consequences.

For example, let's say one baboon decides to move away from his neighbors because he

AFRICA   Mpala
Research
Centre
KENYA
Nairobi

SOURCES: MARGARET CROFOOT, UNIVERSITY OF CALIFORNIA, DAVIS;
DAMIEN FARINE, MAX PLANCK INSTITUTE FOR ORNITHOLOGY

noticed something particularly tasty across the way. His departure might inspire a few friends to join him. The researchers called this a "pull." But if no baboons followed, the hungry baboon might change his mind and choose to stick with the crowd. They called this "anchoring." Taken together, the individual decisions of whether to pull or anchor dictate where the troop goes. The small diagrams to the right illustrate two troop-wide scenarios. If one baboon gains a small following, others may "choose" to join until eventually he or she has the whole troop in tow. When the baboons disagree only slightly on which direction to go, they take the "path of compromise" and the troop moves as one. As we show in the sequence below, both scenarios can and often do happen in quick succession.

This "shared decision-making" came as a surprise to Crofoot because baboon society is hierarchical. When it comes to feeding and mating, dominant individuals overpower their subordinates. But in the case of day-to-day governance, no single baboon—not even the alpha male or female—called the shots. As Crofoot says, "all group members have a voice."

With such a large dataset, her team has many more questions to ask. Perhaps, too many to answer themselves. So they shared ten million data points on an animal-data-sharing platform called Movebank (see p. 30). Other researchers around the world can now study them too—without having to collar more baboons.

In future studies, Crofoot and Farine hope to figure out 1) how baboon troops decide *when* to move and 2) whether individuals ever use circumstances to exert their influence on the troop. After all, compromise may not be the best approach when faced with a hungry leopard.

| 8:00 am | 8:03 | 8:06 | 8:09 | 8:12 | 8:15 |

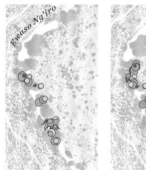 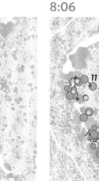 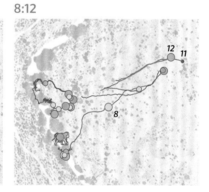 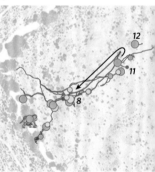

8:00-8:03 Waking between 7 and 8 a.m., the first baboons climb down from their sleeping trees. Adults sit and groom each other while juveniles play nearby.

8:06-8:09 An adult female (ID #12) and a juvenile (11) from the northern group of trees start foraging in the open field. They're soon followed by three more baboons.

8:12-8:15 Despite relatively low status in the troop, 11 and 12 are on to something. All except four decide to follow them. Halfway across the field, 11 turns back. The troop pauses. An adult male from the southern trees (8) runs back to gather the stragglers.

Morning Commute

On August 1, 2012, a troop of 46 baboons began their daily forage with a river-to-river dash across the pastoral land of a nearby village. Below we show the tracks of 13 adults, 10 subadults and 2 large juveniles, each fitted with a GPS collar that recorded their positions every second. Males are colored blue; females are red. Circle size indicates age. To the researchers' surprise, a dominant male or female did not lead the way. A mother and her juvenile did.

Baboon troop movements by sex, age, and status
August 1, 2012 at 8:21 a.m.

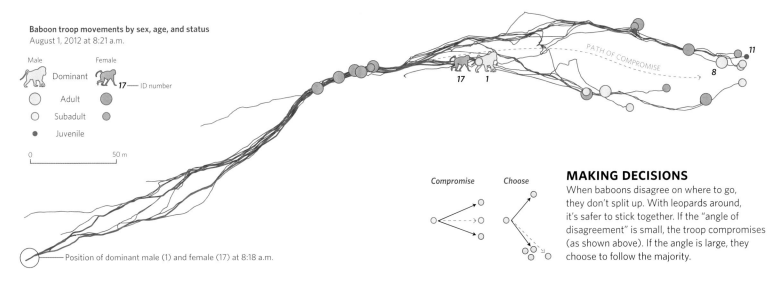

Male   Female
Dominant
17 — ID number
Adult
Subadult
Juvenile

0   50 m

Position of dominant male (1) and female (17) at 8:18 a.m.

PATH OF COMPROMISE

11

8

MAKING DECISIONS

Compromise   Choose

When baboons disagree on where to go, they don't split up. With leopards around, it's safer to stick together. If the "angle of disagreement" is small, the troop compromises (as shown above). If the angle is large, they choose to follow the majority.

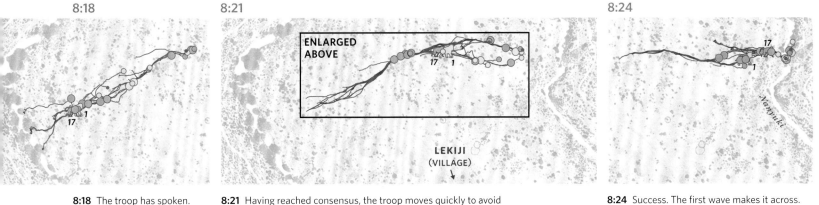

8:18   8:21   8:24

ENLARGED ABOVE

LEKIJI
(VILLAGE)

Nanyuki

8:18 The troop has spoken. Majority rules. The dominant pair (1 & 17) stop grooming and hurry to join the rest.

8:21 Having reached consensus, the troop moves quickly to avoid being harassed by local herders from Lekiji village. With 11 still in front and the dominant pair in the middle, the troop aims for one of the few sites where they can cross the Nanyuki River.

8:24 Success. The first wave makes it across. From here, the troop will forage further south before returning to their sleeping trees along the Ewaso Ng'iro by sundown.

SOURCES: MARGARET CROFOOT, UNIVERSITY OF CALIFORNIA, DAVIS; DAMIEN FARINE, MAX PLANCK INSTITUTE FOR ORNITHOLOGY

Here we show the "lawnmower pattern" described by two flights over a piece of Sumatra's Leuser Ecosystem, where 75% of the island's orangutans live. The drone collected 2,238 images, which the researchers stitched together to form this 27,000-megapixel mosaic. Initially, Wich and Pin Koh sifted through the photos looking for brown nests in the green trees. They have since trained algorithms to do this automatically.

SOURCES: SERGE WICH, LIVERPOOL JOHN MOORES UNIVERSITY; LIAN PIN KOH, UNIVERSITY OF ADELAIDE; WDPA

Drone flight path

Location of photo

Orangutan nests
October 2013

● Detected by drone
● Observed on foot

0   100 m

Launch Site

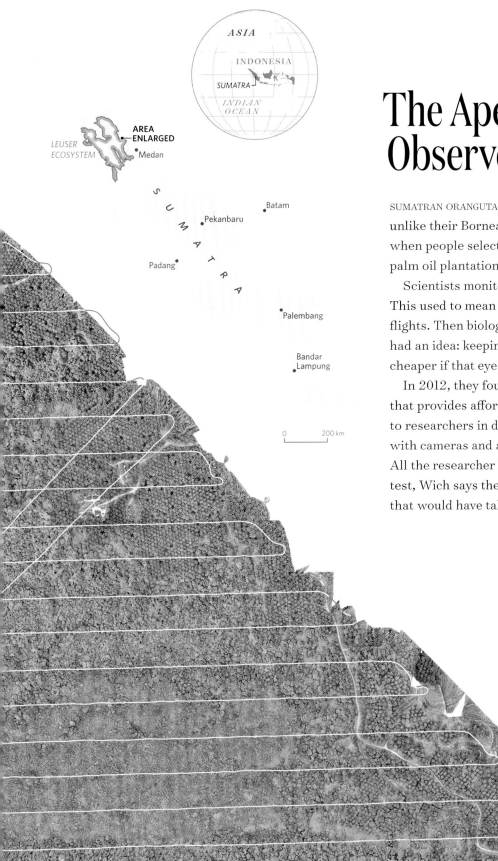

ASIA

INDONESIA

SUMATRA

INDIAN OCEAN

AREA ENLARGED

LEUSER ECOSYSTEM

Medan

S U M A T R A

Batam

Pekanbaru

Padang

Palembang

Bandar Lampung

0   200 km

The Apes Observed from Above

SUMATRAN ORANGUTANS NEED TREES. They nest in the canopies and, unlike their Bornean cousins, rarely descend to the ground. So when people selectively fell trees—or worse, clear forest for palm oil plantations—the population plummets.

Scientists monitor orangutan numbers by counting their nests. This used to mean arduous ground surveys or costly manned flights. Then biologist Serge Wich and ecologist Lian Pin Koh had an idea: keeping an eye on the apes might be easier and cheaper if that eye weren't human.

In 2012, they founded Conservation Drones, an organization that provides affordable, easy-to-use unmanned aerial vehicles to researchers in developing countries. The drones, equipped with cameras and a GPS, fly autonomously along a preset path. All the researcher has to do is throw it in the air. On their first test, Wich says the drone surveyed an area in twenty minutes that would have taken three days to cover on foot.

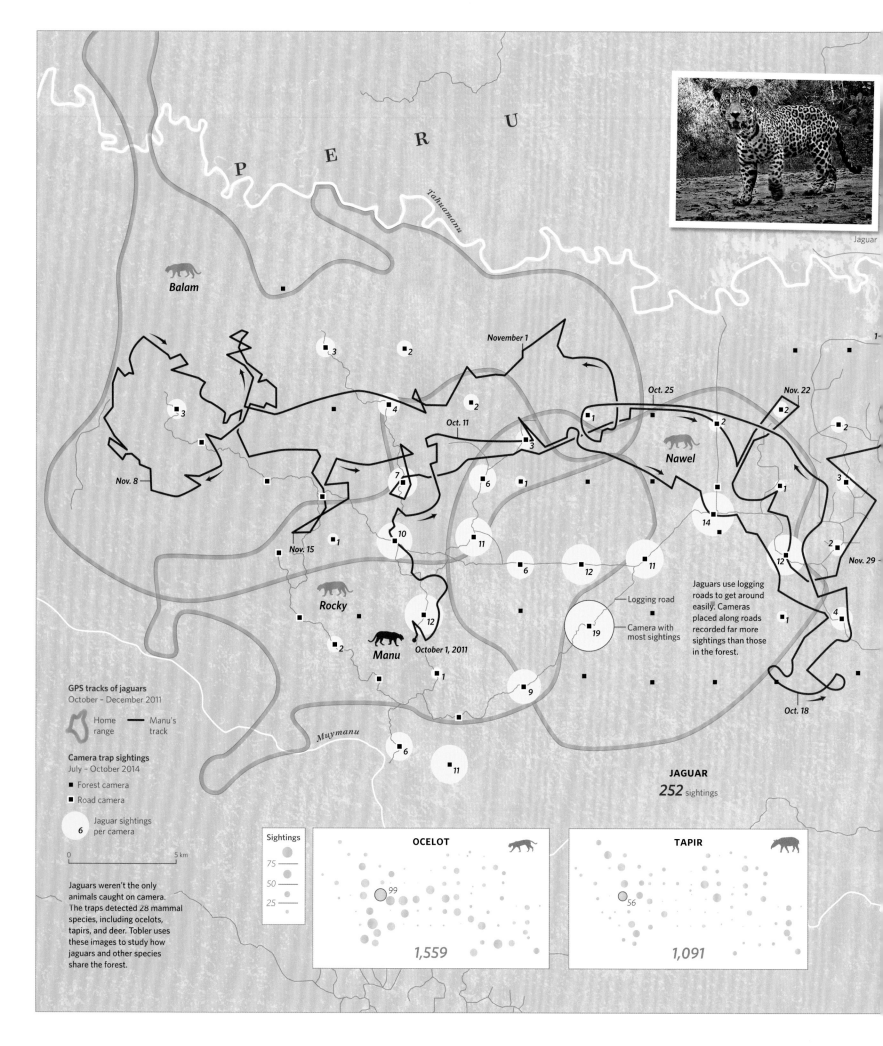

P E R U

Tahuamanu

Jaguar

Balam

November 1

Oct. 25

Nov. 22

Oct. 11

Nawel

Nov. 8

Nov. 15

Rocky

Manu

October 1, 2011

Jaguars use logging roads to get around easily. Cameras placed along roads recorded far more sightings than those in the forest.

— Logging road
— Camera with most sightings

Oct. 18

Nov. 29

GPS tracks of jaguars
October – December 2011

Home range — Manu's track

Camera trap sightings
July – October 2014

■ Forest camera
■ Road camera

◯ 6 Jaguar sightings per camera

0 ———————— 5 km

Jaguars weren't the only animals caught on camera. The traps detected 28 mammal species, including ocelots, tapirs, and deer. Tobler uses these images to study how jaguars and other species share the forest.

Muymanu

JAGUAR
252 sightings

Sightings
75 ———
50 ——
25 —

OCELOT
99
1,559

TAPIR
56
1,091

Red brocket deer (*Mazama americana*)

Ocelot (*Leopardus pardalis*)

Jaguar (*Panthera onca*)

Tapir (*Tapirus terrestris*)

IBERIA

60 km²
Typical size of
camera trap studies

December 1

The Jaguars Taking Selfies

JAGUARS EVOLVED TO BE INVISIBLE. They're quiet, camouflaged, largely nocturnal and live in some of the most remote forests on Earth. About twenty years ago, scientists began using motion-activated "camera traps" to catch the cats in action. From these sightings, in study areas the size of Manhattan, they reasoned they could estimate how many jaguars lived within the surrounding forests.

Then in 2011, Mathias Tobler attached GPS collars to five jaguars in the Peruvian Amazon. One male named Manu (purple) had a range of 600 km²—*ten times* the size of Manhattan. Tobler was stunned. He began reviewing every camera trap study on jaguars, including his own. "90 percent of the studies people have done totally overestimated jaguar densities," he says. "Our camera trap grids were too small." The implications, however, were huge. Populations that scientists had deemed safe might actually be in need of protection.

Tobler returned to Peru in 2014, this time to install 89 cameras across 650 km². The larger grid encompassed entire jaguar ranges (blue) and identified 41 individuals, more than any study had ever seen.

AREA
ENLARGED

Lima ★ | SOUTH
PERU | AMERICA

RED BROCKET DEER

42

567

SOURCES: MATHIAS TOBLER; SAN DIEGO ZOO GLOBAL; GEORGE POWELL, WORLD WILDLIFE FUND; GLCF; OSM

Oxnard

SIMI HILLS
VENTURA
L.A.
101

405

Griffith Park
Zoo
Hollywood Sign

Liberty Canyon
Corridor

SANTA MONICA MOUNTAINS
NAT. REC. AREA

1

LOS
ANGELES

Malibu

Santa Monica

Los Angeles
International Airport ✈

Plans are underway for
a vegetated overpass across
Highway 101. This will give
mountain lions in the Santa
Monica Mountains an escape
route to the Simi Hills.

Long
Beach

The Mountain Lions
Trapped by Roads

PACIFIC

OCEAN

MOUNTAIN LIONS IN SOUTHERN CALIFORNIA are having what Hollywood might call a "moment." The A-lister among them is P-22, a 6-year-old male who lives alone in the hills of Griffith Park. In the past three years, he's been photographed walking past the HOLLYWOOD sign; hiding under a house; and prowling the Los Angeles Zoo, where, the next day, keepers also discovered a dismembered koala.

Thirty years ago, such close encounters would have resulted in a dead cat. Today, L.A. residents are becoming more comfortable with the idea of an apex predator in the neighborhood. "When people see P-22, they treat him like a celebrity," says Winston Vickers, a wildlife veterinarian at University of California, Davis. As people learn more about these animals—also known as pumas, cougars, and panthers—they begin to think of them less like marauders and more like mascots. You can now buy T-shirts with P-22's likeness or follow him on Twitter (@GPMountainLion).

In the late 1980s, scientists began radio tracking and modeling the movements of mountain lions in the Santa Ana Mountains, southeast of L.A. They realized the animals were effectively marooned on an island, surrounded by freeways and ever-encroaching human development. Vickers and his

*NORTH
AMERICA* U.S.

☐
AREA
ENLARGED MEXICO

Mountain lions are wide-ranging animals. In Southern California, freeways restrict their movements. Here we show five of the 74 cats that researchers have tracked since 2001. Only one has ever crossed Interstate 15.

M56
On March 7, 2010, this young male left the Santa Ana Mountains in search of a new home territory. He traveled south along the beach and up Route 76 before crossing Interstate 15 to explore the Peninsular Ranges.
In late April, M56 killed eight sheep in Jatapul Valley. The landowner obtained a depredation permit. On the night of April 28, a trapper captured and shot M56.

M122
Adult males will kill or threaten males that do not leave their home ranges. M122 was born near Murrieta and dispersed to claim territory in the northwestern foothills.

F50
F50 was living with her offspring in the western Santa Ana Mountains until she was hit by a car on Highway 74 near where her daughter F62 and a male kitten were also hit.

SAN BERNARDINO
NATIONAL FOREST

SAN BERNARDINO
RIVERSIDE

CHINO HILLS
STATE PARK

Santa Ana

Riverside

U N I T E D   **S T A T E S**

Jul. 23   Palm
Springs

Jul. 5

Anaheim

Coal
Canyon
Corridor

Irvine L.

M122

Santa Ana

Irvine

June 1

F50

Mission
Viejo

CLEVELAND
NAT.
FOREST

Apr. 29   Murrieta

Temecula

SAN JACINTO MTS.

SAN BERNARDINO
NATIONAL FOREST

SANTA ROSA AND
SAN JACINTO MTS.
NAT. MONUMENT

RIVERSIDE

M56

Mar. 25

Palomar
Linkage

RIVERSIDE
SAN DIEGO

Jun. 25,
2004

RIVERSIDE
IMPERIAL

March 7, 2010

San Clemente

Laguna
Beach

CAMP
PENDLETON
MARINE
CORPS
BASE

Fallbrook

Santa Margarita

PALOMAR
MT.

August 21

F18

M53

*SALTON
SEA*

Mar. 22

April 3

*SANTA
ROSA
MTS.*

IMPERIAL
SAN DIEGO

Oceanside

Apr. 7-13

Escondido

CLEVELAND
NAT.
FOREST

Julian

ANZA-BORREGO
DESERT STATE
PARK

F18

Typically, females
don't disperse as far
as males. F18 is an
exception. She walked
100 kilometers to the
San Jacintos near Palm
Springs and then came
back to reside in San
Diego County.

Ramona

May 10, 2009

November 30

*LAGUNA
MTS.*

M53

In summer 2009, this
young male crossed into
Mexico via the Parque-
to-Park Linkage at least
three times. He roamed
69 kilometers south of
the border before he
was struck and killed by
a car in Mexico.

CLEVELAND
NAT. FOREST

M56 shot
Apr. 28
Japatul Valley

Apr. 25

**S A N
D I E G O**

Jacumba

Parque-to-Park
Linkage

La Rumorosa

Tecate

June 9

T I J U A N A

2D

98

8

2D

GPS tracks of mountain lions
2004–2015

Home range

Wildlife corridor

Existing

Proposed

◇ Successful
highway crossing

July 28

M E X I C O

*Laguna
Salada*

0   25 km

SOURCES: T. WINSTON VICKERS AND WALTER BOYCE, UNIVERSITY OF
CALIFORNIA, DAVIS; BRIAN COHEN, THE NATURE CONSERVANCY; SRTM; USGS

May 26

M86 to the Rescue

To study the connections between California's mountain lions, researchers sample blood from every cat they collar. The DNA shows frequent inbreeding in the Santa Ana Mountains. If lions are to survive there, they need a more diverse gene pool. Fortunately, one outsider did manage to cross Interstate 15 and breed successfully, a male from the Peninsular Ranges named M86.

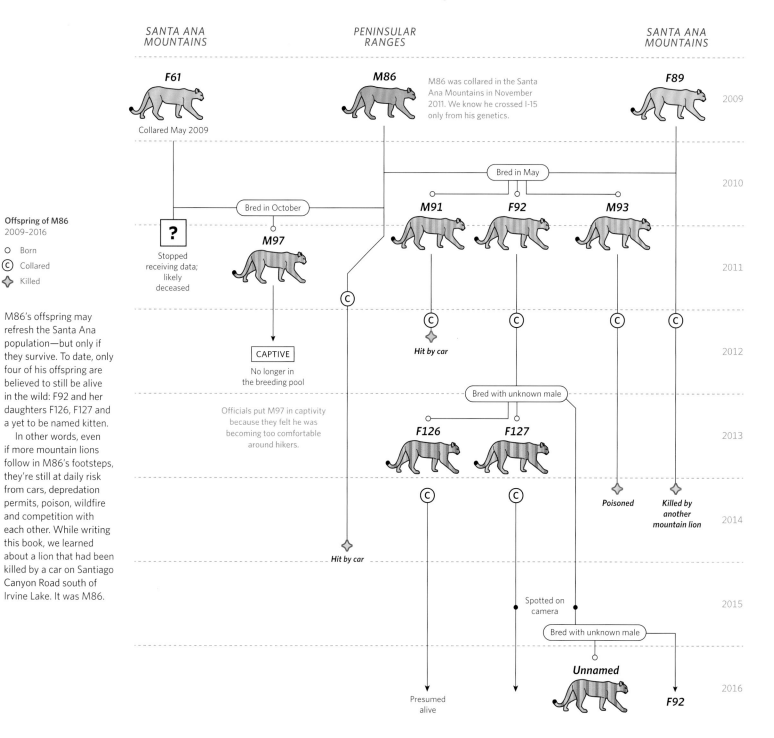

SANTA ANA MOUNTAINS

PENINSULAR RANGES

SANTA ANA MOUNTAINS

F61
Collared May 2009

M86
M86 was collared in the Santa Ana Mountains in November 2011. We know he crossed I-15 only from his genetics.

F89

2009

Bred in May

2010

Bred in October

M91

F92

M93

Offspring of M86
2009–2016

○ Born
Ⓒ Collared
◈ Killed

M97

?
Stopped receiving data; likely deceased

2011

M86's offspring may refresh the Santa Ana population—but only if they survive. To date, only four of his offspring are believed to still be alive in the wild: F92 and her daughters F126, F127 and a yet to be named kitten.

In other words, even if more mountain lions follow in M86's footsteps, they're still at daily risk from cars, depredation permits, poison, wildfire and competition with each other. While writing this book, we learned about a lion that had been killed by a car on Santiago Canyon Road south of Irvine Lake. It was M86.

Ⓒ

Ⓒ

◈
Hit by car

Ⓒ

Ⓒ

Ⓒ

2012

CAPTIVE
No longer in the breeding pool

Officials put M97 in captivity because they felt he was becoming too comfortable around hikers.

Bred with unknown male

F126

F127

2013

Ⓒ

Ⓒ

◈
Poisoned

◈
Killed by another mountain lion

2014

◈
Hit by car

Spotted on camera

2015

Bred with unknown male

Unnamed

2016

Presumed alive

F92

collaborators brought those studies into the twenty-first century with GPS technology and genetic analysis (left). Since these methods were introduced in 2001, only one tagged lion—a male named M56 (purple, on map)—has managed to cross Interstate 15 in either direction, but he was killed 25 days later for preying on a rancher's sheep. Without the ability to breed with other gene pools, the Santa Ana population is in jeopardy.

To Vickers, the region's mountain lions are symbolic. "They're the signal that we've gone too far," he says. "They're naturally wide-ranging and can survive in most places, but they're telling us that the freeways are much more substantial barriers than we presumed." From decades of tracking data, he and his collaborators have identified potential passageways across these barriers. In the Santa Ana Mountains, there are only two. We visited both.

In 2003, the California Department of Transportation converted CA-91's exit 42 into a wildlife crossing called Coal Canyon Corridor, which sounds like a densely thicketed trail but is, in fact, a gravel underpass decorated with boulders and six withered saplings. Recently, the state repaved the corridor's west half for use as a highway patrol turn-around. "It's maddening," says Vickers. "They tore pavement out and then put pavement back." Of the 33 cats he has tracked in the Santa Ana Mountains, not one has used the crossing. "Even though people think Coal Canyon is a nice, wide corridor, the cats don't think so," he says. "They're approaching across open area at eye level with drivers on the highway. They're secretive animals. They need vegetation or culverts for cover."

At the opposite end of the mountain range, a proposal exists to build a vegetated bridge over I-15 just south of Temecula. It would give the Santa Ana lions an escape hatch to Palomar Mountain and the Peninsular Ranges. It's their only hope short of translocation—but it's a long shot. While an ecological reserve exists west of the interstate, the land east of it is split between homes, golf courses, and other private holdings. Purchasing land one plot at a time is expensive and takes time. To put the predicament in perspective, the Coal Canyon Corridor required ten acquisitions; the Palomar Linkage could require dozens.

From a lot beside the road, an unmarked trail led to a rise overlooking the passing cars. At the top, it was easy to see a mountain lion's point of view: *right there*, 100 meters away, lay a continuous chain of wilderness all the way to Mexico. All that

To Vickers, the mountain lions are symbolic. "They're the signal that we've gone too far … they're telling us that the freeways are more substantial barriers than we presumed."

stood in the way were eight lanes of traffic. Behind us, a billboard welcomed drivers to Temecula with the words, "Old Traditions, New Opportunities." To the left of the text, an artist had painted the city's seal, in which a stagecoach passed between two hills. If this signified the old, where was the new? In the semi-circle of blue above the scene, there seemed to be more than enough space to add a bridge with a mountain lion strolling across.

SOURCES: HOLLY ERNEST, UNIVERSITY OF WYOMING;
T. WINSTON VICKERS, UNIVERSITY OF CALIFORNIA, DAVIS

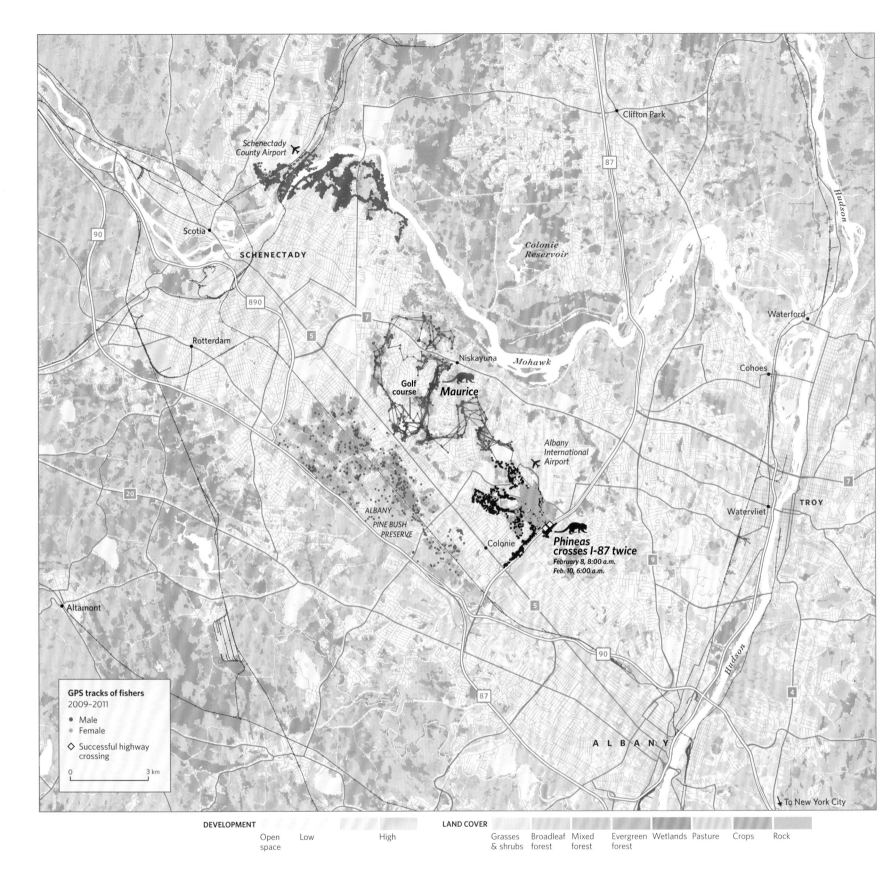

GPS tracks of fishers
2009–2011

• Male
• Female

◇ Successful highway
crossing

0   3 km

Schenectady
County Airport

Scotia

SCHENECTADY

890

5

Rotterdam

7

Niskayuna

Mohawk

Golf
course

Maurice

Albany
International
Airport

ALBANY
PINE BUSH
PRESERVE

Colonie

*Phineas
crosses I-87 twice*
February 8, 8:00 a.m.
Feb. 10, 6:00 a.m.

Altamont

20

Clifton Park

87

*Colonie
Reservoir*

Waterford

Cohoes

Watervliet

TROY

7

9

5

90

87

4

ALBANY

↓ To New York City

Hudson

Hudson

DEVELOPMENT

Open   Low   High
space

LAND COVER

Grasses   Broadleaf   Mixed   Evergreen   Wetlands   Pasture   Crops   Rock
& shrubs   forest   forest   forest

The Fishers
Sneaking Through Suburbia

MOUNTAIN LIONS aren't the only animals moving to the city. Two thousand coyotes now reside in Chicago; leopards prowl downtown Mumbai; and, in 2015, a wolf walked into a Dutch village for the first time in 120 years.

Three hours north of New York City in the suburbs of Albany, another carnivore is living alongside humans. They're members of the weasel family called fishers. You may not have heard of them because, for a long time, there weren't many left. Until a ban in the 1930s, trappers hunted these mink-like mammals to near extinction; deforestation drove them further toward the brink. Today, with few natural predators, fishers are reclaiming their historic range, one scrap of forest at a time.

Fishers remain hard to spot. They hunt at night and avoid open space. To find out how they're getting by, zoologists Roland Kays and Scott LaPoint tracked some for a few winters with methods new and old. Their cutting-edge GPS collars recorded a position every two minutes when the fishers were active and once an hour when they were sleeping.

But to verify *how* the animals got from point to point, they strapped on snowshoes and followed the footprints. For example, GPS data showed that a fisher they'd named Phineas had somehow crossed Interstate 87—twice. "We went to that point ourselves," says Kays, "and found he had been using a small drainage culvert."

Such ingenuity isn't always enough to survive in an unnatural habitat. To assist animals, conservationists sometimes create paths between patches of forest. But how do they decide where best to put them? Typically, they eyeball it. Some use algorithms to simulate the safest, easiest routes through a landscape, much like a GPS navigation system does in your car. Kays and LaPoint tried a third approach: studying the GPS tracks. The differences were striking. Many of the simulated routes went unused. Of the routes the fishers *did* take between forest patches, only six matched the models. There's a valuable lesson here: animals know what's best for animals. We need to accommodate what they're doing, not the other way around.

NORTH AMERICA
U.S.
•Albany

To the left, we show data from eight fishers: five male, three female. While males require room to disperse, these females showed they could survive in a square kilometer.

A male named Maurice (red) wove his way between the fairways of a golf course. After crossing I-87 twice, Phineas (purple) crossed under access ramps to hunt within a highway cloverleaf junction. Kays says, "Getting out in the forest ourselves is the only way to learn these details; the GPS data just show us exactly where to look."

SOURCES: ROLAND KAYS, NORTH CAROLINA MUSEUM OF NATURAL SCIENCES; SCOTT LaPOINT, MAX PLANCK INSTITUTE FOR ORNITHOLOGY; USGS

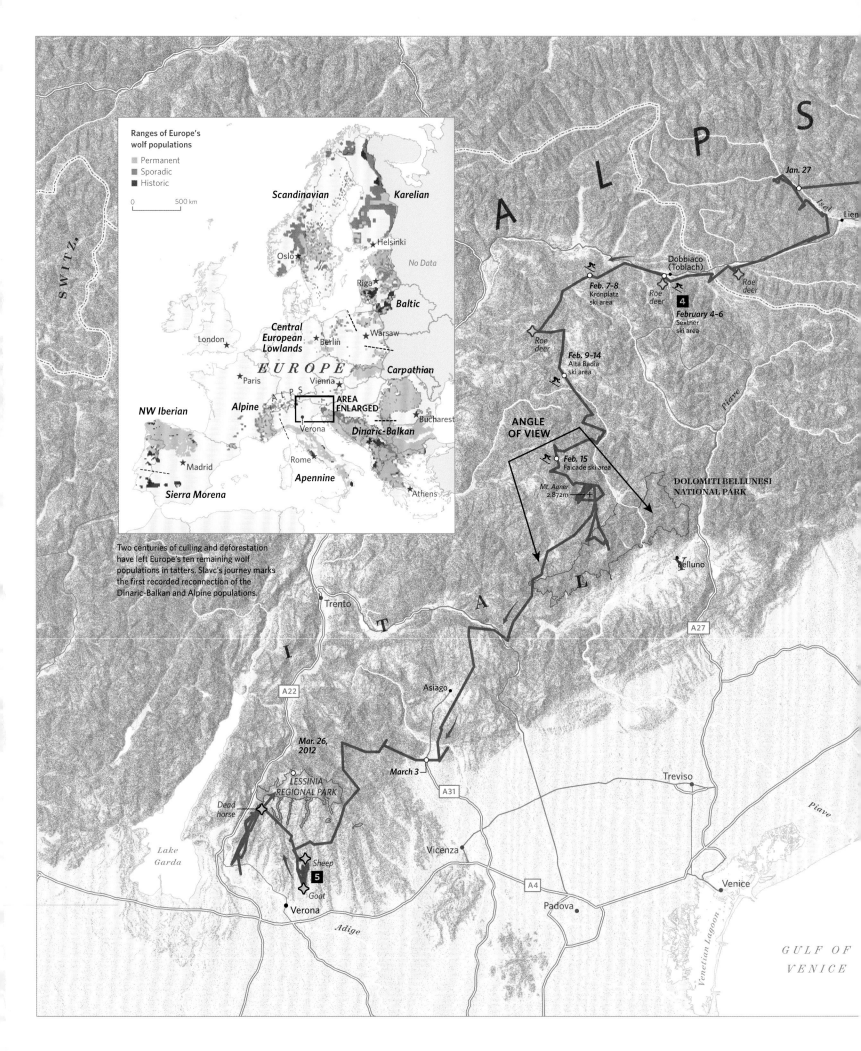

Ranges of Europe's
wolf populations

Permanent
Sporadic
Historic

0   500 km

SWITZ.

Scandinavian   Karelian

★ Helsinki

Oslo ★

Riga ★   No Data

Baltic

London ★   Central
                  European   ★ Warsaw
                  Lowlands

                  ★ Berlin   Carpathian

          E U R O P E

          ★ Paris   Vienna ★

NW Iberian   ALPS   AREA
                              ENLARGED
          Alpine
                  Verona ★   ★ Bucharest

          ★ Madrid   Dinaric-Balkan

                  Rome ★

          Sierra Morena   Apennine   ★ Athens

Two centuries of culling and deforestation
have left Europe's ten remaining wolf
populations in tatters. Slavc's journey marks
the first recorded reconnection of the
Dinaric-Balkan and Alpine populations.

A L P S

Jan. 27

Isel

Lien

Dobbiaco
(Toblach)

Feb. 7–8   Roe
Kronplatz   deer   Roe
ski area   deer

          Roe   4
          deer   February 4–6
                         Sextner
Feb. 9–14   ski area
Alta Badia
ski area

Roe
deer   Piave

ANGLE
OF VIEW

Feb. 15   DOLOMITI BELLUNESI
Falcade ski area   NATIONAL PARK

Mt. Agner
2,872m

          Belluno

I T A L

Trento   A27

          Asiago

A22

Mar. 26,
2012   March 3   A31

LESSINIA
REGIONAL PARK   Treviso

Dead
horse   Piave

Lake   Sheep
Garda   5   Vicenza

          Goat   A4   Venice

Verona   Padova

Adige   GULF OF

          Venetian Lagoon   V E N I C E

Dispersal Mode

Between ten months and two years of age, wolves leave their maternal pack and strike out on their own. What's remarkable about Slavc's dispersal is not just the distance he covered but also his determination. He crossed major rivers, worked his way out of a high valley in the depths of winter (see below), and ran the gauntlet of Verona's suburbs. Then the dispersal switch flicked off, and the journey was over as quickly as it began.

A Slavc Enters the Col
With its high numbers of red deer and chamois, the area surrounding Col di Prá might have seemed promising. Slavc secures a kill on arrival.

B Lost in the Dolomites
Slavc seems to be seeking a way out. After a failed attempt to cross a mountain to the east, he takes an uncharacteristically long rest at high altitude.

C Back for the Kill
Slavc returns to feed on what's left of his only kill in five days. He didn't give up though, making a second kill the following night.

D Slavc Finds a Way
Ten days after entering the Col, Slavc makes his way south in the direction of Fiera di Primiero and Verona beyond.

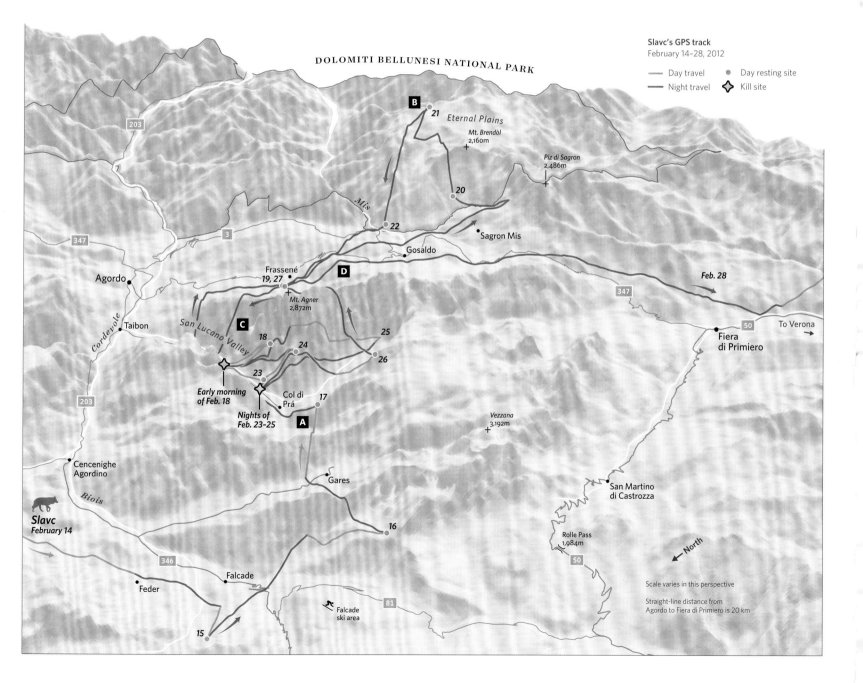

Slavc's GPS track
February 14–28, 2012

— Day travel   ● Day resting site
— Night travel   ✦ Kill site

DOLOMITI BELLUNESI NATIONAL PARK

Eternal Plains

Mt. Brendòl
2,160m

Piz di Sagron
2,486m

Mis

Sagron Mis

Gosaldo

Frassené
19, 27

Agordo

Cordevole

Taibon

San Lucano Valley

Mt. Agner
2,872m

Feb. 28

To Verona

Fiera di Primiero

Early morning
of Feb. 18

Col di Prá

Nights of
Feb. 23–25

Vezzana
3,192m

Cencenighe
Agordino

Biois

Slavc
February 14

Gares

San Martino
di Castrozza

Rolle Pass
1,984m

North

Feder

Falcade

Falcade
ski area

Scale varies in this perspective

Straight-line distance from
Agordo to Fiera di Primiero is 20 km

The Wolf
Who Traversed the Alps

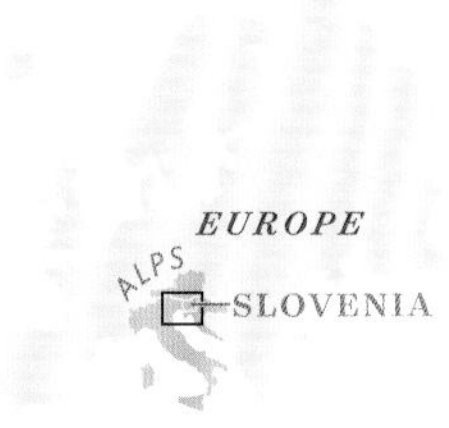

EUROPE
ALPS
SLOVENIA

WHEN HUBERT POTOČNIK and his colleagues collared a wolf near Trieste, Italy, in July 2011, they expected to see the movements of a young male staking out territory. And that's what they saw for the first six months. Then, on December 19, something changed. The wolf, whom the team had named Slavc, had suddenly moved from his home range to the village of Vipava, 25 kilometers north. When Potočnik zoomed in and saw Slavc's latest GPS point in a back garden, his heart sank. "I called the wildlife manager," he recalls, "and said, 'Probably, Slavc is killed.'"

Fortunately, this was a false alarm. The reality was far more exciting. Slavc had switched into dispersal mode. For the next 98 days, Potočnik followed his every move—from Ljubljana to Verona by way of Austria, a country where shooting stray dogs is permitted. A wolf with a GPS collar may not look so different. For Potočnik, this was a real concern. "We were scared that some hunter would shoot him, so we were wondering how to inform people." He assembled a group of wildlife experts and park wardens, who watched over Slavc when he walked through their neck of the woods. They annotated his tracks, investigated his kills, and got local media to raise awareness and keep hunters at bay.

Four months and 1,000 kilometers later, Slavc had not only linked two wolf populations (see inset on foldout), but he had also enchanted the public and reminded them that throughout Europe, large carnivores once roamed.

   SOURCES: HUBERT POTOČNIK, UNIVERSITY OF LJUBLJANA; SRTM; OSM; NE; GADM

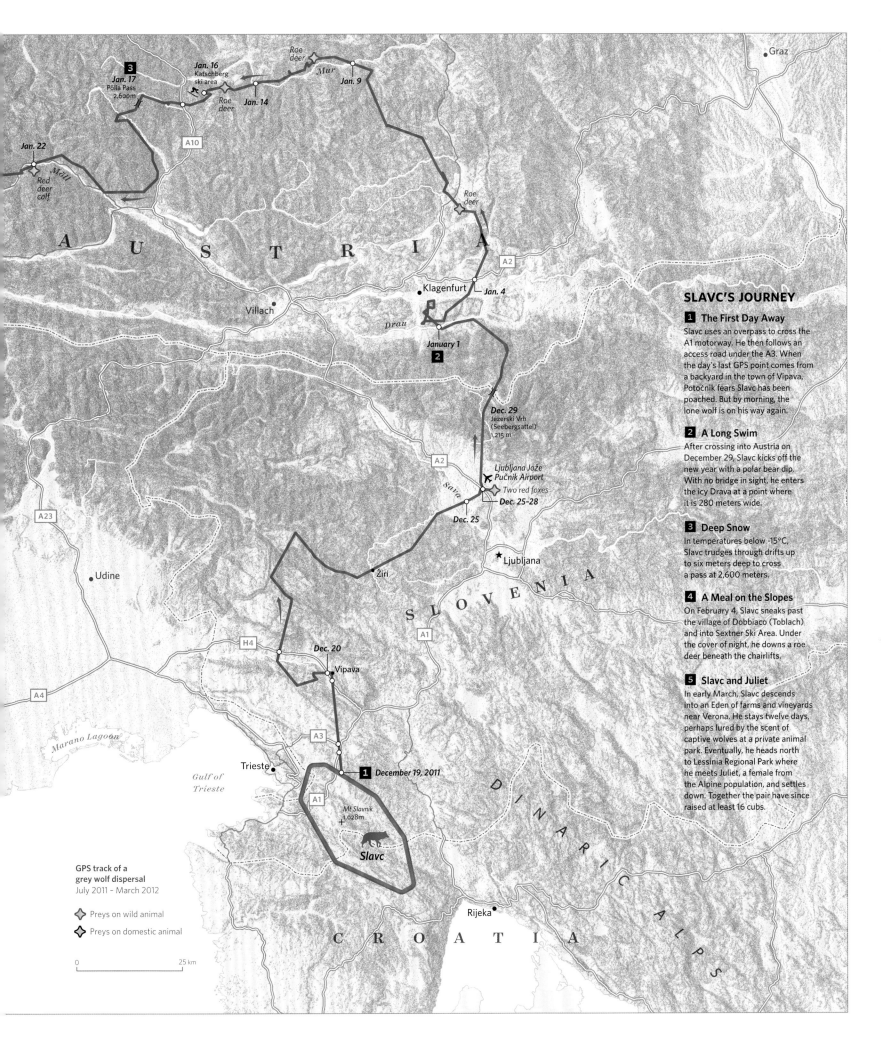

Graz

3 Jan. 17 Pölla Pass 2,600m

Jan. 16 Katschberg ski area

Roe deer

Mur

Jan. 9

Jan. 14

Roe deer

Jan. 22

Möll

Red deer calf

A10

A U S T R I A

Roe deer

Villach

A2

Klagenfurt

Jan. 4

Drau

SLAVC'S JOURNEY

1 The First Day Away

Slavc uses an overpass to cross the A1 motorway. He then follows an access road under the A3. When the day's last GPS point comes from a backyard in the town of Vipava, Potočnik fears Slavc has been poached. But by morning, the lone wolf is on his way again.

2 A Long Swim

After crossing into Austria on December 29, Slavc kicks off the new year with a polar bear dip. With no bridge in sight, he enters the icy Drava at a point where it is 280 meters wide.

3 Deep Snow

In temperatures below -15°C, Slavc trudges through drifts up to six meters deep to cross a pass at 2,600 meters.

4 A Meal on the Slopes

On February 4, Slavc sneaks past the village of Dobbiaco (Toblach) and into Sextner Ski Area. Under the cover of night, he downs a roe deer beneath the chairlifts.

5 Slavc and Juliet

In early March, Slavc descends into an Eden of farms and vineyards near Verona. He stays twelve days, perhaps lured by the scent of captive wolves at a private animal park. Eventually, he heads north to Lessinia Regional Park where he meets Juliet, a female from the Alpine population, and settles down. Together the pair have since raised at least 16 cubs.

January 1

2

Dec. 29 Jezerski Vrh (Seebergsattel) 1,215 m

A2

Sava

Ljubljana Jože Pučnik Airport

Two red foxes
Dec. 25-28

Dec. 25

Žiri

★ Ljubljana

S L O V E N I A

A1

A23

A4

Udine

H4

Dec. 20

Vipava

A3

Trieste

Gulf of Trieste

Marano Lagoon

1 December 19, 2011

A1

Mt Slavnik +1,028m

Slavc

D I N A R I C   A L P S

Rijeka

C R O A T I A

GPS track of a grey wolf dispersal
July 2011 – March 2012

◆ Preys on wild animal

◇ Preys on domestic animal

0 ————— 25 km

The Elk of Greater Yellowstone

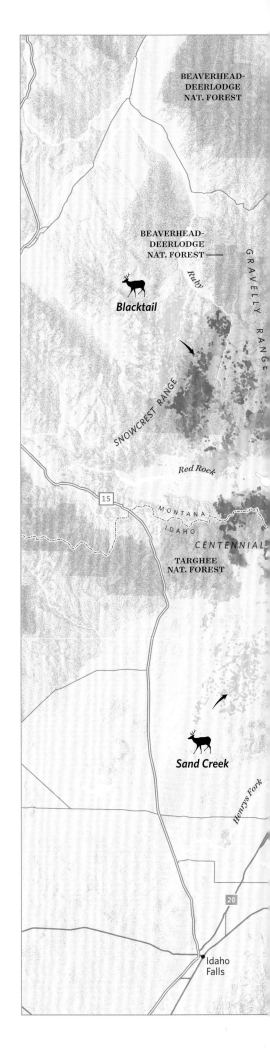

To the right we show the annual summer migration of nine elk herds. Though there's debate as to the exact number of distinct herds, ecologist Arthur Middleton says, "In a way, it's the same mega-herd."

FOUR MILLION PEOPLE visit Yellowstone National Park each year. They come to see erupting geysers, bubbling mud, and sulfurous springs, but many may leave unaware of another natural wonder happening before their eyes.

Each May, as rising temperatures dry the land at lower elevations, 25,000 elk begin to move. With newborn calves in tow, they brave rushing rivers and snow-filled passes to reach plateaus where summer rain keeps the grass thick and green. "The summer elk migration is the heartbeat of greater Yellowstone," says Arthur Middleton, an ecologist at University of California, Berkeley. "It's what feeds other species and the local economies." In Montana alone, elk hunters spent $138 million in 2014. They're not the only ones investing in the region. Beyond the national park and national forest boundaries, private landowners are leasing away land at astonishing rates. Where the herds once found forage, they are now finding vacation homes. Without clear paths to grass in summer and out of deep snow in winter, elk will suffer. In turn, so will predators that eat them, as well as the animals they'll eat instead.

For people to grasp the geographic extent of this ecosystem, Middleton needed them to see the migrations. That's easier said than done. "You can park at Old Faithful," he says, "but not

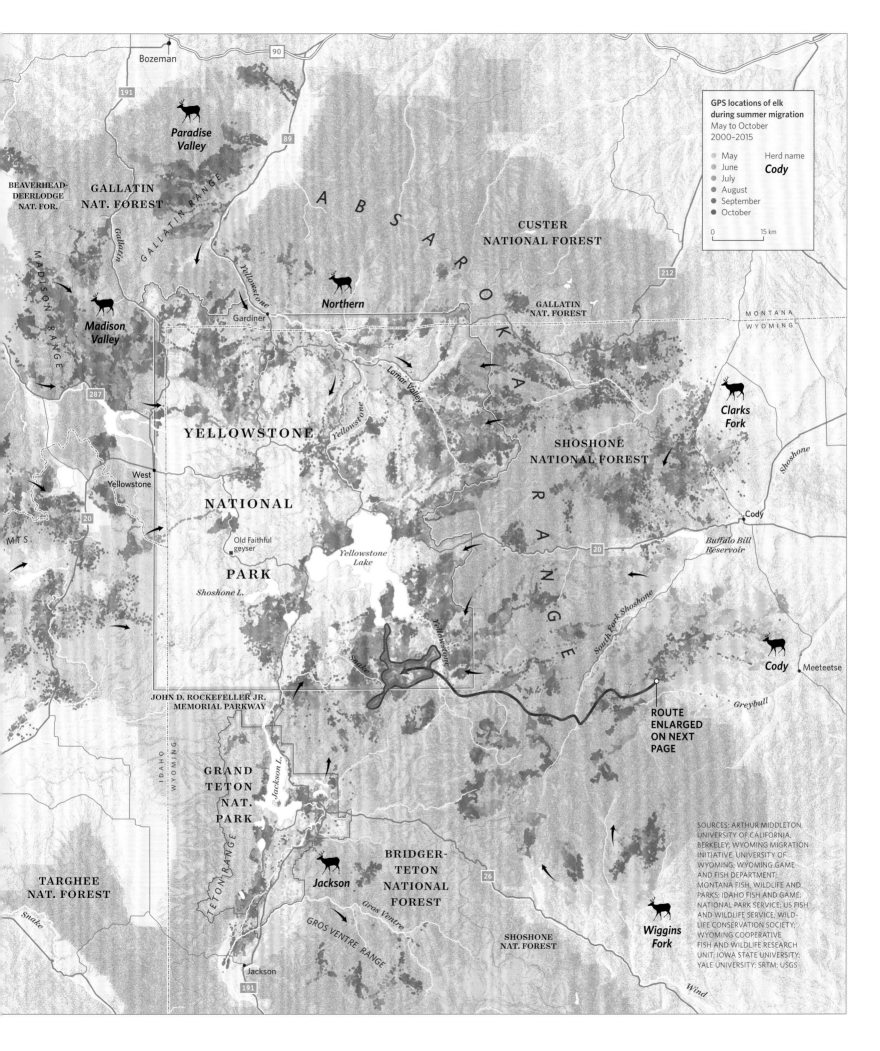

Bozeman

90

191

89

Paradise
Valley

GALLATIN RANGE

BEAVERHEAD-
DEERLODGE
NAT. FOR.

GALLATIN
NAT. FOREST

A B S A R O K A

CUSTER
NATIONAL FOREST

212

MADISON RANGE

Gallatin

Yellowstone

MONTANA
WYOMING

Madison
Valley

Northern

Gardiner

GALLATIN
NAT. FOREST

287

Lamar Valley

Clarks
Fork

Shoshone

YELLOWSTONE

Yellowstone

SHOSHONE
NATIONAL FOREST

West
Yellowstone

NATIONAL

R A N G E

Cody

M T S.

20

20

Old Faithful
geyser

Yellowstone
Lake

PARK

Buffalo Bill
Reservoir

Shoshone L.

South Fork Shoshone

Cody   Meeteetse

Yellowstone

Greybull

Snake

ROUTE
ENLARGED
ON NEXT
PAGE

JOHN D. ROCKEFELLER JR.
MEMORIAL PARKWAY

IDAHO
WYOMING

GRAND
TETON
NAT.
PARK

Jackson L.

TETON RANGE

BRIDGER-
TETON
NATIONAL
FOREST

26

TARGHEE
NAT. FOREST

Jackson

Snake

Gros Ventre

GROS VENTRE RANGE

SHOSHONE
NAT. FOREST

Wiggins
Fork

Jackson

191

Wind

**GPS locations of elk
during summer migration**
May to October
2000–2015

- May
- June
- July
- August
- September
- October

Herd name
Cody

0 ————— 15 km

SOURCES: ARTHUR MIDDLETON,
UNIVERSITY OF CALIFORNIA,
BERKELEY; WYOMING MIGRATION
INITIATIVE, UNIVERSITY OF
WYOMING; WYOMING GAME
AND FISH DEPARTMENT;
MONTANA FISH, WILDLIFE AND
PARKS; IDAHO FISH AND GAME;
NATIONAL PARK SERVICE; US FISH
AND WILDLIFE SERVICE; WILD-
LIFE CONSERVATION SOCIETY;
WYOMING COOPERATIVE
FISH AND WILDLIFE RESEARCH
UNIT; IOWA STATE UNIVERSITY;
YALE UNIVERSITY; SRTM; USGS

at these wildlife spectacles." Mapping big data offered a solution.

In the past two decades, 28 separate agencies have been using GPS collars to track elk around Yellowstone. Middleton, who came to Wyoming in 2007 for a tracking study of his own on elk-wolf interactions, discovered that few were sharing data and that some herds had never been tracked at all. He decided to bring everyone together to create an ecosystem-scale portrait. On these pages, we share the result of their collaboration.

For the first time, we can see how the lifeblood of the world's first national park also depends on protecting land *outside* its borders. And once you see that—once you see that twice a year elk are hoofing across 23 million acres of state, private, tribal, and federal boundaries on trails that predate them all—it's hard not to question our reasons for rending wilderness into so many scraps, each with its own agenda and regulations. Elk use the land as one big, interconnected system. Perhaps we might learn to do the same.

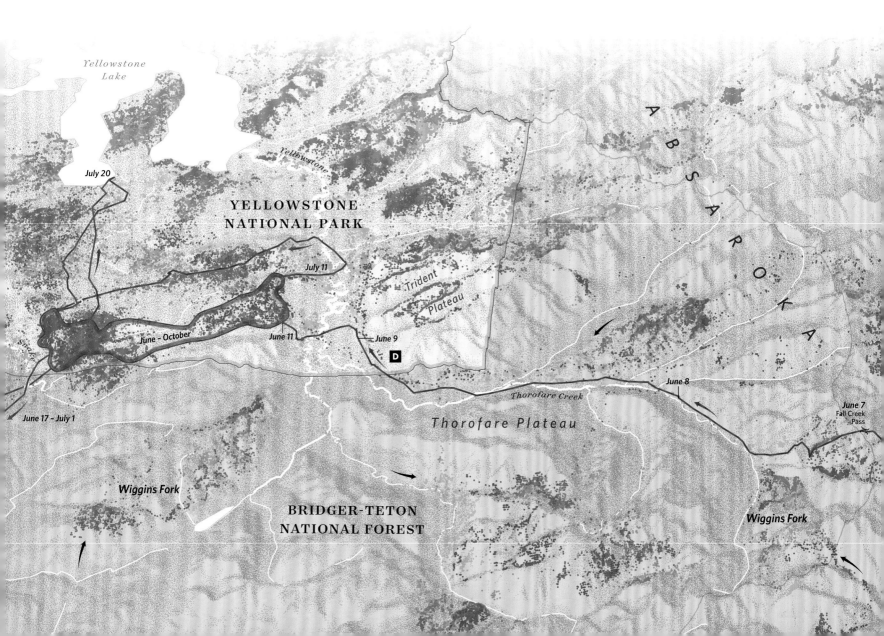

The Hard Way

When researchers first started tracking elk in 2000, GPS collars recorded one location per day. That was sufficient for an ecosystem-scale view. Now their collars sample once every thirty seconds, which gives the precision they need to follow movements of a single elk. Of all the routes elk take into Yellowstone, the one used by this member of the Cody herd may be the hardest.

A Winter Range

Starting in the high plains south of Cody, Wyoming, on May 1, an adult female elk—#35342—began an 80-kilometer trek from her winter feeding grounds east of Carter Mountain to her summer range in Yellowstone National Park.

B Shoshone National Forest

After ascending to 3,000 meters, she stopped for two weeks on May 4. She stopped again on Boulder Ridge, most likely to give birth and wait for her newborn calf to get its legs. Calving time peaks around June 1.

C Needle Mountain

On June 6, mother and calf descended 1,500 meters, forded the South Fork Shoshone, and climbed to Fall Creek Pass in one 18-hour slog. Calves learn these routes from their mothers, often during their first weeks of life.

D Summer Range

Once through the pass, #35342 followed Thorofare Creek for two days, entering Yellowstone National Park at 10 p.m. on June 8. She remained here until October, when deep snow prompted the herd to retrace its steps.

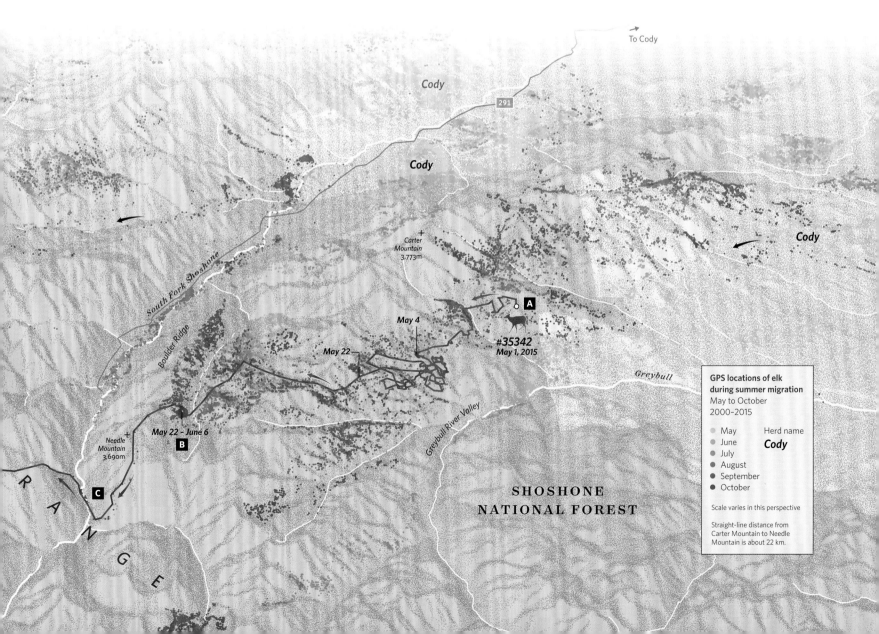

To Cody

Cody

291

Cody

Cody

Carter Mountain 3,773m

South Fork Shoshone

A

#35342 May 1, 2015

May 4

May 22

Boulder Ridge

Greybull

Greybull River Valley

May 22 – June 6

B

Needle Mountain 3,690m

C

R A N G E

SHOSHONE NATIONAL FOREST

GPS locations of elk during summer migration
May to October
2000–2015

- May
- June
- July
- August
- September
- October

Herd name
Cody

Scale varies in this perspective

Straight-line distance from Carter Mountain to Needle Mountain is about 22 km.

The Pheasants Who Walk the Himalayas

SEARCH FOR "TRAGOPAN MATING DANCE" on YouTube and you'll see why these horned pheasants were named, in part, after Pan, the promiscuous Greek god of the wild. When aroused, the male raises his wings and begins shaking violently. A pair of blue fleshy horns pop from his bobbing head. He emits angry clacks. A wide blue bib unfurls from his red neck like a ceremonial banner. This frenzy of bird bravado intensifies until he finally rears up and puffs out his chest. At that point, he lowers, deflates his horns, retracts his bib, and goes back to pecking the ground as if nothing ever happened.

"I am afraid anything I can say will quite fail to give an adequate idea of the extraordinary aspect of the bird whilst this display is at its height," wrote tragopan owner C. Barnby Smith in the April 1912 edition of *The Avicultural Magazine.* "Anyone coming suddenly upon the spectacle," he continued, "would scarcely believe they were looking at a bird, it is so demoniacal." A century later, GPS tracking in Bhutan has revealed a new set of inexplicable behaviors.

Satyr tragopans perform their dances each spring in high valleys of the Himalayas. Come September, many of these flightless birds begin walking to lower elevations for the winter, much like Yellowstone's elk (see previous pages).

But after analyzing GPS data from thirty birds over a three-year period, researchers found the migrations weren't so straightforward. "Some go up, some go down," says Martin Wikelski, one of the study's co-authors. Some don't migrate at all. One even switched from being a migrant one year to a resident the next.

For species living at altitude, the great worry has been that climate change will force them into a corner. Warming temperatures will drive animals farther uphill until there is no more hill left to climb. In these data, Wikelski sees hope. "Everybody claimed that these shifts happen and that species drop out. They should study animals on an individual level." If tragopans can survive a Himalayan winter by going lower *or* higher, then clearly they're even stranger than we thought.

SOURCE: MARTIN WIKELSKI, MAX PLANCK INSTITUTE FOR ORNITHOLOGY; UGYEN WANGCHUCK INSTITUTE FOR CONSERVATION AND ENVIRONMENT; SRTM; OSM; WDPA

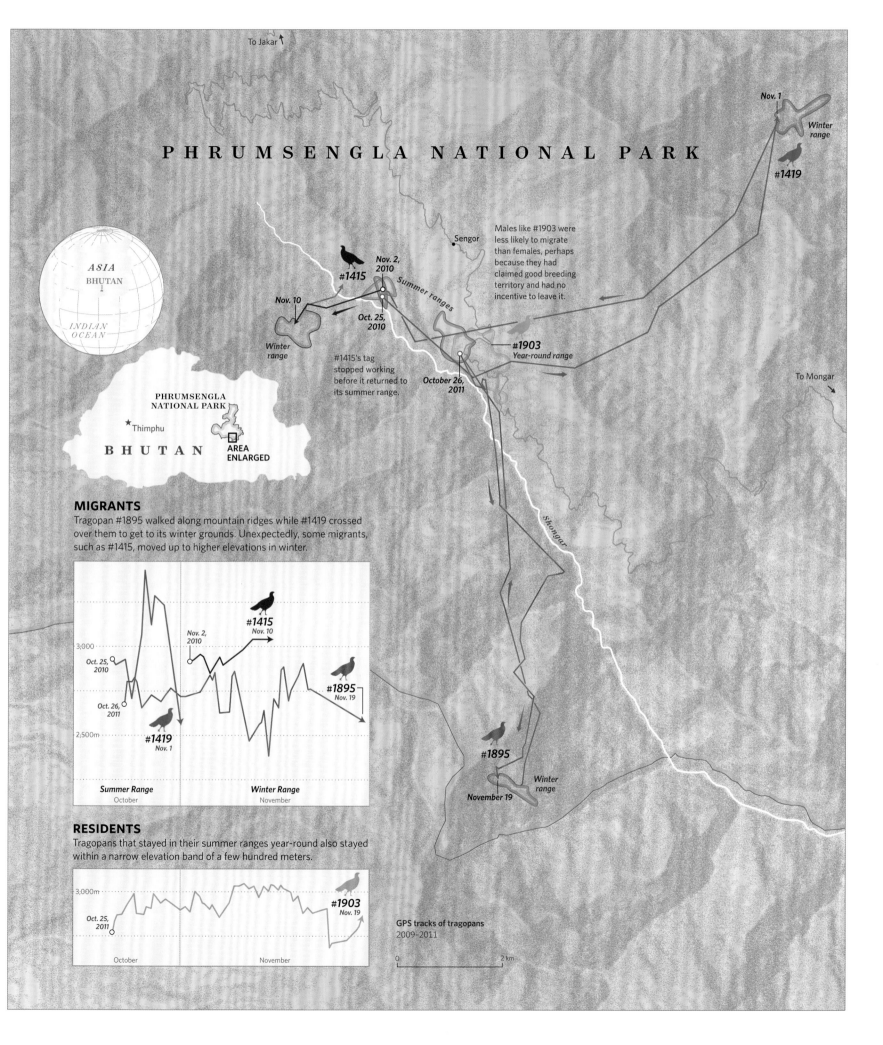

PHRUMSENGLA NATIONAL PARK

ASIA
BHUTAN

INDIAN
OCEAN

PHRUMSENGLA
NATIONAL PARK

★ Thimphu

B H U T A N

AREA
ENLARGED

To Jakar ↑

Sengor

Males like #1903 were
less likely to migrate
than females, perhaps
because they had
claimed good breeding
territory and had no
incentive to leave it.

Nov. 1

Winter
range

#1419

Nov. 2,
2010

#1415

Summer ranges

Nov. 10

Oct. 25,
2010

Winter
range

#1415's tag
stopped working
before it returned to
its summer range.

October 26,
2011

#1903
Year-round range

To Mongar →

Shongar

#1895

Winter
range

November 19

MIGRANTS

Tragopan #1895 walked along mountain ridges while #1419 crossed
over them to get to its winter grounds. Unexpectedly, some migrants,
such as #1415, moved up to higher elevations in winter.

Nov. 2,
2010

#1415
Nov. 10

3,000

Oct. 25,
2010

Oct. 26,
2011

#1895
Nov. 19

2,500m

#1419
Nov. 1

Summer Range
October

Winter Range
November

RESIDENTS

Tragopans that stayed in their summer ranges year-round also stayed
within a narrow elevation band of a few hundred meters.

3,000m

Oct. 25,
2011

#1903
Nov. 19

October

November

GPS tracks of tragopans
2009–2011

0   2 km

The Pythons in the Everglades

BURMESE PYTHONS EVOLVED in southern Asia. When the large constrictors began appearing in southern Florida and local bobcats, raccoons, and other mammals started disappearing, residents and ecologists were rightfully alarmed.

In January 2016, a thousand people came to the Everglades for the fourth annual Python Challenge. For cash prizes up to $5,000, they tried to bag as many pythons as possible in a month. Based on where pythons have been seen in Florida and knowledge of detection rates for other snakes, experts estimate at least tens of thousands of pythons now live in the state. Python Challenge participants caught 106.

Shannon Pittman, a postdoctoral fellow at Davidson College, took a different approach. As a specialist in invasive species, she was curious as to how far the pythons might be willing to spread, so she implanted radio tags in twelve snakes in August 2006. She released six where she tagged them (blue, on the map) and the rest at two locations more than 20 kilometers away (orange and purple). Over the next three to ten months, all six translocated snakes slithered back whence they came, most within five kilometers of their capture locations; they also moved faster and straighter than the control snakes, who had no urgency to get anywhere in particular.

How many of us could navigate so precisely through unfamiliar terrain, let alone the tangles of a Floridian swamp? Perhaps we shouldn't be so quick to dismiss reptilian brains. The pythons clearly had some form of internal map and compass. A map sense helps you determine your position in relation to where you want to go; the compass sense keeps you on that heading until you get there. Pigeons and sea turtles have such senses. What directs them is one of the great mysteries of animal migration. It could be smell, stars, polarizing light, magnetic fields, or some combination of these. Whatever the method, the ability to avoid getting lost empowers animals to take risks and settle in new areas, regardless of what the native species might think.

NORTH AMERICA
U.S.
Miami

Marquesas
Keys

Key West

FLORIDA

BIG CYPRESS
NATIONAL
PRESERVE

EVERGLADES
NATIONAL PARK

Ground
covered
before
first data
point

Release
site

Release
site

9336

5

MIAMI

Miami International
Airport

Miami Beach

Tamiami

Coral Gables

BISCAYNE
BAY

BISCAYNE
NATIONAL
PARK

Homestead

Key Largo

FLORIDA BAY

CAPE SABLE

FLORIDA KEYS

Marathon

**Radio tracks
of Burmese pythons**
August 2006 –
September 2007

Translocated snakes

◇ Captured
○ Released
◖◗ Recaptured

Control snakes

✦ Captured and released
   in the same location

0 —————————— 15 km

SOURCE: SHANNON PITTMAN,
DAVIDSON COLLEGE; GLCF; GSHHG; USGS

The Ants That Change Jobs

HOW DO YOU TRACK AN INDIVIDUAL ANT, let alone a full colony? Tiny transmitters exist, but they aren't precise enough to show how ants interact, and that's precisely what Danielle Mersch wanted to observe. Instead, she and her team at the University of Lausanne engineered a sort of reality show for insects. She glued tiny barcodes to the backs of carpenter ants and placed them inside climate-controlled boxes no larger than this page. Then, after filming them at two frames per second for forty days, she used software to reconstruct the movements of their barcodes.

From more than two billion data points, Mersch discovered three patterns of behavior in the artificial nest. Some ants stayed close to the queen and her brood. She called them "nurses" (yellow). Others—dubbed "cleaners" (red)—roamed the nest, often visiting a garbage pile. Lastly, there were "foragers" (blue), who left the nest to gather food.

These "working groups" weren't immutable. Mersch watched individuals rise through ant society over the course of their short lives. Young ants started out as nurses before becoming cleaners and, finally, foragers in old age. In the absence of central command, they used age and spatial segregation to delegate tasks.

In human society, we may exert more choice in the matter, but for many of us, first jobs may likewise include babysitting or chores before we graduate to careers that take us away from home and ultimately put food on the table.

Some companies already use ant-inspired software to cut the cost of transporting their products. Ants need to get to food as efficiently as possible; delivery drivers need to get to customers. It's the classic traveling salesman problem. Rather than try to figure it out with some centralized plan, ant colonies simply send out thousands of "salesmen." Faster routes are reinforced by use until they become *the* route. Computer models can now replicate this behavior to optimize delivery routes. As autonomous vehicles join our ranks, it's not a stretch to imagine a day when those machines, like ants, will manage themselves.

SOURCE: DANIELLE MERSCH, UNIVERSITY OF LAUSANNE

Garbage pile

CLEANERS

— Edge of artificial nest

NURSES

Brood

FORAGERS

Nest entrance

To track how information flows from ant to ant, Mersch selected 27 individuals from each colony to be "information carriers." Whenever two were close enough for their antennae to touch, she assumed a hypothetical message had been passed on.

News traveled fast. 89% of the colony got word within an hour. Because nurses and foragers work close together, they spread information among themselves quickly. Cleaners, who are somewhat more segregated, took longer to learn the news.

Spatial distribution of a carpenter ant colony
40 days

A pixel's color indicates the working group that spent the most time in that area.

▪ Nurses
▪ Cleaners
▪ Foragers

0   20 mm

Consider the subtleness of the sea; how its most dreaded creatures glide under water, unapparent for the most part, and treacherously hidden beneath the loveliest tints of azure.

—HERMAN MELVILLE

The Whales We Watch on Facebook

by James Cheshire

AS A TEENAGER, I was lucky enough to visit Iceland with my school. The highlight was a short flight to the Westman Islands off its south coast. On Heimaey, the largest island, I remember climbing Eldfell—its rocks still warm from the 1973 eruption—and standing in awe of the view from the summit: an icefield on the mainland to the north and a string of steep-sided islands to the south. It was enough to inspire me to study geography at university. I always hoped to return one day.

Thirteen years later, I was back enjoying the same view. This time my eyes were not drawn to the ice or the islands but the ocean in between. I had come to join Filipa Samarra from the Marine Research Institute in Reykjavík and her team on a search for the killer whales who spend summers

here, feeding on spawning herring. I found out about Samarra's research via her team's Facebook page, Icelandic Orcas, where they share their fieldwork and photos with thousands.

On my first morning, a message came through from Samarra: her lookouts had spotted whales off Stórhöfði, the southernmost point on the island. We were all to meet on the quayside at 9:30 a.m. Before long, we were motoring out of the harbor and into the swell. Skippering the *Marvin* was Volker Deecke (University of Cumbria), an expert in whale acoustics. "You don't get seasick do you?" he asked, as he dropped a hydrophone over the side of the boat. I steadied myself enough to answer "no" before he mused, "Well, there's a ship and a sea that gets everyone." That day the North

ICELAND

★Reykjavík

◇AREA
ENLARGED

• Vestmannaeyjar
+
Heimaey *Eldfell*
200m

— *Stórhöfði*

*ATLANTIC
OCEAN*

WESTMAN ISLANDS

0 ____ 1 km

Atlantic was calm. Deecke shut off the motor, and the hydrophone spluttered to life with the clicks and whistles of killer whales. After years of listening, Deecke knew what they meant: "They're feeding," he said, "over to the northwest!" There was a commotion on the horizon. Diving seabirds drew our eyes and cameras to a set of black fins rising and falling in the waves.

We maneuvered alongside them and started taking pictures. Astrid M. van Ginneken (Orca Survey) was in charge of cataloging every whale we saw. She is a veteran photographer and it showed. Unlike my scattergun approach, each click of her shutter was considered. Trained in the days of film when each frame cost money and time, she said, "The more pictures taken on the water, the more work there is back on shore." Getting a useable shot is harder than it sounds.

It's hard to believe now, but the earliest whale-tracking devices were essentially giant, barbed drawing pins, each engraved with a unique number and address.

The speed of the whales, their frequent dives, and their changes of direction made it tricky to keep track of them. To me, the morning passed in a blur of black fins, white spray, and blue sea, which is pretty much how killer whales looked to researchers prior to 1970.

Back then, whales were counted as they swam past boats or lookout stations on shore. Because they weren't counted as individuals, population numbers were fuzzy. It was not until the 1970s that Michael Bigg and his colleagues at the Canadian Department of Fisheries and Oceans brought population figures into focus along the Pacific coast of North America. They realized you could identify individual killer whales by looking at details on their dorsal fins and saddle patches. For example, IS086 has a chunk missing from her fin, while IS045 has a saddle patch that tapers into a long vapor trail (see p. 89).

Photos of individual whales could be checked against catalogs of other sightings to map a whale's movements and social interactions over time. This revealed two things: 1) not all killer whales migrate and 2) not all killer whales eat the same prey. In the North Pacific, for example, there are "residents" who stick to the waters off British Columbia and eat fish, and there are "transients" who roam between California and Alaska in search of whales and seals. The two groups don't interact and show clear genetic differences; some have suggested they're separate species. In Iceland, Samarra's team was using photo-identification to investigate the extent to which these migratory and dietary differences exist in North Atlantic whales.

A CENTURY AGO, researchers were not aiming cameras at the whales they were trying to study. They were shooting harpoons. It's hard to believe now, but the earliest whale-tracking devices were essentially giant, barbed thumbtacks, each engraved with a unique number and address. In return for cash, whalers would post these back to the researchers along with approximate details

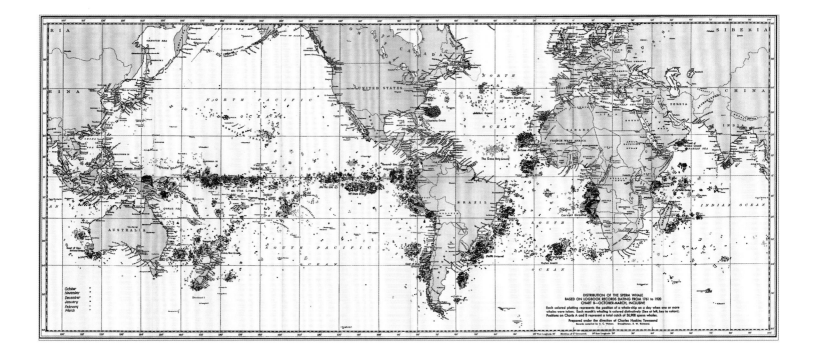

DISTRIBUTION OF THE SPERM WHALE
BASED ON LOGBOOK RECORDS DATING FROM 1761 to 1920
CHART B—OCTOBER-MARCH, INCLUSIVE

of where and when they killed the whales. While a few returns demonstrated the great distances whales could travel, the intensity of commercial whaling at the time meant many whales were killed within days of tagging. And unlike bird-banding rings, which can be identified many times in different locations, the harpoons provided only two data points: where they struck live whales and where they were extracted from dead ones.

Whalers generated a larger but no less lethal dataset in the logbooks they kept. After leafing through a number of them on the shelves of the New Bedford Public Library in Massachusetts in 1931, Charles Townsend, then director of the New York Aquarium, surmised that by mapping "the positions where large numbers of whales had been taken, much could be learned of their distribution and something of their migrations."

Over the next few years, Townsend set about sourcing as many logbooks as he could. Traveling along the coast of New England to whaling towns straight from the pages of *Moby Dick*—Nantucket, Salem, Stonington—he acquired dozens from libraries and historical societies, even personal collections. In total, Townsend trawled through records from more than 1,600 voyages by 744 ships between 1761 and 1920. He enlisted R. W. Richmond, a draftsman in New York, to draw circles at the locations of all 53,877 kills. The circles, colored by month of kill, required four maps: two for sperm whales (36,908); one for right whales (8,415); and one for both humpbacks (2,883) and bowheads (5,114). On the following pages, we have merged them into a single map.

This is one of the four original maps from Charles Townsend's 1935 report. Entitled "Distribution of the Sperm Whale," it depicts 36,908 kills between October and March as detailed by North American whaling logbooks.

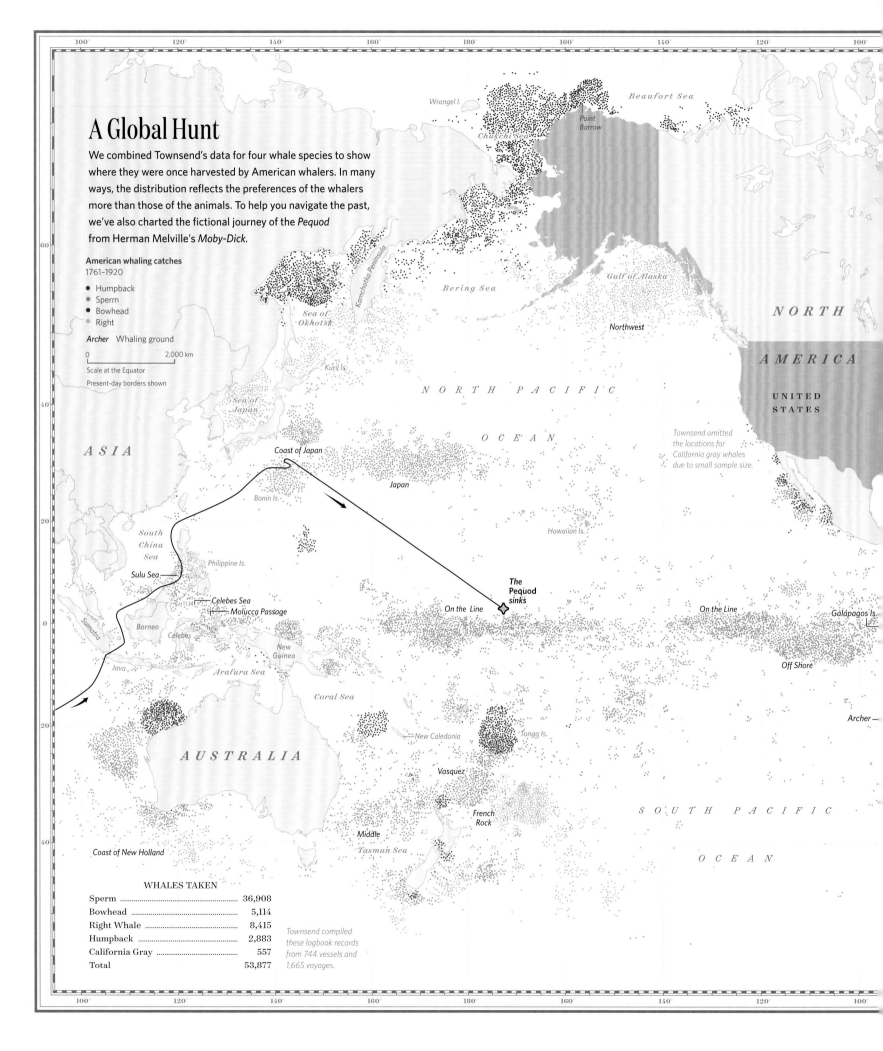

A Global Hunt

We combined Townsend's data for four whale species to show where they were once harvested by American whalers. In many ways, the distribution reflects the preferences of the whalers more than those of the animals. To help you navigate the past, we've also charted the fictional journey of the *Pequod* from Herman Melville's *Moby-Dick*.

American whaling catches
1761–1920

- Humpback
- Sperm
- Bowhead
- Right

Archer Whaling ground

0 ————————— 2,000 km

Scale at the Equator

Present-day borders shown

Beaufort Sea

Wrangel I.

Chukchi Sea

Point
Barrow

Kamchatka Peninsula

Gulf of Alaska

Bering Sea

NORTH

Northwest

AMERICA

UNITED
STATES

*Sea of
Okhotsk*

Kuril Is.

*Sea of
Japan*

NORTH PACIFIC

OCEAN

ASIA

Coast of Japan

Bonin Is.

Japan

Townsend omitted
the locations for
California gray whales
due to small sample size.

Hawaiian Is.

South
China
Sea

Philippine Is.

Sulu Sea

The
Pequod
sinks

On the Line

On the Line

Galápagos Is.

Celebes Sea

Molucca Passage

Borneo

Sumatra

Celebes

On the Line

Off Shore

*New
Guinea*

Java

Arafura Sea

Coral Sea

Archer

AUSTRALIA

New Caledonia

Tonga Is.

Vasquez

SOUTH PACIFIC

*French
Rock*

Middle

OCEAN

Tasman Sea

Coast of New Holland

WHALES TAKEN

Sperm	36,908
Bowhead	5,114
Right Whale	8,415
Humpback	2,883
California Gray	557
Total	53,877

*Townsend compiled
these logbook records
from 744 vessels and
1,665 voyages.*

80°   60°   40°   20°   0°   20°   40°   60°   80°

ARCTIC   OCEAN

GREENLAND

Baffin Island

Bowhead

Townsend omitted the
locations for North Atlantic
right whales and bowhead
whales due to small sample size.

N   O   R   T   H

British Isles

A   T   L   A   N   T   I   C

Commodore
Morris

EUROPE

The Shoals

O   C   E   A   N

ASIA

New Bedford

Nantucket

Azores

Voyage of the Pequod

Western
Islands

Mediterranean Sea

Steen

Southern

Charleston   Western

St. Antonio

Coast of Arabia

Caribbean Sea

Cape
Verde Is.

Arabian Sea

The Twelve Forty

A   F   R   I   C   A

•Panama Bay

Cornell

EQUATOR

Zanzibar   Seychelles

S   O   U   T   H

Mahe Banks

I   N   D   I   A   N

St. Helena   Carroll

A   M   E   R   I   C   A

Coast of
Africa

Collao

Woolwich
Bay

O   C   E   A   N

Coast of Brazil

Pigeon

Madagascar

Coast of Chile

S   O   U   T   H

Tristan

Delagoa.
Bay

Platte

A   T   L   A   N   T   I   C

Cape of Good Hope

Brazil
Banks

O   C   E   A   N

False Banks

Crozet

*Falkland Islands
(Islas Malvinas)*

Desolation

Cape Horn

80°   60°   40°   20° West   Meridian of 0° Greenwich   20° East   40°   60°   80°

These plots were the first to demonstrate the general movements and extents of whales, and thanks to the Wildlife Conservation Society of Canada's efforts to digitize them, they're still used by researchers to compare where the animals go, then and now.

By the 1950s, attempts to gather data from *live* whales were increasing, although—as it'll soon be clear—they still fell well short of modern ethical standards. Perhaps one of the best publicized at the time was Paul Dudley White's expedition to record a whale's heartbeat. When he was not performing his duties as President Eisenhower's cardiologist, White took a keen interest in how mammals' heart rates varied according to their size. A human's resting heart rate ranges from 60–100 beats per minute, though rates of 40 or slower have been recorded in athletes. White knew that hearts of bigger mammals beat more slowly. He was curious as to just how slowly they could go.

In 1953, White had been part of a team that recorded a heart rate of 12–20 beats per minute from a beluga whale in the Bering Sea. Their methods weren't pretty. To hold the animal still alongside the boat, they stuck a harpoon head into its side, all while the whale was "alternately diving, blowing and frantically trying to escape." In spite of the whale's distress, White concluded that "it is possible to obtain an electrocardiogram of a whale in its natural environment," and three years later, he led an expedition to the coast of Baja California in search of gray whales. The plan was "to place two electrodes beneath the tough black hide of an adult whale, penetrating its blubber layer but not enough to cause serious injury."

From these electrodes trailed two wires that attached to a sea sled carrying the electrocardiograph. Things didn't go as planned.

In White's record of the trip, published in *National Geographic*, he vividly recalls how, on their final attempt to attach the electrodes, "both harpoon guns cracked simultaneously. Lines flashed outward from the reels at the muzzles. The upright whale gave a massive shudder and fell away to one side in a white flash of water." The whale broke free from the wires immediately after being struck, which led White to admit that "our heartbeat-hunting weapons were not yet adequate for their job."

As time went on, the hard line of the fifties gave way to a more compassionate view of the natural world in the sixties and seventies. Perhaps the biggest catalyst for this shift, at least in respect to whales, was Roger Payne, founder of Ocean Alliance. In 1967, he began working with Scott McVay at Princeton University to analyze the sounds of humpbacks. The pair weren't seasoned cetologists. Payne had been researching how bats and owls used sound for echolocation, while McVay worked in administration. As relative outsiders, they heard with fresh ears what many at the time had overlooked: the whales were singing. Their underwater utterances weren't random but long, elaborate, rhythmic sequences. In 1971, they presented their findings in a legendary *Science* paper entitled, "Songs of Humpback Whales."

As Payne wrote in his book *Among Whales*, there was no technical reason why less invasive methods such as photo-identification could not have been adopted back in the 1920s. "Nobody used it, simply, I suspect, because of the mind-set of the times: the major body of valid research had always involved examining dead animals—that was automatically the approach scientists took. It seems never to have seriously occurred to anyone that if the whole thing were done benignly, it would also mean far more data per animal."

By 1979, *National Geographic* had shifted from reporting the harpooning exploits of Paul Dudley White to being one of Payne's biggest supporters in his quest to save the whales. The magazine commissioned the largest one-time pressing in the history of the recording industry: 10.5 million plastic discs of whale song for readers to enjoy while reading the accompanying article, "Humpbacks: Their Mysterious Songs."

TO FIND OUT JUST HOW FAR cetology has progressed since then, I paid a visit to Mark Johnson and René Swift at the University of St Andrews' Sea Mammal Research Unit (SMRU) in Scotland. Overlooking the North Sea, Johnson's office resembled an inventor's workshop. Electronics in various stages of completion covered every available surface. Downstairs, Swift sat at a desk surrounded by machinery and tanks of saltwater. Together, they've developed some of the most advanced marine tracking devices for researchers around the world. Johnson crams the latest technology into them; Swift then puts them through the ringer to ensure they can withstand the wind, water, and extreme pressure and temperature changes of life in the sea.

Johnson showed me a sensor about the size of a computer mouse. Known as DTAGS (short for digital sound recording tags), these get suction-cupped to whales for a couple of days before they detach and float to the surface for collection. Each has an on-board magnetometer and accelerometer to record the animal's every pitch and roll. What sets DTAGS apart from many marine tags is their ability also to record the clicks, buzzes, and whistles of sonar-generating toothed whales. In a process known as echolocation, these sounds bounce off nearby objects and surfaces and back to the whale, whose brain translates the echoes into a radar-like sense of its environment and possible prey. DTAGS can collect 64 gigabytes of data in a few hours. Since our human brains lack a whale's audio processing power, converting these enormous sound files into a format that we can understand has been one of the major challenges

"Originally we were using harpoons to attach things because we wanted to know where a resource was going. Now we deploy tags for conservation purposes."

for Johnson. A few years ago, he adapted a visualization form called an "echogram" (see p. 86) to represent how a whale sees with sound.

Having looked at hundreds of these, Johnson has become an expert in interpreting avoidance strategies for prey. "Imagine someone is gunning at you in a car. What should you do? How do you stay alive with the minimum amount of energy? You wait till the last moment and then jump to one side." For a fish, the last minute swim to the

Clicking

Buzzing →

Clicking

4 meters

Sonar beam

Echoes off fish

A

B

C

D

2

E

0

Echo strength

Strong

Weak

0   1 second   2   3   4   5

Hunting in the Deep

This is an echogram. It shows the intensity of sound returning to an echolocating Blainville's beaked whale. Wide columns represent infrequent clicks; narrow ones indicate a "buzz" or period of rapid clicking. Objects farthest from the whale appear at the top; time runs left to right. Dark, crisp areas indicate strong echoes off static obstacles, while more diffuse areas indicate echoes off moving objects, such as a fleeing fish. Here we show the whale homing in on one.

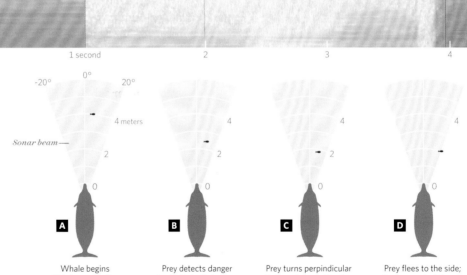

-20°   0°   20°

4 meters

Sonar beam —

2

0

A
Whale begins a high-frequency buzz to locate prey.

B
Prey detects danger and coils its body to prepare for a speedy escape.

C
Prey turns perpindicular to the whale and begins swimming away.

D
Prey flees to the side; as it moves out of the sonar beam, the echo weakens.

E
The whale gives up and reorients itself for a new chase.

side works because a whale's beam of sound is narrow. When a fish leaves the beam, from the whale's point of view, it might as well have disappeared (see D, left).

The development of new devices and techniques reveals how our appreciation of animals has changed. "Originally," Swift says, "we were using harpoons to attach things because we wanted to know where a resource was going. Now we deploy tags for conservation purposes." For example, DTAGS can also help researchers assess the impacts of ocean noise on whale behavior. It may not grab as many headlines as an oil spill, but the noise created by human activities can be just as disruptive—even fatal—for animals that map their world through sound. In 2014, Patrick Miller (SMRU) led an international team to observe the impacts of sound exposure on beaked whales, the species group most clearly linked to sonar-related strandings. They selected a group near the island of Jan Mayen in the Arctic Ocean and attached a DTAG to one of them. They then pumped noise into the ocean for 35 minutes. At a volume of 98 decibels underwater—about the sound of a passing submarine—the whale appeared to turn and move toward their ship. When they raised the volume to 130 decibels the whale changed its mind. It made a near 180° turn and performed the longest and deepest dive ever recorded for its species: 94 minutes, 2,339 meters.

The whale continued to behave differently until its tag fell off seven hours later. Not once in the period after the sound exposure did it emit a click or buzz, something it was doing frequently beforehand. The researchers also saw fewer whales in

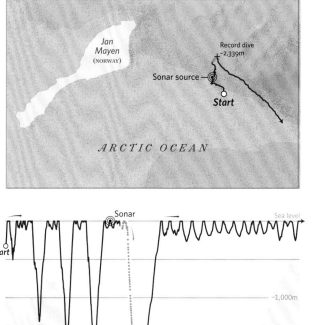

Northern bottlenose whale before, during, and after sonar exposure
June 25, 2013

—— Before and after
—— During

0   3 km

Prior to sound exposure, this northern bottlenose whale was performing deep and regular dives. Once the noise began, it stopped feeding and undertook the deepest dive ever recorded for the species. It then fled the area in a streak of short, shallow dives.

the area in the following days, an indication that the noise disturbed other whales, too.

It's not just echolocating whales that seem to be affected by sound. Northern right whales in Massachusetts Bay struggle to hear each other over the constant din of passing ships. This breakdown in communication forces many to forage alone and reduces their chances to breed. And in an experiment similar to Miller's, Jeremy Goldbogen (Cascadia Research Collective) found that even relatively low levels of military sonar caused a blue whale to stop feeding for 62 minutes. For the

SOURCES: MARK JOHNSON, SMRU; NATACHA AGUILAR DE SOTO, UNIVERSITY OF LA LAGUNA (ECHOGRAM); PATRICK MILLER, SMRU; GEBCO; GSHHG (SONAR)

world's biggest animal, even the slightest pause has a big calorific impact. Goldbogen estimated that the whale was consuming 19 kilograms of krill *per minute* prior to sound exposure. Losing an hour cost the whale over one metric ton of food—enough calories to power all its organs for a day.

BACK AT HER DESK ONSHORE, Filipa Samarra sat surrounded by cameras, wetsuits, and a few dozing researchers adjusting to the perpetual daylight of an Icelandic summer. She was reviewing van Ginneken's photos from the previous day. For a photo to be useful for identification, it needs to show the full dorsal fin plus the whale's saddle patch in sharp focus. Ideally, there will be a shot taken from both sides for each whale since the markings on each side are unique. Watching her edit down the images, it was clear that good photos require an experienced photographer and boat driver who can both anticipate where the whale will next surface. Perhaps to make me feel better about my blurry shots, Samarra said North Atlantic whales have a reputation for being tricky to photograph. "Some days they just don't want us near them."

Successful days can lead to surprising findings. For example, in July 2014, Samarra saw a male that seemed strangely familiar. She thought to herself, "I know this whale. I know I've seen these marks." After hunting through an old catalog of photos, she discovered who it was: IS038, last seen in 1994. Researchers presume a whale has died if years pass without a sighting, so Samarra did not take this resight for granted. "When you realize you've matched a whale that hadn't been

seen for *twenty* years, it's such an amazing feeling."

I was barely able to match the whales I'd photographed the previous day to the shortlist she had given me. I reassured myself that this is a complex task. Photos are taken at different distances and angles. The same fin can look sharp in one image and blunt in another. To add to the complexity, whales pick up marks at sea. For example, Samarra warned me that one of the males, IS011, always seems to get nicks with bits of skin hanging off.

Thanks to all these photographs, a more complete picture is beginning to emerge of the lives of North Atlantic whales. It seems their diets and social groupings are more complex than the resident and transient pods studied by the likes of Bigg in the North Pacific. Icelandic whales overwinter to the west of Iceland, near Grundarfjörður, where they feed on herring. Most then follow the herring to the Westman Islands in the summer. However, one group heads south to summer off Scotland, where the fish are *less* plentiful. Samarra had a hunch that these whales might be changing their diets to eat seals in Scottish waters. Because she cannot be in two places at once, she has turned to Facebook for help.

The whales come close to shore and close to ferry routes near the Orkney and Shetland Islands, so it's easy for the public to take photos and post them online. "I did not have Facebook," Samarra said. "Then a colleague told me he thought he saw the Icelandic whales on there. I decided I'd better join to find out." Sure enough, people were photographing the very whales Samarra had studied in Iceland the previous winter. This was

IS086

IS011

IS038

IS045

Photo-identification sites of killer whales
April 2011 – January 2015

◉ Winter
● Summer
→ Summer migration

0   200 km

Photo-identification helps researchers connect whale sightings in different seasons at different locations. In the summer, IS086's group has been seen in Scotland eating seals; her overwintering companions, IS011 and IS045, prefer to follow spawning herring to the Westman Islands.

confirmed by a shot of a female named Mousa (IS086) with a distinctive chunk missing from her dorsal fin. Curiously, the photos showed her and her group trying to wash seals off rocks along the Scottish coast. Were they, in fact, eating both fish and mammals?

On my third day in the Westman Islands, the *Marvin*'s engine failed. We drifted in the North Atlantic for a few hours before the second research boat could tow us ashore. The next day, that boat's engine failed too. Field days were lost and frustrations ran high, but the Icelandic Orcas Facebook page meant the science could continue. Samarra checked it regularly to see what was happening in Scotland while we were stuck ashore. Then around

midday on Monday, July 11th, she saw that the Fair Isle Bird Observatory and Guesthouse had posted photos of killer whales. It was Mousa's group—and they were devouring two gray seals. Samarra was overjoyed. "It's incredible! It confirms what we thought all along. We now have definitive proof that the whales are changing their diets."

Because North Atlantic fish stocks are diminishing, it's not yet clear if these whales do this out of choice or necessity. Either way, with the horrors of industrial whaling still in living memory of both humans and whales, it is remarkable to think that a photo or video posted to Facebook by a tourist could now offer the missing piece to a puzzle that researchers have been assembling for a century.

PHOTOS: SARA TAVARES, ICELANDIC ORCAS PROJECT
MAP SOURCES: FILIPA SAMARRA, MARINE RESEARCH INSTITUTE, REYKJAVÍK; GEBCO; GSHHG

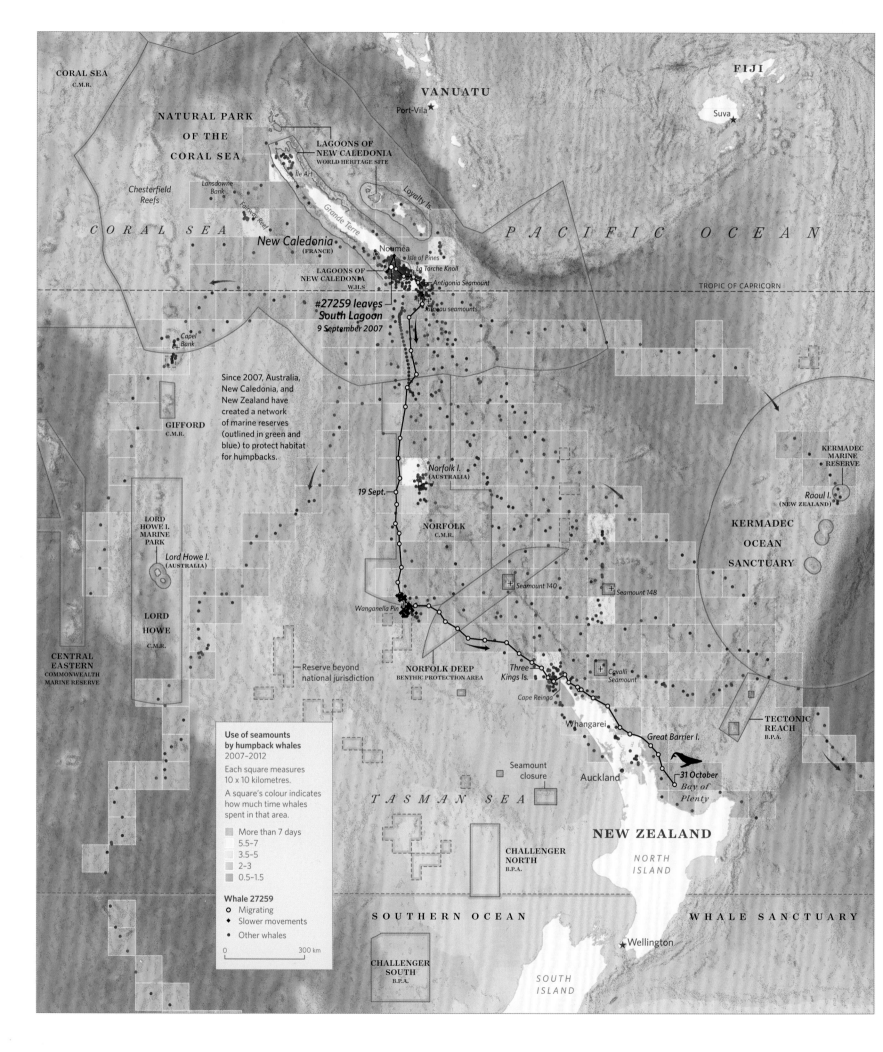

FIJI

Suva ★

VANUATU
Port-Vila ★

CORAL SEA
C.M.R.

NATURAL PARK

OF THE

CORAL SEA

Chesterfield Reefs

Lansdowne Bank

LAGOONS OF
NEW CALEDONIA
WORLD HERITAGE SITE

Île Art

Fairway Reef

Grande Terre

Loyalty Is.

C O R A L   S E A

P A C I F I C   O C E A N

New Caledonia
(FRANCE)

Nouméa

Isle of Pines

Lg Torche Knoll

LAGOONS OF
NEW CALEDONIA
W.H.S

Antigonia Seamount

Jumeau seamounts

TROPIC OF CAPRICORN

**#27259 leaves
South Lagoon**
9 September 2007

Capel Bank

Since 2007, Australia,
New Caledonia, and
New Zealand have
created a network
of marine reserves
(outlined in green and
blue) to protect habitat
for humpbacks.

GIFFORD
C.M.R.

KERMADEC
MARINE
RESERVE

Norfolk I.
(AUSTRALIA)

Raoul I.
(NEW ZEALAND)

19 Sept.

NORFOLK
C.M.R.

KERMADEC

OCEAN

SANCTUARY

LORD HOWE I.
MARINE
PARK

Lord Howe I.
(AUSTRALIA)

LORD
HOWE
C.M.R.

+ *Seamount 140*

+ *Seamount 148*

CENTRAL
EASTERN
COMMONWEALTH
MARINE RESERVE

Wanganella Pin

Reserve beyond
national jurisdiction

NORFOLK DEEP
BENTHIC PROTECTION AREA

*Three
Kings Is.*

+ *Cavalli
Seamount*

Cape Reinga

TECTONIC
REACH
B.P.A.

Whangarei

Great Barrier I.

Seamount
closure

Auckland

★ *31 October*
*Bay of
Plenty*

**Use of seamounts
by humpback whales**
2007–2012

Each square measures
10 x 10 kilometres.

A square's colour indicates
how much time whales
spent in that area.

T A S M A N   S E A

NEW ZEALAND

NORTH
ISLAND

CHALLENGER
NORTH
B.P.A.

More than 7 days
5.5–7
3.5–5
2–3
0.5–1.5

Whale 27259
○ Migrating
◆ Slower movements
• Other whales

SOUTHERN OCEAN

WHALE SANCTUARY

0 ——— 300 km

★ Wellington

CHALLENGER
SOUTH
B.P.A.

SOUTH
ISLAND

The Humpbacks Seeking Seamounts

THE IUCN RED LIST OF THREATENED SPECIES labels humpback whales as a species of "least concern." From this designation, you might think the whales have been sufficiently saved. For Claire Garrigue, it's not so simple. The subpopulation she studies in New Caledonia only numbers in the hundreds. There's ample reason for concern.

To find out how best to protect them, she began tracking them in 2007. She started with twelve that were breeding in the French territory's South Lagoon. All but two swam south, suggesting that this subpopulation and New Zealand's might be strongly connected. There was another surprise. Seven whales visited a large undersea mountain called the Antigonia Seamount; one stayed for

three weeks. Garrigue, who has been studying these whales since 1991, had never known they did this anywhere. Nor had anyone else. She conducted follow-up studies with more whales, most of which slowed their migrations around seamounts too. But why? Are they rest stops, road signs, or social venues? There's still a lot we don't know.

Using satellites and sonar, the Global Seamount Census estimates more than 25 million of these subsurface islands exist worldwide. At least a hundred thousand taller than 1,000 meters remain uncharted. In fact, in 2005, a nuclear submarine crashed into one southeast of Guam, killing a crew member. Not even the US Navy knows where they all are. Perhaps the whales do.

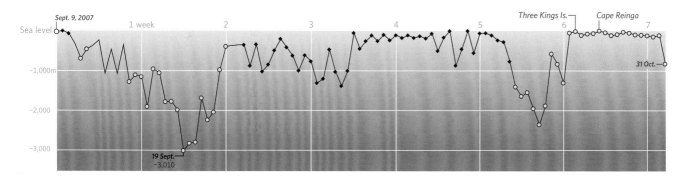

Whale #27259's activity
Sept. 9 – Oct. 31, 2007

o Migrating
♦ Slower movements

Whale #27259 and her calf stopped at Waganella Pin for seventeen days during their 3,340-kilometer journey to New Zealand.

SOURCES: CLAIRE GARRIGUE, OPÉRATION CÉTACÉS AND INSTITUT DE RECHERCHE POUR LE DÉVELOPPEMENT; GEBCO; GSHHG

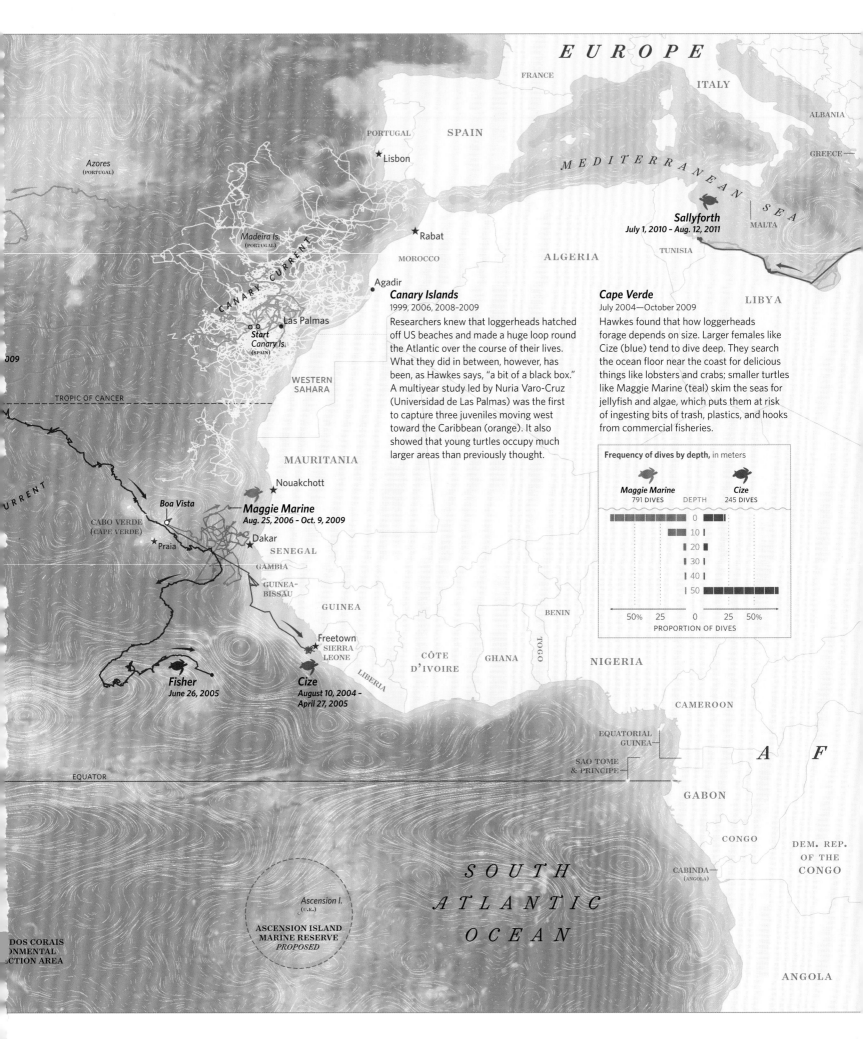

EUROPE

FRANCE

ITALY

ALBANIA

GREECE

M E D I T E R R A N E A N *S E A*

MALTA

PORTUGAL

SPAIN

★ Lisbon

Azores
(PORTUGAL)

Madeira Is.
(PORTUGAL)

★ Rabat

Sallyforth
July 1, 2010 - Aug. 12, 2011

MOROCCO

ALGERIA

TUNISIA

LIBYA

Agadir

CANARY CURRENT

Las Palmas

*Start
Canary Is.*
(SPAIN)

Canary Islands
1999, 2006, 2008–2009

Researchers knew that loggerheads hatched
off US beaches and made a huge loop round
the Atlantic over the course of their lives.
What they did in between, however, has
been, as Hawkes says, "a bit of a black box."
A multiyear study led by Nuria Varo-Cruz
(Universidad de Las Palmas) was the first
to capture three juveniles moving west
toward the Caribbean (orange). It also
showed that young turtles occupy much
larger areas than previously thought.

Cape Verde
July 2004—October 2009

Hawkes found that how loggerheads
forage depends on size. Larger females like
Cize (blue) tend to dive deep. They search
the ocean floor near the coast for delicious
things like lobsters and crabs; smaller turtles
like Maggie Marine (teal) skim the seas for
jellyfish and algae, which puts them at risk
of ingesting bits of trash, plastics, and hooks
from commercial fisheries.

TROPIC OF CANCER

WESTERN
SAHARA

MAURITANIA

Nouakchott

Boa Vista

Maggie Marine
Aug. 25, 2006 - Oct. 9, 2009

CABO VERDE
(CAPE VERDE)

Dakar ★

SENEGAL

★ Praia

GAMBIA

GUINEA-
BISSAU

GUINEA

CURRENT

Frequency of dives by depth, in meters

Maggie Marine
791 DIVES   DEPTH

Cize
245 DIVES

	0	
	10	
	20	
	30	
	40	
	50	

50%   25   0   25   50%
PROPORTION OF DIVES

BENIN

NIGERIA

Freetown
SIERRA
LEONE

Fisher
June 26, 2005

Cize
August 10, 2004 -
April 27, 2005

LIBERIA

CÔTE
D'IVOIRE

GHANA

TOGO

CAMEROON

EQUATORIAL
GUINEA

SAO TOME
& PRINCIPE

A   F

EQUATOR

GABON

CONGO

DEM. REP.
OF THE
CONGO

S O U T H

A T L A N T I C

O C E A N

Ascension I.
(U.K.)

**ASCENSION ISLAND
MARINE RESERVE**
PROPOSED

CABINDA
(ANGOLA)

009

DOS CORAIS
ONMENTAL
CTION AREA

ANGOLA

NORTH
AMERICA

UNITED
STATES

★ Washington

NORTH
CAROLINA

■ *June 12, 2004*
North Carolina
Aquarium at
Fort Fisher

Bermuda
(U.K.)

GULF STREAM

U
Apr. 21, 2010 –
Mar. 16, 2012

North Carolina
June 2004—June 2005

Instead of using the Gulf Stream and
other currents to circle the Atlantic,
Fisher cut straight across, logging
11,600 kilometers in 350 days.

NORTH
ATLANTIC
OCEAN

Mid-Atlantic Ridge

P
Apr. 1 – July 11,

BAHAMAS

ANTILLES CURRENT

CUBA

Cayman Is.
(U.K.)

HAITI

DOMINICAN
REPUBLIC

*Puerto
Rico*
(U.S.)

British Virgin Is.
(U.K.)

JAMAICA

ST. KITTS & NEVIS
Montserrat
(U.K.)

ANTIGUA &
BARBUDA

Guadeloupe
(FRANCE)

CARIBBEAN SEA

DOMINICA

NORTH EQUATORIAL C

HONDURAS

ST. LUCIA

ST. VINCENT &
THE GRENADINES

BARBADOS

T
*October 25, 2009 –
March 22, 2010*

After this study ended, T's tag
appeared on land in St. Lucia.
Varo-Cruz fears T may have
been hooked and eaten.

NICARAGUA

GRENADA

COSTA
RICA

TRINIDAD &
TOBAGO

PANAMA

VENEZUELA

GUYANA

COLOMBIA

SURINAME

FRENCH
GUIANA
(FRANCE)

ECUADOR

SOUTH AMERICA

Satellite tracks of sea turtles
2004-2013

O Nesting beach

0 —————————— 1,000 km
Scale at the Equator

BRAZIL

PERU

Recife •

COST
ENV
PRO

SOURCES: LUCY HAWKES, UNIVERSITY OF
EXETER; GRAEME HAYS, DEAKIN UNIVERSITY
(CHAGOS); NURIA VARO-CRUZ, UNIVERSIDAD
DE LAS PALMAS (CANARY ISLANDS); ANNETTE
BRODERICK AND BRENDAN GODLEY, UNIVERSITY
OF EXETER (CYPRUS); GEBCO; GSHHG; NE; GADM

White lines and swirls show
average ocean currents for
November. Researchers model
their speed and direction to
predict how turtles will move
across the seas.

The Turtle Who
Swam Against the Current

"MY GOD, THERE'S A LOT OF TURTLES on here," said Lucy Hawkes, a member of the Marine Turtle Research Group at the University of Exeter. She was scrolling through a database of their active tracking projects: "We've got Ascension, North Carolina, British Virgin Islands, Cape Verde, Cayman Islands, Mexico, Cyprus, Dominican Republic, Equatorial Guinea, Gabon, Israel, Kuwait, Lampedusa—that's Italy—Mozambique, Guadalupe, Montserrat, Oman, Peru, [she takes a breath] Scotland, Turkey, Sri Lanka, and Greece." Total number of tags deployed: 443 and counting.

One of her first traveled on a loggerhead turtle named Fisher. In 1995, biologists from the North Carolina Aquarium at Fort Fisher found him on a nearby beach. He was weak and underweight, so they brought him to the aquarium's rehabilitation center. Eight years later, Fisher was 40 kilograms and outgrowing his adoptive home. His caretakers loaned him to Newport Aquarium in Kentucky for an exhibit presciently titled *Turtles: Journey of Survival*. By his tenth birthday, Fisher tipped the scales at 70 kilograms. He was ready to hunt in the wild.

On June 12, 2004, Hawkes stuck a tag on Fisher's shell and released him into the Atlantic. She expected him to ride the Gulf Stream to Spain. But Fisher had other plans. "He did a straight line to Cape Verde," Hawkes said, "which, bizarrely, is exactly where he should be at ten years old. It was as if he thought, 'I've got to catch up with everyone.'" Imagine that. After ten years in captivity, Fisher knew where he needed to be, at what time, and how to get there. On this foldout, you'll find a few more ways that sea turtles are defying expectations.

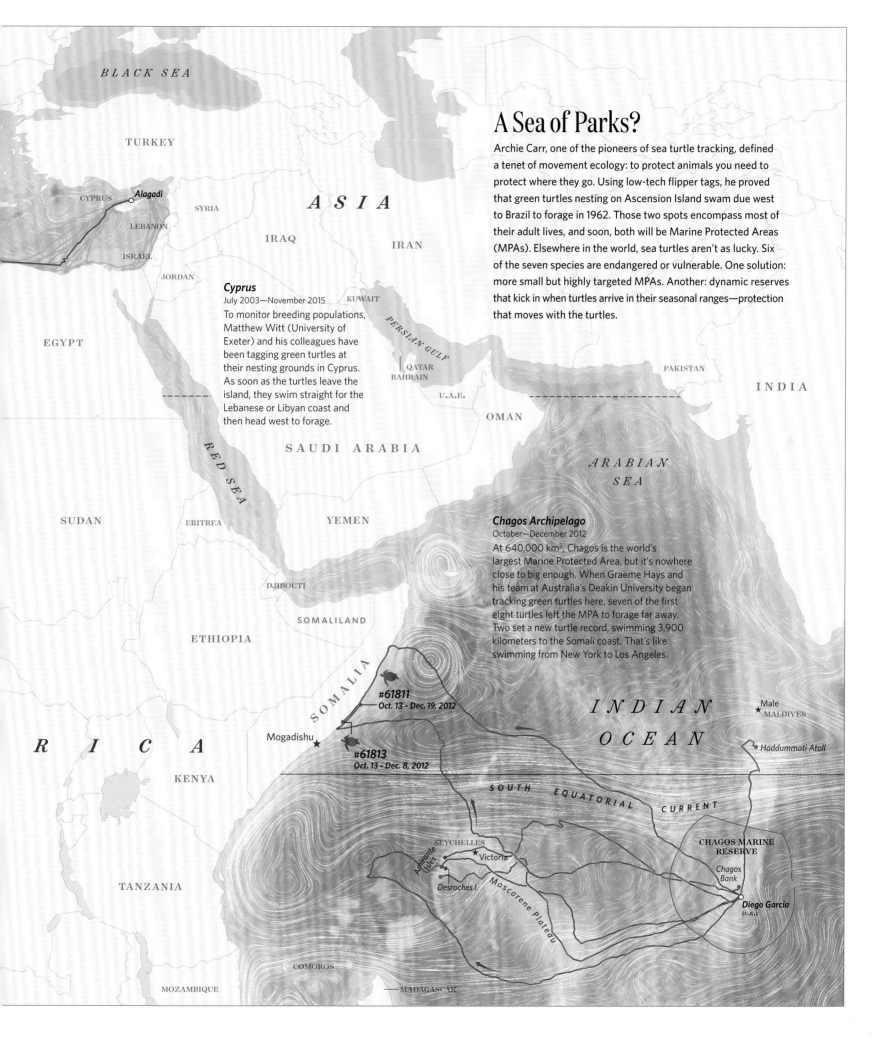

A Sea of Parks?

Archie Carr, one of the pioneers of sea turtle tracking, defined a tenet of movement ecology: to protect animals you need to protect where they go. Using low-tech flipper tags, he proved that green turtles nesting on Ascension Island swam due west to Brazil to forage in 1962. Those two spots encompass most of their adult lives, and soon, both will be Marine Protected Areas (MPAs). Elsewhere in the world, sea turtles aren't as lucky. Six of the seven species are endangered or vulnerable. One solution: more small but highly targeted MPAs. Another: dynamic reserves that kick in when turtles arrive in their seasonal ranges—protection that moves with the turtles.

BLACK SEA

TURKEY

CYPRUS ○ *Alagadi*

ASIA

SYRIA

LEBANON

ISRAEL

JORDAN

IRAQ

IRAN

Cyprus
July 2003—November 2015
To monitor breeding populations, Matthew Witt (University of Exeter) and his colleagues have been tagging green turtles at their nesting grounds in Cyprus. As soon as the turtles leave the island, they swim straight for the Lebanese or Libyan coast and then head west to forage.

KUWAIT

PERSIAN GULF

QATAR
BAHRAIN

U.A.E.

PAKISTAN

INDIA

EGYPT

OMAN

SAUDI ARABIA

ARABIAN SEA

RED SEA

SUDAN

ERITREA

YEMEN

Chagos Archipelago
October—December 2012
At 640,000 km², Chagos is the world's largest Marine Protected Area, but it's nowhere close to big enough. When Graeme Hays and his team at Australia's Deakin University began tracking green turtles here, seven of the first eight turtles left the MPA to forage far away. Two set a new turtle record, swimming 3,900 kilometers to the Somali coast. That's like swimming from New York to Los Angeles.

DJIBOUTI

SOMALILAND

ETHIOPIA

INDIAN

Male
MALDIVES

OCEAN

SOMALIA

#61811
Oct. 13 - Dec. 19, 2012

Haddummati Atoll

Mogadishu ★

#61813
Oct. 13 - Dec. 8, 2012

RICA

KENYA

SOUTH EQUATORIAL CURRENT

CHAGOS MARINE RESERVE

SEYCHELLES

Chagos Bank

Amirante Islets

★ Victoria

Mascarene Plateau

Desroches I.

TANZANIA

○ *Diego Garcia*
(U.K.)

COMOROS

MOZAMBIQUE

MADAGASCAR

Sharks, Turtles, and the Landscape of Fear

ANIMALS MOVE to eat and to avoid getting eaten. That's the gist of a one-size-fits-all model that ecologists call "the landscape of fear." According to that theory, animals learn which parts of their range are risky and evade them as those risks increase. It makes sense, but what if it's not always true?

Neil Hammerschlag, director of the Shark Research and Conservation Program at the University of Miami, is one of the theory's skeptics. He was curious as to how it might apply to animals in a landscape as large and fluid as the ocean. To see predators and prey interact at that scale, he merged two sets of satellite tracks from prior studies: 68 loggerhead turtles (whose summer range we show in green) and 31 tiger sharks (in gray). He was looking for areas where their ranges overlapped (yellow) to see if turtles acted differently in shark-infested waters.

Sea turtles come to the surface to forage and to breathe. Tiger sharks attack from below. If the fear theory held true, Hammerschlag expected to see turtles surfacing less frequently in high-risk areas. But that's not what happened. The turtles kept swimming as usual; it was the sharks who changed behavior. In the presence of turtles, tiger sharks spent more time at depth, presumably to position themselves for an ambush.

Why then, weren't the turtles more afraid? Hammerschlag has his own theories: perhaps the need to eat and nest outweighed the risks. Perhaps overfishing has rendered the sharks "functionally extinct." Or perhaps, from a turtle's point of view, there are now bigger worries in the water: fishing nets and boat propellers.

LAKE ERIE

NEW YORK

New York

PENNSYLVANIA

Philadelphia

Wilmington

NEW JERSEY

Atlantic City

Cape May

Delaware Bay

DEL.

MARYLAND

Baltimore

Washington, D.C.

Chesapeake Bay

VIRGINIA

Norfolk

Virginia Beach

UNITED STATES

OUTER BANKS

Pamlico Sound

NORTH CAROLINA

Wilmington

SOUTH CAROLINA

Myrtle Beach

Charleston

ATLANTIC OCEAN

Tiger shark #68554

27 June - 22 Aug.

17 June

Tiger shark #68555

Apr. 11 – Oct. 10

11 June

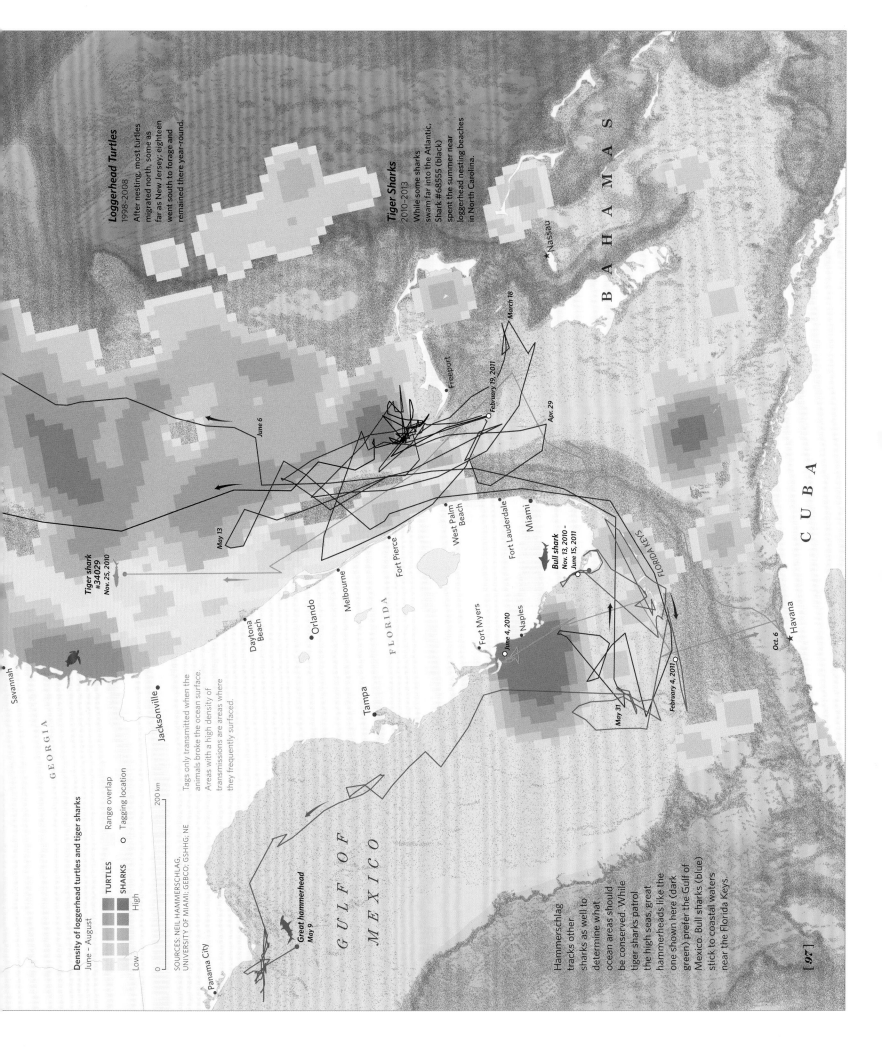

Density of loggerhead turtles and tiger sharks
June – August

TURTLES
SHARKS

Low   High

Range overlap

○ Tagging location

0   200 km

SOURCES: NEIL HAMMERSCHLAG,
UNIVERSITY OF MIAMI; GEBCO; GSHHG; NE

Tags only transmitted when the
animals broke the ocean surface.
Areas with a high density of
transmissions are areas where
they frequently surfaced.

Loggerhead Turtles
1998-2008

After nesting, most turtles
migrated north, some as
far as New Jersey; eighteen
went south to forage and
remained there year-round.

Tiger Sharks
2010-2013

While some sharks
swam far into the Atlantic,
Shark #68555 (black)
spent the summer near
loggerhead nesting beaches
in North Carolina.

Tiger shark
#34029
Nov. 25, 2010

May 13

June 6

March 18

February 19, 2011

Freeport

Apr. 29

★ Nassau

B A H A M A S

West Palm Beach

Fort Pierce

Fort Lauderdale

Miami

Bull shark
Nov. 13, 2010 -
June 15, 2011

F L O R I D A   K E Y S

Melbourne

•Orlando

Daytona Beach

Jacksonville•

F L O R I D A

Tampa•

Savannah•

G E O R G I A

Fort Myers

June 4, 2010

Naples•

February 4, 2011

May 31

Oct. 6

★ Havana

C U B A

Great hammerhead
May 9

Panama City•

G U L F   O F
M E X I C O

Hammerschlag
tracks other
sharks as well to
determine what
ocean areas should
be conserved. While
tiger sharks patrol
the high seas, great
hammerheads like the
one shown here (dark
green) prefer the Gulf of
Mexico. Bull sharks (blue)
stick to coastal waters
near the Florida Keys.

[*97*]

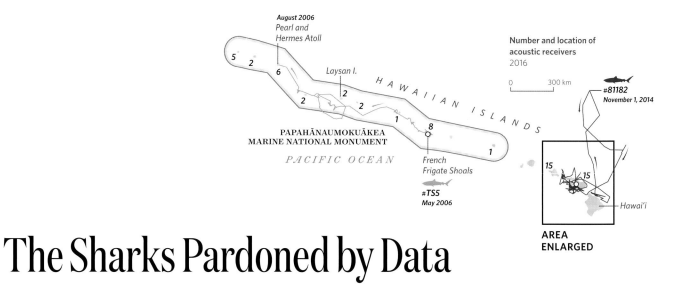

August 2006
Pearl and
Hermes Atoll

5 2
   6

Laysan I.

H A W A I I A N   I S L A N D S

Number and location of acoustic receivers
2016

0   300 km

2

2

2

1

8

**PAPAHĀNAUMOKUĀKEA
MARINE NATIONAL MONUMENT**

1

PACIFIC OCEAN

French
Frigate Shoals

#81182
November 1, 2014

#TS5
May 2006

15
   15

**AREA
ENLARGED**

Hawai'i

The Sharks Pardoned by Data

In May 2006, researchers tagged a 3.9-meter female tiger shark (orange) at the French Frigate Shoals, where she had come to feed on young albatrosses. Once fledgling season ended, her satellite tag showed her traveling 1,000 kilometers along the island chain, arriving at Pearl and Hermes Atoll in August. Though the tag stopped working soon after, acoustic receivers detected her again near the island of Hawai'i in March 2007 and at Laysan Island in July before she returned to the Shoals in October. To connect these points, she would have had to travel 3,480 kilometers.

IN RESPONSE TO A FATAL SHARK BITE in 1958, the state of Hawaii killed 4,668 sharks over the next 17 years. It was a tactic driven by fear, not facts. More fatalities in the 1990s prompted Hawaii to consider culling once more. This time, the Hawaiian people pushed back, insisting that killing sharks wasn't the solution. "That was our opening to see what sharks are really doing," says Kim Holland, a research professor at the Hawai'i Institute of Marine Biology. His team helped convince the state to fund a study, not a slaughter.

Over the years, their ongoing investigation has used multiple tracking technologies, often simultaneously. Early on, they implanted tiger sharks with acoustic transmitters. Each emitted a unique sequence of "pings," which the researchers could follow by boat for short distances. For a wider view, in 2005 they installed underwater listening stations throughout the archipelago that recorded whenever a pinging shark passed by (above). Meanwhile, fin-mounted satellite tags were capturing sharks' routes between them.

Before this research began, people thought that sharks weren't common and that the few seen near beaches were permanent residents. "From the very first tracks, we saw those assumptions were completely wrong," says Holland. "Tiger sharks are incredibly nomadic." Once the team added the acoustic array and satellite tags to their toolbox, the behavior became even clearer. The sharks were traveling thousands of kilometers between islands and often making long trips out to sea.

"Tiger sharks are around the Hawaiian Islands, fairly close to shore, all the time," says Holland. When you consider the thousands of people entering the water each year, "the astounding thing is that there are so *few* attacks." On average, there are three to four bites per year in Hawaii, compared to more than 50 ocean drownings. In the rare event of a fatal bite, he says the state now takes a more scientific stance. "They will not endorse culling unless they have evidence that a rogue shark is really hanging out in one particular spot. And that's never been the case."

SOURCES: CARL MEYER AND KIM HOLLAND, HAWAI'I
INSTITUTE OF MARINE BIOLOGY; GEBCO; GSHHG

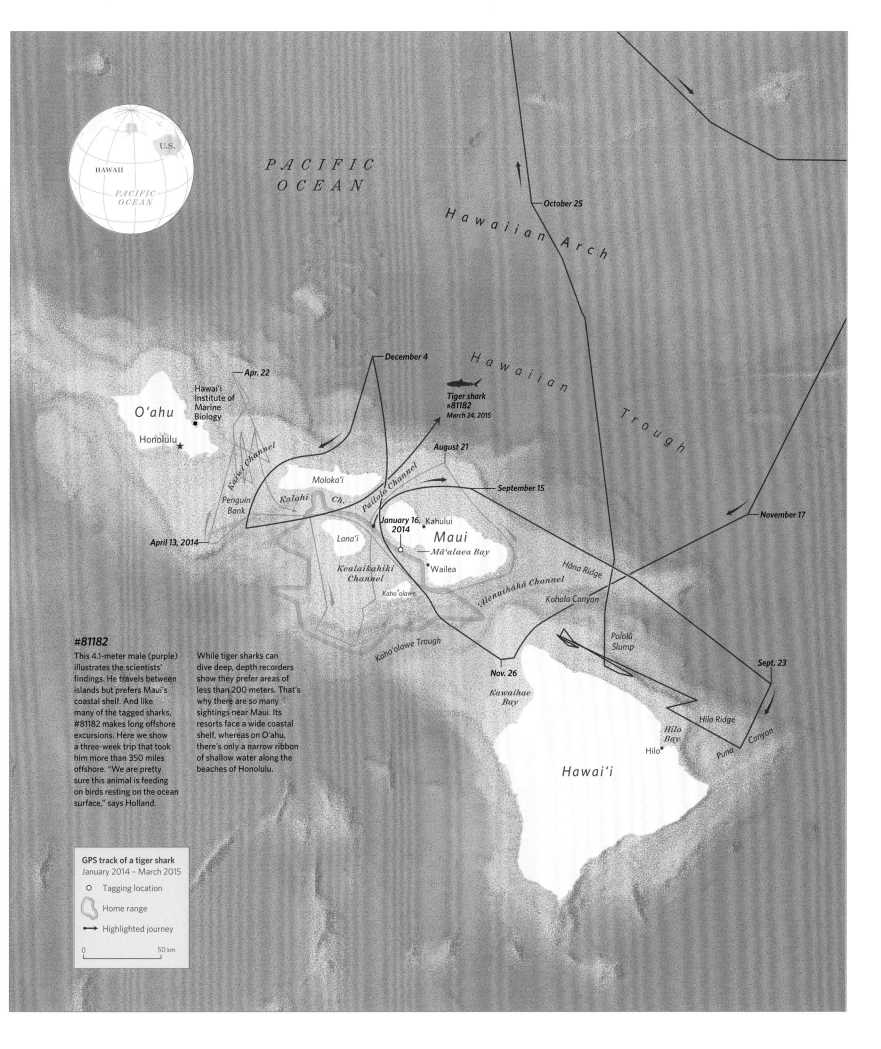

PACIFIC
OCEAN

U.S.

HAWAII

PACIFIC
OCEAN

Hawaiian Arch

— October 25

Hawaiian Trough

— Apr. 22

Hawai'i
Institute of
Marine
Biology

O'ahu

Honolulu ★

December 4

Tiger shark
#81182
March 24, 2015

Kaiwi Channel

Moloka'i

August 21

Paiolo Channel

September 15

November 17

Penguin
Bank

Kalohi
Ch.

April 13, 2014 —

Lana'i

January 16,
2014

Kahului

Maui

Mā'alaea Bay

Kealaikahiki
Channel

Wailea

Kaho'olawe

Hāna Ridge

ʻAlenuihāhā Channel

Kohala Canyon

Pololū
Slump

Sept. 23

Kaho'olawe Trough

Nov. 26

Kawaihae
Bay

Hilo Ridge

Hilo
Bay

Puna
Canyon

Hilo •

Hawai'i

#81182

This 4.1-meter male (purple) illustrates the scientists' findings. He travels between islands but prefers Maui's coastal shelf. And like many of the tagged sharks, #81182 makes long offshore excursions. Here we show a three-week trip that took him more than 350 miles offshore. "We are pretty sure this animal is feeding on birds resting on the ocean surface," says Holland.

While tiger sharks can dive deep, depth recorders show they prefer areas of less than 200 meters. That's why there are so many sightings near Maui. Its resorts face a wide coastal shelf, whereas on O'ahu, there's only a narrow ribbon of shallow water along the beaches of Honolulu.

GPS track of a tiger shark
January 2014 – March 2015

○ Tagging location

   Home range

→ Highlighted journey

0 ————————— 50 km

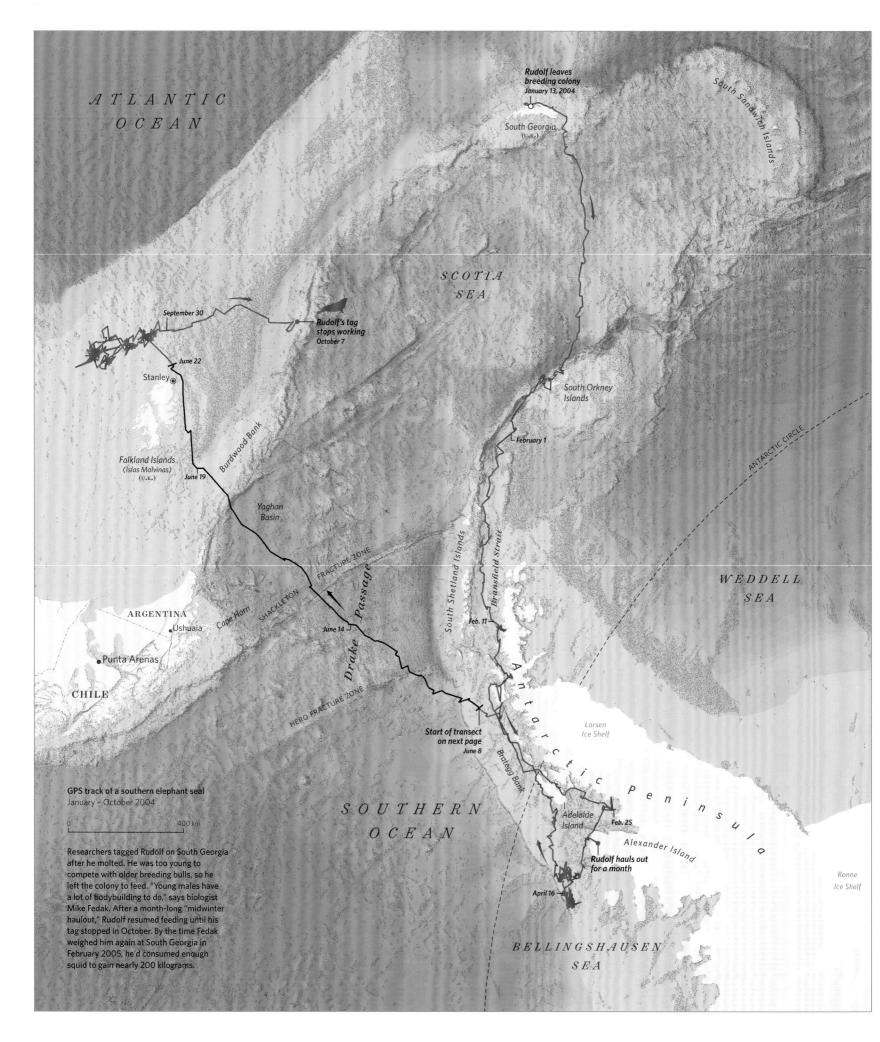

ATLANTIC
OCEAN

**Rudolf leaves
breeding colony**
January 13, 2004

South Sandwich Islands

South Georgia
(U.K.)

SCOTIA
SEA

September 30

Rudolf's tag
stops working
October 7

June 22

Stanley

*South Orkney
Islands*

February 1

ANTARCTIC CIRCLE

Falkland Islands
(Islas Malvinas)
(U.K.)

June 19

Burdwood Bank

*Yaghan
Basin*

South Shetland Islands

Bransfield Strait

WEDDELL
SEA

ARGENTINA
Ushuaia

Cape Horn

SHACKLETON

FRACTURE ZONE

June 14

Drake Passage

Feb. 11

Punta Arenas

HERO FRACTURE ZONE

*Larsen
Ice Shelf*

CHILE

**Start of transect
on next page**
June 8

Antarctic Peninsula

GPS track of a southern elephant seal
January – October 2004

0 ————————— 400 km

Brategg Bank

SOUTHERN
OCEAN

*Adelaide
Island*

Feb. 25

Alexander Island

*Ronne
Ice Shelf*

Researchers tagged Rudolf on South Georgia
after he molted. He was too young to
compete with older breeding bulls, so he
left the colony to feed. "Young males have
a lot of bodybuilding to do," says biologist
Mike Fedak. After a month-long "midwinter
haulout," Rudolf resumed feeding until his
tag stopped in October. By the time Fedak
weighed him again at South Georgia in
February 2005, he'd consumed enough
squid to gain nearly 200 kilograms.

**Rudolf hauls out
for a month**

April 16

BELLINGSHAUSEN
SEA

The Seals Who
Map the Southern Ocean

TO GET YOUR BEARINGS in a new city, you might wander the streets, consult a guidebook, or seek recommendations from locals. Often the best approach is to try all three. When it comes to understanding our world's polar seas, oceanographers find themselves in a similar boat; they have deployed sensing buoys to drift in the currents and used nautical charts to study specific areas. However, the one thing they have always lacked is local knowledge.

Step forward Mike Fedak of the Sea Mammal Research Unit (SMRU) at the University of St Andrews in Scotland. He and his colleagues have been conversing with seals about their neighborhoods for years. They may not do much talking, but the sensors glued to their fur—which fall off when they molt every six months or so—give

us information about climate change and seal behavior that we would never have discovered on our own. For instance, an elephant seal named Rudolf (left) was able to collect sea temperature data under the ice along the Antarctic Peninsula, areas oceanographers would find hard to reach.

Lars Boehme, an oceanographer at SMRU, recalls unease from other researchers in the early days of "animal-directed sampling." They said seals aren't as "impartial" as scientists. They'll only visit parts of the oceans that are important to them. For those at SMRU, however, that's exactly the point. "We're trying very hard to learn about the animals," says Fedak, "and, as a by-product, deliver information to oceanography in general."

It's unlikely that one seal will transform our understanding of the Southern Ocean, but

Weddell seals stay close to ice shelves and provide researchers with many readings from a few areas; southern elephant seals like Rudolf (opposite) produce long transects as they roam the oceans.

Rudolf's long track and deep dives mean he's "the first seal I introduce students to," says Clint Blight, the technical brains behind much of SMRU's seal-tracking visualization software.

Southern elephant seal tracks
by tagging location

○ Breeding colony
— South Georgia
— Marion

— Kerguelen
— Macquarie
— South Shetland

— Weddell seal tracks

0   2,500 km

SOURCES: MIKE FEDAK AND CLINT BLIGHT,
UNIVERSITY OF ST ANDREWS; GEBCO; GSHHG; NE

how about 700 of them? Scientists from eleven countries have joined Fedak's initiative, and between them, their seals have sent back more than 300,000 measurements of temperature and salinity from the southern hemisphere. Researchers make them all public via the MEOP (Marine Mammals Exploring the Oceans Pole-to-pole) data portal.

From this evidence, Fedak says we are beginning to understand the broader state of the "Global Ocean" in the face of climate change. Our oceans are all connected in one big conveyor belt. A key section of it runs down the Atlantic Ocean and along the Antarctic coastline. To keep this running, the polar seas need to stay cold and salty. But as global warming heats the Southern Ocean, melting ice sheets will send more fresh water into the sea, further exacerbating the issue.

Without realizing it, the seals have become our sentinels. Their continual data streams keep

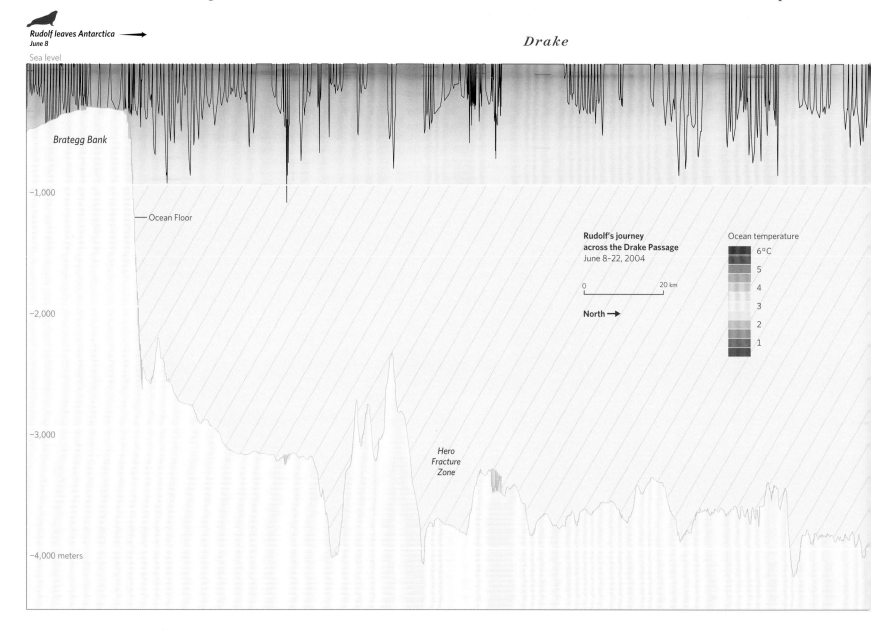

Rudolf leaves Antarctica →
June 8

Drake

Sea level

Brategg Bank

−1,000

— Ocean Floor

Rudolf's journey across the Drake Passage
June 8–22, 2004

0 ———— 20 km

North →

Ocean temperature
6°C
5
4
3
2
1

−2,000

−3,000

Hero
Fracture
Zone

−4,000 meters

researchers up to date on ocean temperatures, while educating us about their daily lives. To date, they can send back only text-message-sized files. The scientists at SMRU are looking forward to a new generation of tags that will be able to handle much of the data processing on-board. In short, they will be turning their data into information before transmitting them back to the lab.

Fedak predicts this will be a breakthrough for marine biology. With today's technology, he has no way to assess the impact of a new offshore wind farm on the seals, for example. The tags tell him that seals moved around the turbines but nothing about how they're affecting the animals' health. Accelerometers on the new tags will measure how quickly speed decays between each of a seal's flipper beats, from which an onboard computer can calculate the seal's mass. That's what Fedak wants—a signal to say whether or not seals like Rudolf are getting fat enough to breed.

Passage

Rudolf reaches the Falkland Islands
June 22

Burdwood Bank

−1,000

−2,000

Deep Dives in a Warming Sea

Elephant seals can dive as deep as 1,500 meters in search of food. This makes them perfect for collecting temperature data since they get to the cool, deep waters that drive ocean currents. The variations in temperature shown here are only a few degrees Celsius, but that's still significant. It takes a lot of energy to heat an entire ocean even by a tenth of a degree.

−3,000

Shackleton Fracture Zone

Yaghan Basin

−4,000

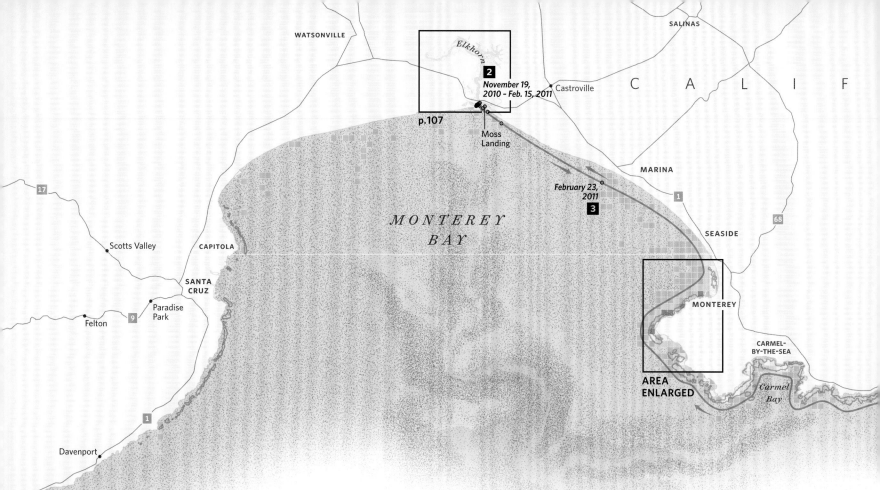

The map shows Monterey Bay and surrounding area, including locations: WATSONVILLE, SALINAS, Elkhorn, CALIF, Castroville, MARINA, Scotts Valley, CAPITOLA, SANTA CRUZ, Paradise Park, Felton, MONTEREY, SEASIDE, CARMEL-BY-THE-SEA, Carmel Bay, Davenport, Moss Landing, MONTEREY BAY. Annotations: **2** November 19, 2010 – Feb. 15, 2011; p.107; **3** February 23, 2011; AREA ENLARGED. Road markers: 17, 9, 1, 68.

The Otters Reclaiming Their Range

The sea otter is such a rare mammal today, so nearly extinct, that there is very little likelihood any of the readers of this handbook will ever see one alive.

—Field Book of North American Mammals, 1928

SEA OTTERS HAVE THE THICKEST FUR on Earth, a fact two centuries of trappers did not overlook. By the time sea otter hunting was banned in 1911, only thirteen remnant populations remained worldwide. In California, it seemed like too little too late.

Then in 1938, local landowner Howard G. Sharpe spotted "objects" with "odd-shaped flippers" floating in the kelp at the mouth of Bixby Creek, 13 miles south of Carmel. He couldn't believe it. Neither could game officials. Sharpe convinced them to come see for themselves, and before long, guards and a patrol boat were dispatched to protect a raft of 50 otters from poachers.

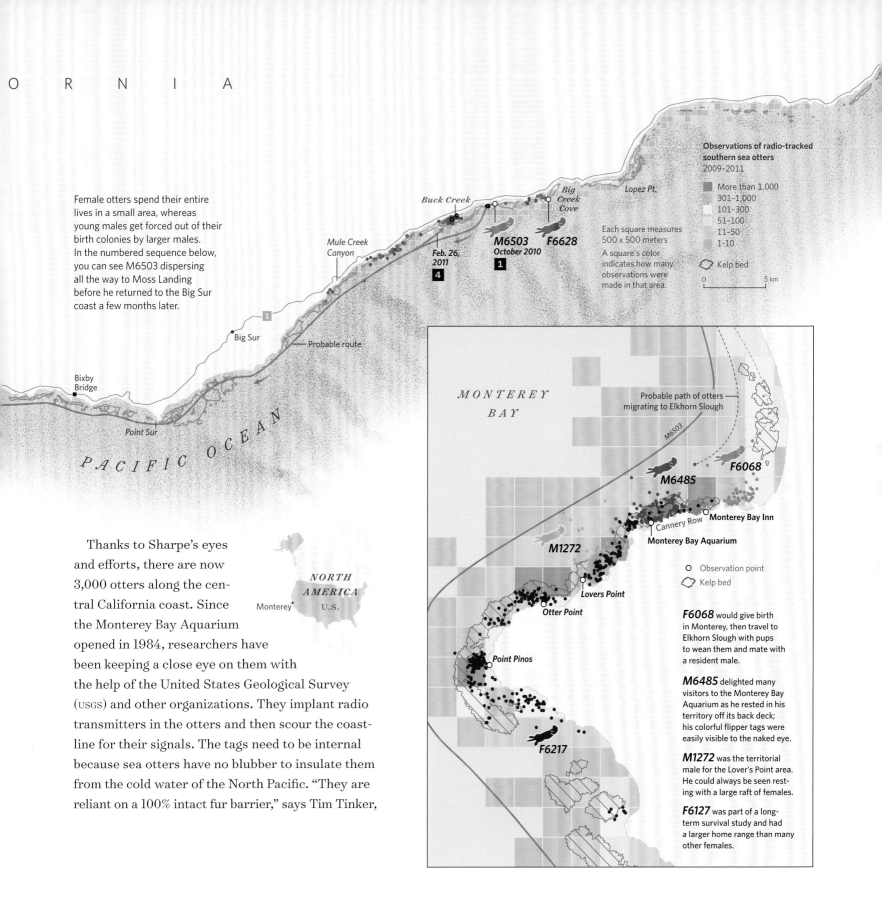

Female otters spend their entire lives in a small area, whereas young males get forced out of their birth colonies by larger males. In the numbered sequence below, you can see M6503 dispersing all the way to Moss Landing before he returned to the Big Sur coast a few months later.

Buck Creek

Big Creek Cove

Lopez Pt.

Observations of radio-tracked southern sea otters 2009-2011

More than 1,000
301-1,000
101-300
51-100
11-50
1-10

Each square measures 500 x 500 meters

A square's color indicates how many observations were made in that area.

Kelp bed

0   5 km

M6503
October 2010
1

F6628

Feb. 26, 2011
4

Mule Creek Canyon

1

Big Sur

Probable route

Bixby Bridge

Point Sur

PACIFIC OCEAN

Thanks to Sharpe's eyes and efforts, there are now 3,000 otters along the central California coast. Since the Monterey Bay Aquarium opened in 1984, researchers have been keeping a close eye on them with the help of the United States Geological Survey (USGS) and other organizations. They implant radio transmitters in the otters and then scour the coastline for their signals. The tags need to be internal because sea otters have no blubber to insulate them from the cold water of the North Pacific. "They are reliant on a 100% intact fur barrier," says Tim Tinker,

NORTH AMERICA
Monterey
U.S.

MONTEREY BAY

Probable path of otters migrating to Elkhorn Slough

M6503

F6068

M6485

Cannery Row

Monterey Bay Inn

Monterey Bay Aquarium

M1272

Lovers Point

Otter Point

Point Pinos

F6217

○ Observation point

Kelp bed

F6068 would give birth in Monterey, then travel to Elkhorn Slough with pups to wean them and mate with a resident male.

M6485 delighted many visitors to the Monterey Bay Aquarium as he rested in his territory off its back deck; his colorful flipper tags were easily visible to the naked eye.

M1272 was the territorial male for the Lover's Point area. He could always be seen resting with a large raft of females.

F6127 was part of a long-term survival study and had a larger home range than many other females.

SOURCES: M. TIM TINKER, SARAH ESPINOSA, JOE TOMOLEONI, USGS; MICHELLE STAEDLER, MONTEREY BAY AQUARIUM; GEBCO; USGS

a biologist at USGS. "When that's compromised [e.g. by a GPS collar], they're like us with a hole in a drysuit. They'll die very quickly."

Radio tracking and behavior monitoring requires researchers to look for otters every day. Sarah Espinosa has been doing so since 2013. We joined her in Elkhorn Slough, an estuary 15 miles north of the Aquarium. Our first stop was Seal Bend (see right). Espinosa set up a spotting scope fitted with a radio antenna/receiver and aimed them at a raft of otters in the main channel. Immediately, the receiver began to beep. "It's 3421," she said. "A subadult female." To confirm the "resight," we peered through the scope and looked for a set of unique, color-coded flipper tags. (These do not compromise an otter's fur.) Soon we spotted an otter with two yellow tags. False alarm. "That's chartreuse," Espinosa noted. Two chartreuse tags meant 3539, an adult female. Her beeps were loud and steady. Beeps stop when an otter dives to forage. "Sounds likes she's resting," Espinosa said and noted the behavior on a chart.

There are 26 tagged otters in the Slough, not including migrants from the bay or the rehabilitated otters that the Aquarium releases here. That morning, we spotted three at Seal Bend. We gave up looking for 3421 there and continued upstream. At Yampah Island, we found dozens of mothers, pups, and territorial males in the tidal creeks, but no 3421. Eventually, we found her at Avila along with Robert Scoles and Ron Eby, the citizen scientists responsible for this study in the first place.

Ten years ago, Scoles, a volunteer at the Aquarium, started noticing something peculiar on his commute home. As he crossed the bridge over Moss Landing Harbor, he saw otter tracks on the beach. Though scientists knew otters "hauled out" to conserve energy, Scoles had never seen it. Together, with Eby, a retired naval officer, they began daily stakeouts, counting otters and documenting their foraging habits. After two years, their data were undeniable. "The Slough is just an ideal environment for otters," said Eby. Compared to those in the bay, "they forage less, rest more, and don't have to dive deep or struggle against ocean swells." Their data inspired Tinker to launch a study in 2013 that has already transformed his approach to sea otter conservation.

For years, otters were managed like other marine mammals—as a big, homogeneous, mobile group. "Turns out, this was about the worst possible way to manage the population," Tinker says. Breeding females spend their entire lives in small areas, which means protective measures must be localized as well. Preserving kelp beds in the bay, for example, won't help the otters in the Slough. "We're only now realizing that otters aren't just outer-coast predators," he says. "Because after the fur trade, otters weren't left in any estuaries."

In the summer, some otters migrate here from Monterey to mate, but none of the residents ever leave. To Tinker, estuary otters and ocean otters are as different as the country mouse and the city mouse. From the diligent data collection of Espinosa and volunteers like Scoles and Eby, it's now clear that estuary otters eat clams, crabs, and snails and rest in seagrass meadows, whereas ocean otters dive for urchins and abalone and rest in kelp forests. "If you had come here five years ago," says Tinker, "we wouldn't have known that."

Safe in the Slough

"The Slough's a weird place," says Sarah Espinosa, who coordinates research in the estuary. Snaking past a natural gas plant, a dairy farm, high-tension power lines, a scrapyard, industrial strawberry and artichoke farms, and a railway, it is one of the most critical marine reserves in the US. Its secluded tidal creeks allow female otters to raise and wean their pups undisturbed. "Kayakers can't come back here," says Espinosa. "Perhaps that's why moms and pups like it."

M3146
September 2013—April 2016

As a youngster, he spent his time at Seal Bend with other males. Now eight years old, he often rests in his territory in the tidal creeks by Yampah Island. To forage, he swims toward Moss Landing in search of large clams.

F3539
April 2015—April 2016

When this 6-year-old is not foraging on large clams near Hummingbird Island, she likes to rest in the tidal creeks near Yampah Island and Avila Hill.

M3183
September 2013—April 2016

This 8-year-old male rests and forages in his territory on the west side of Seal Bend.

F3447
September 2013—April 2016

This 8-year-old female has weaned two pups and is now raising her third since 2013. They stick to the creeks near Yampah Island and Avila Hill.

Observed locations of radio-tracked sea otters

○ Observation point

0 ——— 500 m

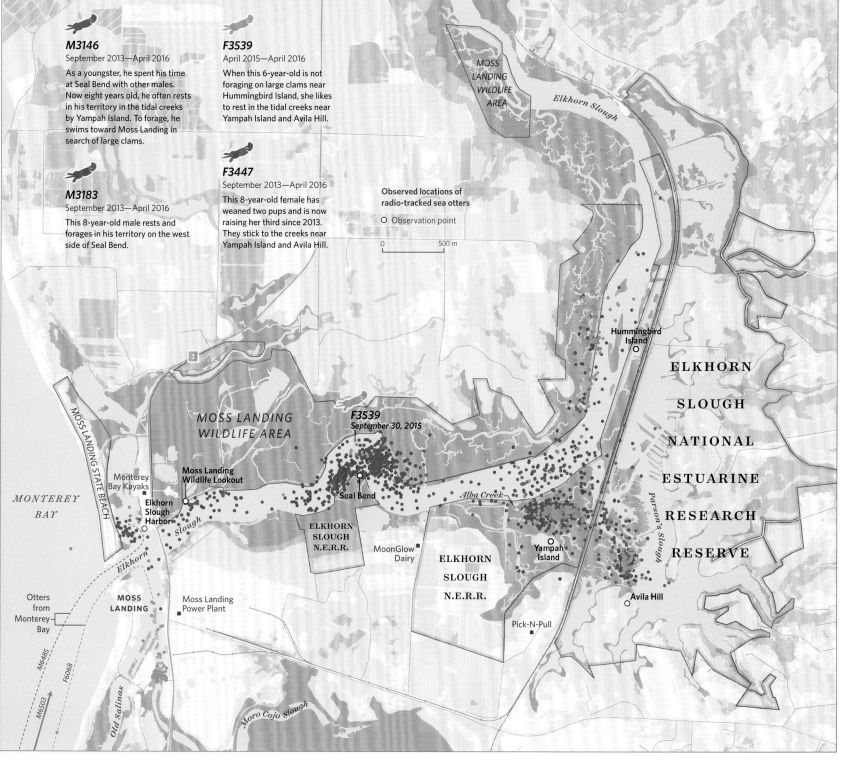

MOSS LANDING WILDLIFE AREA

Elkhorn Slough

MONTEREY BAY

MOSS LANDING STATE BEACH

Monterey Bay Kayaks

Elkhorn Slough Harbor

Slough

Elkhorn

Otters from Monterey Bay

M6485

F6068

M6503

Old Salinas

MOSS LANDING

Moss Landing Power Plant

Moro Cojo Slough

1

MOSS LANDING WILDLIFE AREA

Moss Landing Wildlife Lookout

F3539
September 30, 2015

Seal Bend

Alba Creek

ELKHORN SLOUGH N.E.R.R.

MoonGlow Dairy

ELKHORN SLOUGH N.E.R.R.

Pick-N-Pull

Yampah Island

Avila Hill

Hummingbird Island

Parson's Slough

ELKHORN SLOUGH NATIONAL ESTUARINE RESEARCH RESERVE

OzESauce

Kendall

Aurukun

Embley

The Crocodiles Best Left Alone

ON AVERAGE, fewer than one person a year dies in the jaws of a crocodile in Australia. But to Craig Franklin, Director of Research for the Steve Irwin Wildlife Reserve, that is one too many. "I dread it every time someone is bitten," he says.

Franklin and his team study the movements and physiology of estuarine crocodiles; that is, they motorboat up rivers, wrangle reptiles, and tag them. They hope to show people that crocodiles aren't out to harm them. That's where tracking technology really helps, although Franklin admits this new era of Big Data demands new skills. "I can't deal with it. That's why I bring people in who can."

Ross Dwyer is one of those people. He's tracked everything from kangaroos to cassowaries. "We tag pretty much any croc larger than one meter," he says. Adult crocodiles come in three varieties: females who only move to nest; smaller nomadic males who seek territory to claim; and large males who've already claimed some. From what Dwyer

has seen, these territorial males are all greater than 3.5 meters in length, and they don't care for the little guys hanging around. The smaller males "just get their ass kicked in these rivers," he says. So they go looking for new habitat, which makes them much more visible.

Once spotted, these "problem animals" were often relocated. But as Franklin points out, these are not the crocs that kill people; territorial ones do that. Besides, relocation was futile. Just take a look at Weldon's track on this map (red). This 4.4-meter male returned to where he started. Moving mobile crocs led them to swim farther, which made them easier to spot, and on it went. Today, such animals are killed or sent to farms. Franklin suggests another approach: warn the public about the big crocodiles and let the smaller ones be.

C a p e

Coen

81

G R E A T   D I V I D I N G   R A N G E

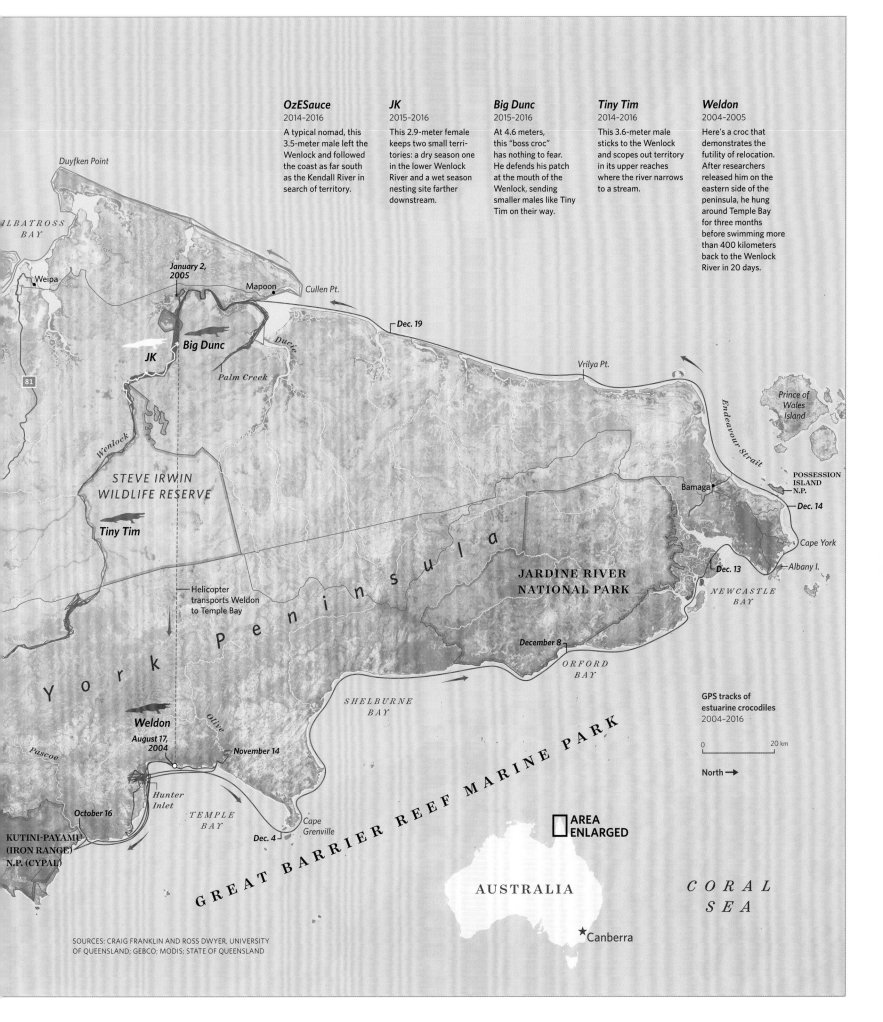

OzESauce
2014–2016

A typical nomad, this 3.5-meter male left the Wenlock and followed the coast as far south as the Kendall River in search of territory.

JK
2015–2016

This 2.9-meter female keeps two small territories: a dry season one in the lower Wenlock River and a wet season nesting site farther downstream.

Big Dunc
2015–2016

At 4.6 meters, this "boss croc" has nothing to fear. He defends his patch at the mouth of the Wenlock, sending smaller males like Tiny Tim on their way.

Tiny Tim
2014–2016

This 3.6-meter male sticks to the Wenlock and scopes out territory in its upper reaches where the river narrows to a stream.

Weldon
2004–2005

Here's a croc that demonstrates the futility of relocation. After researchers released him on the eastern side of the peninsula, he hung around Temple Bay for three months before swimming more than 400 kilometers back to the Wenlock River in 20 days.

Duyfken Point

ALBATROSS BAY

• Weipa

January 2, 2005

Mapoon

Cullen Pt.

Ducie

⌐ *Dec. 19*

Vrilya Pt.

Endeavour Strait

Big Dunc

Palm Creek

JK

81

Wenlock

Prince of Wales Island

STEVE IRWIN WILDLIFE RESERVE

Bamaga •

POSSESSION ISLAND N.P.

⌐ *Dec. 14*

Tiny Tim

Cape York

— Albany I.

JARDINE RIVER NATIONAL PARK

⌐ *Dec. 13*

NEWCASTLE BAY

┐ Helicopter transports Weldon to Temple Bay

Y o r k   P e n i n s u l a

December 8 ⌐

ORFORD BAY

SHELBURNE BAY

GPS tracks of estuarine crocodiles
2004–2016

0 ———— 20 km

North →

Weldon

August 17, 2004

Olive

— November 14

Pascoe

Hunter Inlet

October 16

TEMPLE BAY

Cape Grenville

Dec. 4 ⌐

KUTINI-PAYAMU (IRON RANGE) N.P. (CYPAL)

G R E A T   B A R R I E R   R E E F   M A R I N E   P A R K

☐ **AREA ENLARGED**

AUSTRALIA

C O R A L   S E A

★ Canberra

SOURCES: CRAIG FRANKLIN AND ROSS DWYER, UNIVERSITY OF QUEENSLAND; GEBCO; MODIS; STATE OF QUEENSLAND

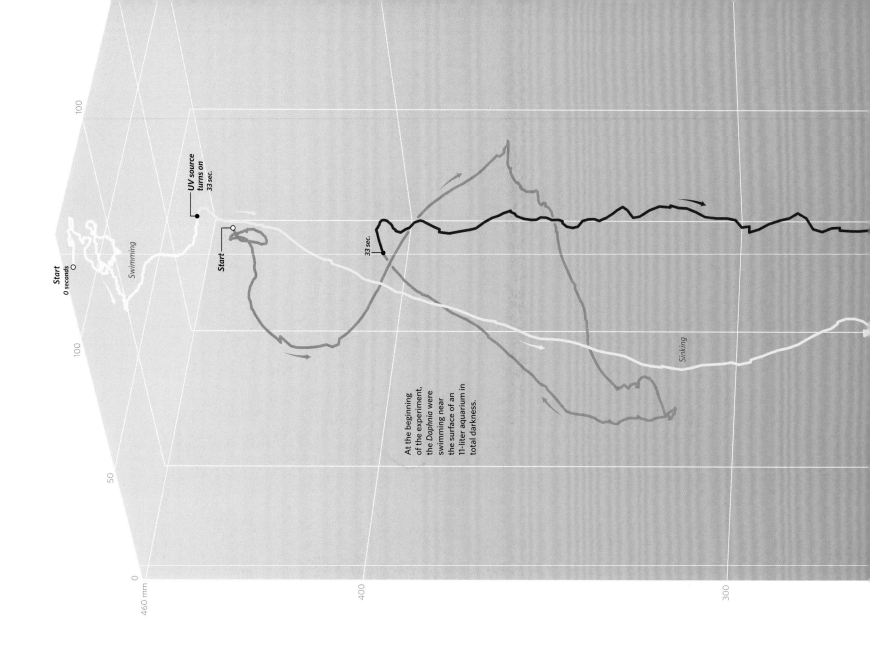

100

UV source
turns on
33 sec.

Start
0 seconds

Swimming

Start

33 sec.

100

At the beginning
of the experiment,
the *Daphnia* were
swimming near
the surface of an
11-liter aquarium in
total darkness.

50

Sinking

400

300

0

460 mm

— ACTUAL SIZE

The Plankton
That Flee the Light

EVERY EVENING, tiny animals called zooplankton travel in their billions from the depths of oceans, lakes, and rivers around the world to feast on microscopic plants at the surface. It's easily the largest migration on Earth in terms of biomass. As soon as day breaks, they do it all in reverse, sinking back into darkness before fish, turtles, and whales can find them. Scientists have known about this "diel vertical migration" for years. And in 2013, a group of researchers from Lund University in Sweden combined biology, chemistry, and physics to track it in exquisite detail.

For this experiment, they chose *Daphnia magna*—transparent freshwater crustaceans less than two millimeters long. These creatures are too small to carry even the smallest electronics, so the scientists coated them with the same fluorescing nanoparticles that surgeons sometimes use to pinpoint cancer cells. Under special lights, these "quantum dots" glow in vibrant colors, enabling cameras to trace their light trails through a dark aquarium. Here, we show the journeys of two sun-sensitive *Daphnia* at actual scale.

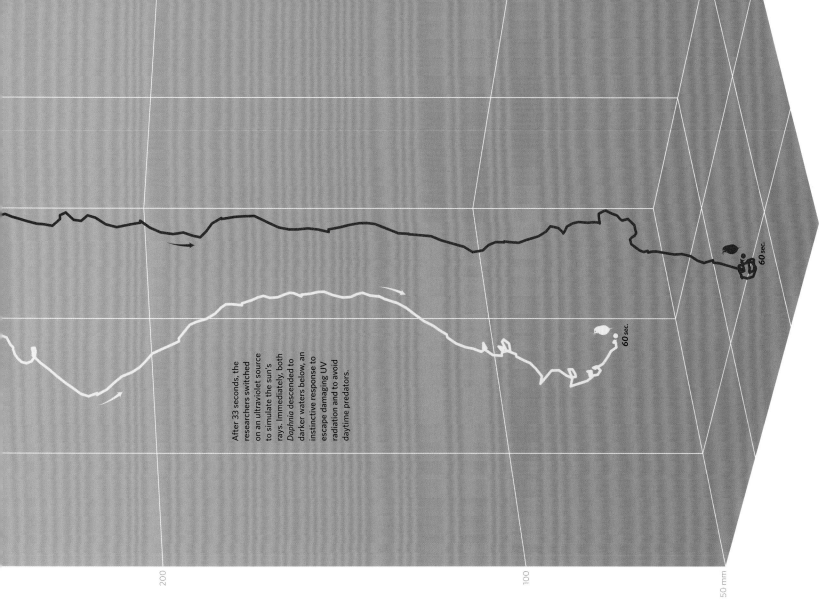

After 33 seconds, the researchers switched on an ultraviolet source to simulate the sun's rays. Immediately, both *Daphnia* descended to darker waters below, an instinctive response to escape damaging UV radiation and to avoid daytime predators.

60 sec.

60 sec.

50 mm

100

200

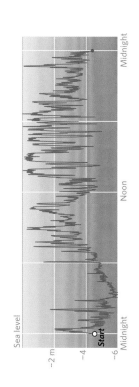

Sea level

-2 m

-4

-6

Start

Midnight

Noon

Midnight

Tracking Jellies

What can't you tag? Between September 2008 and 2009, Graeme Hays of Australia's Deakin University tethered time-depth recorders to the gelatinous waists of 72 jellyfish. It turns out, they're surprisingly active hunters. Over the course of a day, this one swam up and down the water column—at speeds of up to one meter a minute—in search of something to sting.

SOURCES: MIKAEL EKVALL, LUND UNIVERSITY (DAPHNIA); GRAEME HAYS, DEAKIN UNIVERSITY (JELLYFISH)

[THREE]

When the blackbird flew out of sight,
It marked the edge
Of one of many circles.

—WALLACE STEVENS

Birdwatching Through a Wider Lens

by James Cheshire and Oliver Uberti

"IT IS ONE THING TO STUDY in cold blood, as it were, masses of statistics, and quite another to witness these bird-streams actually flowing unceasingly before one, hour after hour." So wrote British ornithologist William Eagle Clarke a little over a century ago while trying to map the seasonal disappearance and reappearance of birds. It was grueling work. To get a clear view of birds in transit, Clarke spent 61 weeks on remote Scottish isles, in lighthouses, and on a lightship moored off the Thames Estuary. Because many birds migrate at night, you have to wonder if he ever slept.

In his two-volume *Studies in Bird Migration*, published in 1912, Clarke asked: *Why do they leave their native lands and set out on long, arduous and dangerous pilgrimages? How are they guided? Is the habit of benefit to those that practise it?* As the natural history curator of the Royal Scottish Museum in Edinburgh, Clarke ranked these among the "greatest mysteries to be found in the animal kingdom." He would not be surprised to hear that they are still being investigated.

This chapter is full of studies where tagging technology has advanced our understanding of bird behavior. However, direct observation remains the foundation of ornithology. For centuries, birders have kept lists of the birds they have seen and heard in their backyards or on their travels. In the 1990s, Steve Kelling, an information scientist at the Cornell Lab of Ornithology, began envisioning a future in which birders could share these lists online.

The Lab has been thinking ahead of its time since ornithologist and Cornell alum Arthur Allen founded it in 1915. He and his colleagues made the first sound recordings of wild birds in 1929, all of which can be heard today—along with many thousands made since—at the Lab's Macaulay Library, the world's largest collection of wildlife sounds. In 2003, the Lab moved to a new headquarters tucked away in Sapsucker Woods, a 230-acre sanctuary on a hill above Ithaca, New York. Kelling greeted us in the lobby. The first thing he showed us was a life-size painting of a wandering albatross, one of 269 birds depicted on the lobby's giant "Wall of Birds." Upstairs in the open-plan offices, you couldn't help but sense the architect's intent to portray the Lab not as a century-old institution but as a 21st-century innovation hub.

Kelling directed us into a conference room with a wall-to-wall window overlooking Sapsucker Pond. "See that big dead tree out there?" he asked.

It was a strategy straight from Silicon Valley. Instead of trying to persuade people to help scientists, Wood wanted to build tools for birders. He wanted to make eBird more *fun*.

"That's a famous tree. In the '60s, Arthur Allen photographed a gyrfalcon in that tree. I recall seeing a western kingbird in that tree. Red-winged woodpecker. Little blue heron. There's probably been more rarities seen over time on that tree than anywhere else, primarily because there's hundreds of birdwatchers here looking at it all day long."

In 1997, Kelling partnered with the National Audubon Society to create a citizen science program called the "Great Backyard Bird Count." The idea was for people around the US to go outside and tally the number and species of birds they could spot in at least 15 minutes and then upload that list to the project's website during the same four-day weekend in February. Kelling will never forget the first count in 1998. "We were working in trailers," he said, pointing to a stand of trees across the pond. "The server was plugged into a real half-assed system over on campus, and on the final night of the count, we had a higher volume of data than the university had ever gotten before. What we realized was that people would actually participate in this stuff." By the end of that first weekend, birders across the country had submitted 15,000 checklists, a huge number in the early days of the internet. But Kelling wasn't satisfied. He wanted to extend the weekend count into a year-round program. He applied for a grant from the National Science Foundation. They rejected it. "They couldn't see the value because we didn't write it right," he said. "The second time we wrote it, they gave us $2.5 million, and that allowed us to build this project called eBird." Fifteen years later, eBird is the most successful citizen science project in the world. As of June 2016, its global community of users had logged 333 million observations. In May 2016 alone, they reported more sightings—11.8 million of them—than in eBird's first six years combined. It won't be long before the total number of observations reaches half a billion (see p. 118).

Given eBird's success, it was surprising to hear that it wasn't an instant hit. "We had all this hype about the project, that, you know, eBird's going to change the world," Kelling recalled. "Then we released eBird in the fall of 2002 and no one

ROUTES TRAVERSED BY MIGRATORY BIRDS
After Prof. Palmen, Dr Menzbier and W. Eagle Clarke

Plate II

William Eagle Clarke included this map in his chapter on "the geographical aspects of British bird migration." He ended the chapter with a line that now seems extremely prescient: "It must be left to local observers to fill in the details—they alone have the opportunities for acquiring the necessary special knowledge."

participated—well, very few. And for the first three years of the project, we actually saw no growth." The Great Backyard Bird Count was still growing each year, but eBird was stalling. Kelling and the entire team at Cornell were stumped. Naysayers insisted that submitting checklists to eBird was too hard. So in 2006, the Lab overhauled the team and hired two prominent members from the birding community, Chris Wood and Brian Sullivan. In two separate presentations to

the entire Lab, both had the same direct advice: "You've got to quit thinking of eBird as a citizen science project."

Early on, many birders would use the site once and rarely return. To keep them engaged, Wood encouraged the Lab to take what birders were already doing—observing birds and making lists—and then help them do it better. It was a strategy straight from Silicon Valley. Instead of trying to persuade people to help scientists, Wood wanted to just build tools for birders. He wanted to make eBird more *fun*. If enough data came pouring in, conservation and research could follow. But first, they needed users.

"My eBird" launched in September 2006. Almost overnight, the website transformed from a place to volunteer your time to a place to share your finds and boast. Birders, an innately competitive lot, could suddenly see how their life lists compared with those of other birders. Rare birds were rewarded as were the volume and quality of their lists. Leaderboards quickly filled with serious birders seeking a top spot in their regions, while eBird's blog named an "eBirder of the month." "It became a huge source of pride for people," said Kelling. "People sign their emails now with *#5 birder on eBird*."

What about users who mistake a cackling goose for a Canada goose? Do such sightings get used in research? Do people submit false reports just for the hell of it? We asked about the bar-headed geese that eBird shows in London's parks, thousands of kilometers from their natural habitat in Asia (see pp. 134–5). Ian Davies, an eBird staff member, pulled up the sighting on his laptop and clicked a button to show every action that had ever happened on that record. "A series of automated data-quality filters initially marked the geese as unconfirmed," he pointed out, "but then our reviewer went in and confirmed the sighting and said that it's an introduced exotic species." eBird has more than 1,400 trusted experts around the world who volunteer their time to vet questionable sightings. But *how* did a reviewer know that the geese in London were valid? "In this case,

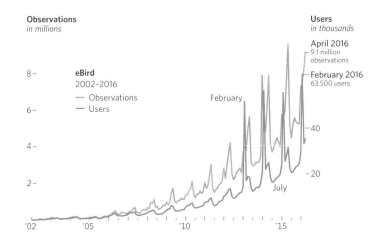

In 2006, a shift in eBird's strategy started a growth rate that hasn't stopped. Activity follows an annual cycle. Every February, the number of users spikes during the Great Backyard Bird Count. Observations remain high through the spring as birds migrate back from the tropics. By July, birds are nesting and less active, so participation dips. Once the autumn migration begins, activity picks up again.

it's a combination of prior knowledge and local expertise," said Davies. "The best way though is through a photo or recording that documents the sighting incontrovertibly." eBird introduced the ability to add media to checklists in November 2015. Users have since uploaded 1,125,000 images. Kelling was beaming as he told us this. "There's 10,000 species of birds in the world. In five months, we'd documented 8,000."

After a few hours with the eBird team, it was clear that they don't come to work every day simply to manage a product. They're among its top users. (Wood currently ranks 17th all-time on the checklist leaderboards; Kelling is 28th.) "We can tell pretty closely whether you're a good birder or a bad birder based on the data you submit. And we use that in our models to improve the quality of the data we use for analysis." "What are the characteristics of a bad birder?" we asked. Without missing a beat, Kelling said, "You stand in a place for an hour and all you see is a pigeon."

AFTER WE SAID GOODBYE TO THE TEAM, we took a walk through Sapsucker Woods to process everything we'd just learned. More than 200 species of birds have been recorded in that sanctuary, so despite our inexperience, we were quietly confident that we would see more than a pigeon. Plus, we had downloaded Cornell's Merlin Bird ID app. It uses eBird data to help people identify the birds they spot. In the process, the app completes a cycle: more eBird data makes the app more useful, which inspires more birders, who with each successful ID collect more data. All it takes is five multiple-choice questions:

Where did you see that bird? Sapsucker Woods

When did you see it? 7 April

What size was it? Robin-sized

What were the main colors? Select from 1 to 3.
Black and red/rufous

What was the bird doing? In trees or bushes

Merlin generated a list of results, each illustrated with a large photo. The first one was our bird: a red-winged blackbird—the very species Arthur Allen wrote his dissertation on in 1911. A year ago, we wouldn't have thought twice about such a bird in the woods. Now for even common birds like robins and sparrows, we found ourselves wanting to learn more.

A few weeks later, warbler aficionado Henry Streby (University of Toledo) encouraged us to attend the "Biggest Week in American Birding" also known as "Warblerstock." This ten-day festival on the southwestern shore of Lake Erie attracts some 2,000 birders each May. There are workshops and eco-tours, karaoke nights and a Birder Prom, but most come just to look for songbirds from the tropics (including as many as 37 species of warbler) that take an annual rest beside the lake before continuing on to summer feeding grounds in Canada. Streby assured us that birds would be "dripping from the trees." He wasn't kidding. It took four hours to walk a kilometer boardwalk because there were flashes of color to see every few steps: American redstarts. Black-throated green warblers. Black-throated *blue* warblers. Yellow warblers. And the tequila-sunrise-breasted blackburnian warbler. We got a short but satisfying glimpse of a black and yellow magnolia warbler, whose migration we knew we wanted to map. It was then that we truly understood the power of eBird: 1) It got us out looking at birds; and 2) By ID'ing that magnolia on Merlin, we were adding to the very data we were going to map. Kelling's team found a way to pull useful data from a world of novices like us instead of relying exclusively on a limited number of experts.

TO STUDY MIGRATION PATTERNS, William Eagle Clarke had just one set of eyes; Kelling now has 320,000 and counting. As you might expect, many eBirders submit observations near where they live or work. Without extra analysis, a map of these sightings would resemble a map of towns and cities. So Kelling's team combines observation data with maps of land cover, population density,

Seasonal Shifts

To map how an entire species moves over time, information scientists at the Cornell Lab of Ornithology create models that interpolate between eBird observations. In other words, these maps are not showing raw data but predictions of how many individuals of a species you'd see at a given location if you went birding between 7 and 8 a.m. and walked at least a kilometer.

"The biggest contribution that eBird is providing," says founder Steve Kelling, "is a way of collecting, visualizing, and then analyzing data to look at entire populations of a species across its entire range across the entire year—and then looking at that across multiple years. Nobody has been able to see that before."

SOURCES: DANIEL FINK, CORNELL LAB OF ORNITHOLOGY; EBIRD; NE

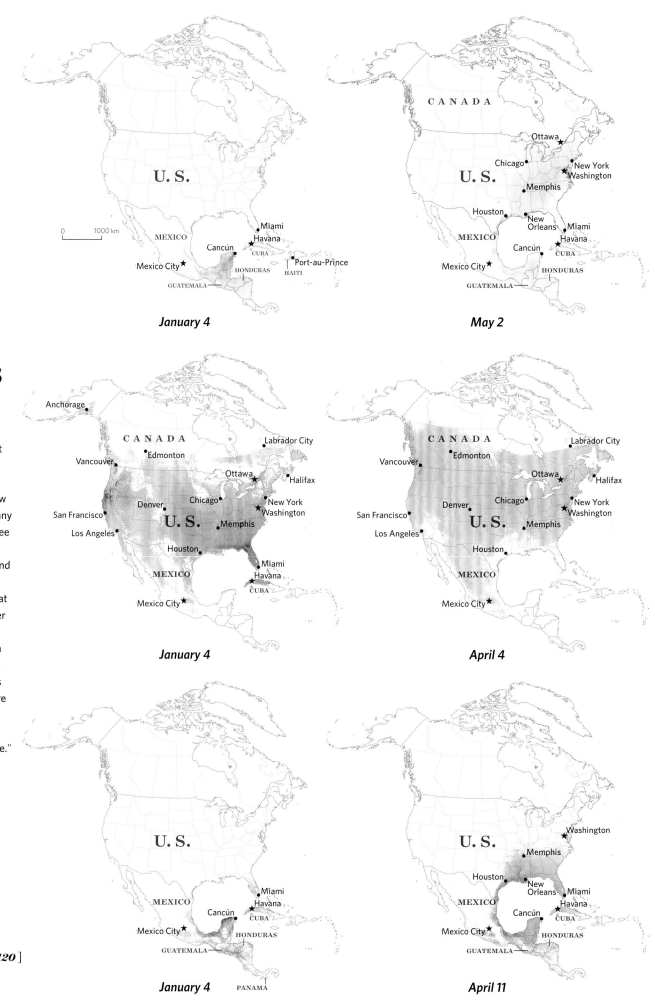

January 4

May 2

January 4

April 4

January 4

April 11

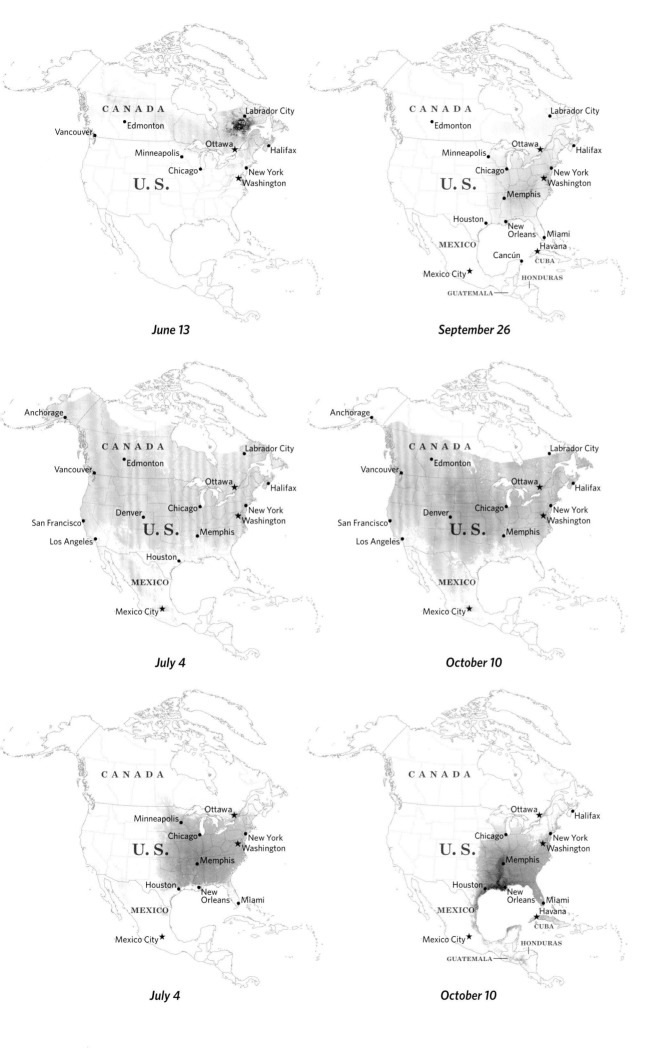

June 13

September 26

Magnolia Warbler

These four maps show the classic pattern of a neotropical migrant. In the winter, they pack into a tiny region of Central America. By early May, the continent ignites as the population flies north to breed, nest, and feed on insects in Canada's boreal forests. Once they've had their fill, as Kelling says, "they haul ass back down as fast as possible."

July 4

October 10

American Robin

This is a bird that's common in the hundreds of millions. Every winter, much of the population concentrates near the Gulf Coast. In the spring, they migrate north and distribute themselves such that every eBirder who goes out sees two robins. As the weather warms, robins switch from eating berries to worms, which also makes them more visible.

July 4

October 10

Indigo Bunting

In the summer, birds feed their young insects and protein to get them strong enough to leave the nest and flee from predators. But once they're out, for many migrant species like indigo buntings, the objective changes. They switch to eating seeds in order to gain enough fat to sustain them on their flights back to the tropics.

elevation, and climate to identify the kinds of places that each species likes to inhabit at different times of the year. For instance, they have enough data from sightings to know that, in June, magnolia warblers thrive in areas with lots of spruce trees. To fill in areas with no sightings, eBird's algorithms search for similar areas and assume these warblers will be there too. For the first time *for any animal*, this process makes it possible to track an entire species.

eBird's maps account for what a bird needs on the ground. Bart Kranstauber, a computational ecologist at the University of Zurich, has been working on an algorithm to replicate their needs in the sky. His thinking is that migratory birds will expend less energy—and therefore will be more likely to survive—if they follow favorable winds to their destination rather than the most direct route. To test this theory, he and his colleagues selected 102 locations in the higher latitudes of the northern hemisphere and 65 locations closer to the equator. Kranstauber's team then used global wind data from 1990 to 2010 to calculate the path of least resistance between these locations, southbound in autumn (August–October) and northbound in the spring (March–May). Their resulting map of "bird highways" (right) exemplifies the increasing value of computer science to ecology: they did not need to see a single bird in flight to create it.

One of the busiest flyways passes through Israel at the junction of three continents: Europe, Asia, and Africa. Twice a year, roughly 500 million birds pass through its narrow airspace, making life hazardous for pilots and deadly for the birds.

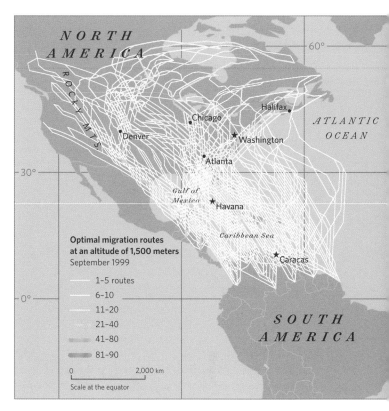

Optimal migration routes
at an altitude of 1,500 meters
September 1999

	1–5 routes
	6–10
	11–20
	21–40
	41–80
	81–90

0   2,000 km

Scale at the equator

White swirls represent the average wind conditions at 1,500 meters. Longer lines indicate stronger winds.

0   1,000 km

September 2, 1999

Sept. 3

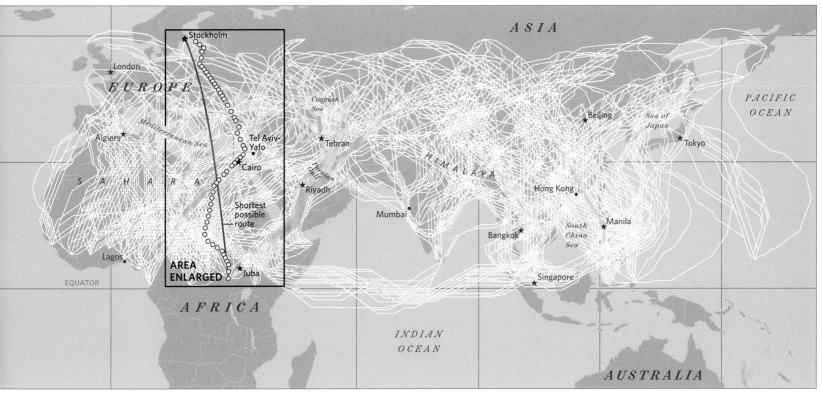

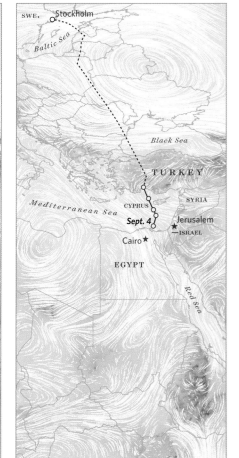

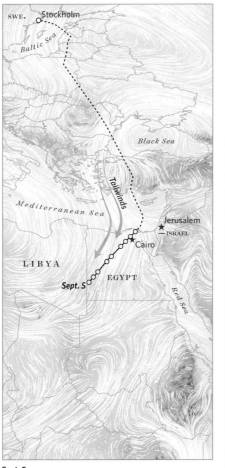

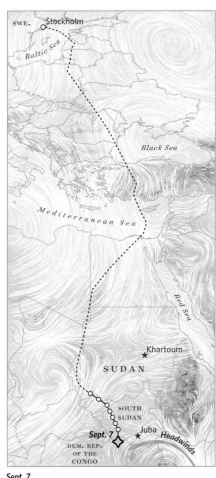

Sept. 4

Sept. 5

Sept. 7

Global Flyways

By compiling 21 years of wind data, researchers discovered that it was faster—and therefore more energy-efficient— for migrating birds to follow favorable winds to their destinations even if it meant flying longer distances. In this sequence, we highlight the optimal route for a bird flying from Sweden to South Sudan, given the wind conditions on September 2–7, 1999. The red line shows the most direct route in terms of distance.

SOURCES: BART KRANSTAUBER, UNIVERSITY OF KONSTANZ; TCR; NE

Between 1972 and 1982, the Israeli Air Force (IAF) lost five aircraft to bird strikes.

The IAF knew the general route and timing of migrations, but they had no way to anticipate the risk of collision at a given time and place. In the early '80s, two researchers at Tel Aviv University had an idea: what if you could adapt radar stations to see where birds are and where they're heading? As part of his doctoral work, Yossi Leshem convinced the IAF to purchase two weather radars for the north and south of Israel. To scan the skies above central Israel, his colleague Leonid Dinevich brought a weather radar back from Russia and set about converting it to detect birds.

A radar station sends out radio waves in a 360° sweep. Anything that reflects the waves back to the station lights up on screen, be they clouds, buildings, hills, trees, aircraft, insects, or birds. Dinevich and a team of Russian scientists funded

If all the world's airports were equipped with avian radar and connected together, we could monitor intercontinental migrations in real-time without tagging a single bird.

by the Ministry of Defence wrote an algorithm to separate bird signals from the noise. The solution is brilliantly simple. Most radar "clutter" is stationary; migrating birds are not. By compiling consecutive radar scans, they could identify which objects moved and then eliminate those that didn't. Categorizing the moving objects by speed and direction added further clarity. For instance,

migrating birds tend to fly between 20 and 80 kilometers per hour. Whatever moved in a straight line at those speeds they considered a single bird. Straight flyers at constant speed were migrating songbirds; straight flyers at fairly steady speeds were waterfowl like ducks and pelicans; those with variable speed were usually the bigger birds such as eagles or white storks (see pp. 144–5) that cause the most damage to aircraft.

While this detail is great for an ornithologist, a pilot just needed to know whether it was safe to fly. Using the algorithm, the converted radar station in central Israel could detect a white stork up to 100 kilometers away or a nocturnally migrating sparrow-sized bird from 25 kilometers away. Most important, it could show the density of migrating birds at a given moment, day or night. If numbers hit unsafe levels, air traffic controllers could delay takeoff until the birds passed or direct the pilot to take off in a different direction. Plus, because the whole process of scanning, analyzing, mapping, and transmitting takes less than 30 minutes, you could conceivably have near-continuous coverage of the conditions overhead. Since the IAF implemented this technology in 1984, the total number of bird strikes in Israel has dropped 76 percent.

Three civilian airports in the US are testing the technology: Seattle-Tacoma, Dallas/Fort Worth, and Chicago's O'Hare. Dinevich and Leshem hope for more. If all the world's airports were equipped with avian radar and connected into a global network, not only would it reduce collisions and save lives, but we could also monitor intercontinental migrations in real-time without tagging a single bird—or spending a single night in a lighthouse.

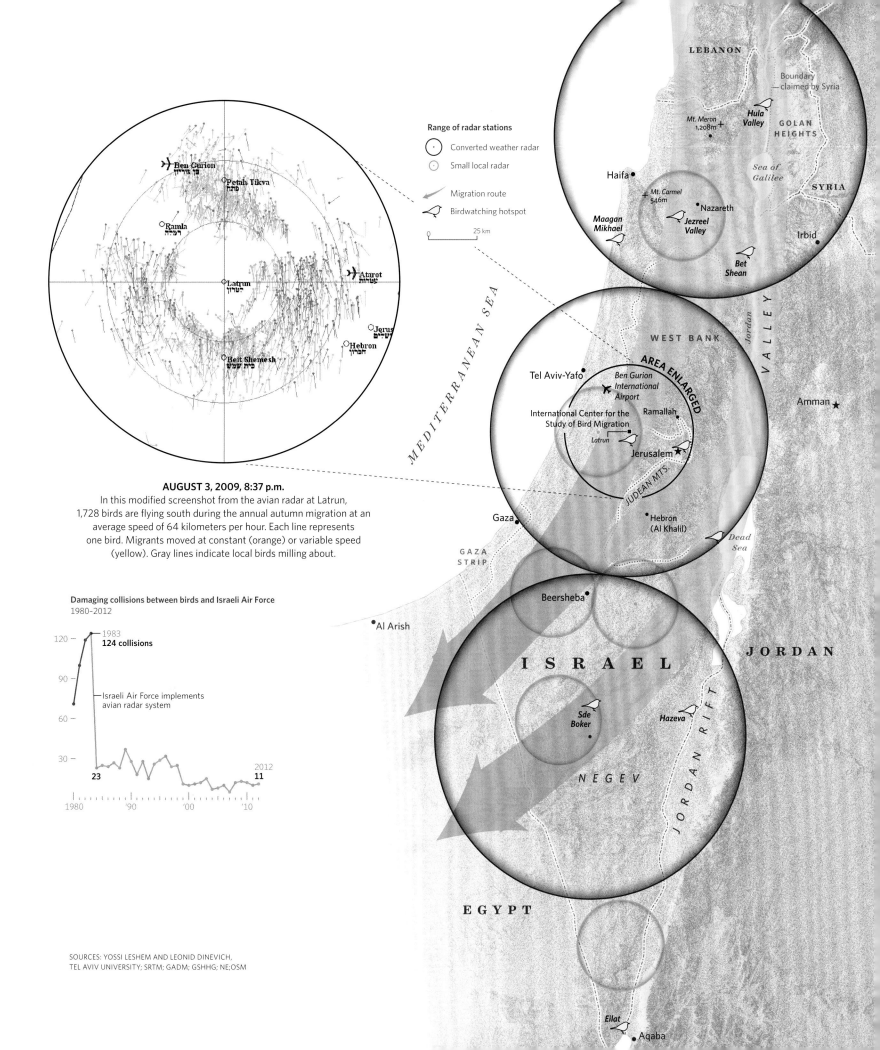

Range of radar stations

◯• Converted weather radar

◯ Small local radar

↗ Migration route

🐦 Birdwatching hotspot

0 ——— 25 km

AUGUST 3, 2009, 8:37 p.m.
In this modified screenshot from the avian radar at Latrun, 1,728 birds are flying south during the annual autumn migration at an average speed of 64 kilometers per hour. Each line represents one bird. Migrants moved at constant (orange) or variable speed (yellow). Gray lines indicate local birds milling about.

Damaging collisions between birds and Israeli Air Force
1980–2012

1983
124 collisions

120 —
90 —

Israeli Air Force implements avian radar system

60 —

30 —

23   2012
                                          11

1980   '90   '00   '10

Ben Gurion · בן גוריון
Petah Tikva · פתח
Ramla · רמלה
Latrun · יטרון
Atarot · עטרות
Jerus · שלי
Hebron · חברון
Beit Shemesh · בית שמש

LEBANON

Boundary claimed by Syria

Mt. Meron 1,208m
Hula Valley
GOLAN HEIGHTS

Haifa
Mt. Carmel 546m
Nazareth
Jezreel Valley
Sea of Galilee
SYRIA
Irbid

Maagan Mikhael
Bet Shean

MEDITERRANEAN SEA

WEST BANK
AREA ENLARGED

Tel Aviv-Yafo
Ben Gurion International Airport
Ramallah

International Center for the Study of Bird Migration
Latrun
Jerusalem
Amman ★

JUDEAN MTS.

Gaza
Hebron (Al Khalil)
Dead Sea

GAZA STRIP

Al Arish

Beersheba

ISRAEL   JORDAN

Sde Boker
Hazeva

NEGEV
JORDAN RIFT

EGYPT

Eilat
Aqaba

SOURCES: YOSSI LESHEM AND LEONID DINEVICH, TEL AVIV UNIVERSITY; SRTM; GADM; GSHHG; NE;OSM

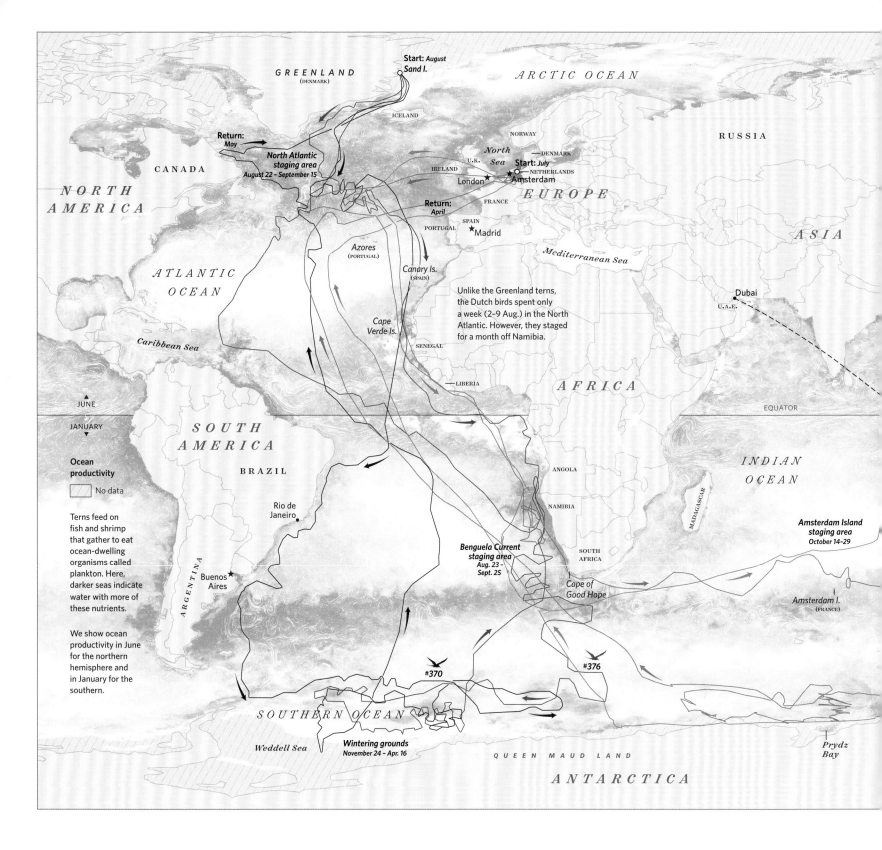

Ocean productivity

No data

Terns feed on fish and shrimp that gather to eat ocean-dwelling organisms called plankton. Here, darker seas indicate water with more of these nutrients.

We show ocean productivity in June for the northern hemisphere and in January for the southern.

Unlike the Greenland terns, the Dutch birds spent only a week (2–9 Aug.) in the North Atlantic. However, they staged for a month off Namibia.

Start: *August* Sand I.

Return: *May*

North Atlantic staging area August 22 – September 15

Start: *July* Amsterdam

Return: *April*

Azores (PORTUGAL)

Canary Is. (SPAIN)

Cape Verde Is.

Rio de Janeiro

Buenos Aires

Benguela Current staging area Aug. 23 – Sept. 25

Cape of Good Hope

Amsterdam Island staging area October 14–29

Amsterdam I. (FRANCE)

#370

#376

Dubai

Prydz Bay

Wintering grounds November 24 – Apr. 16

Weddell Sea

QUEEN MAUD LAND

ANTARCTICA

THE RECORD ROUTES

Here we show four birds, two from each dataset. All four stopped in the North Atlantic to feed at a previously unknown "staging area" where cold, nutrient-rich water collides with less-productive seas. After refueling, the terns headed to Africa. South of Cape Verde, one of the Greenlanders (#370) crossed to Brazil while the rest followed the African coast to a feeding spot in the Benguela Current. Eventually Egevang's terns ended up in the Weddell Sea for the winter. Fijn's birds, however, banked east past the Cape of Good Hope and flew as far as Australia after a rest in the Indian Ocean. For both groups, the southbound trip took three to four months. The dash home? About 40 days.

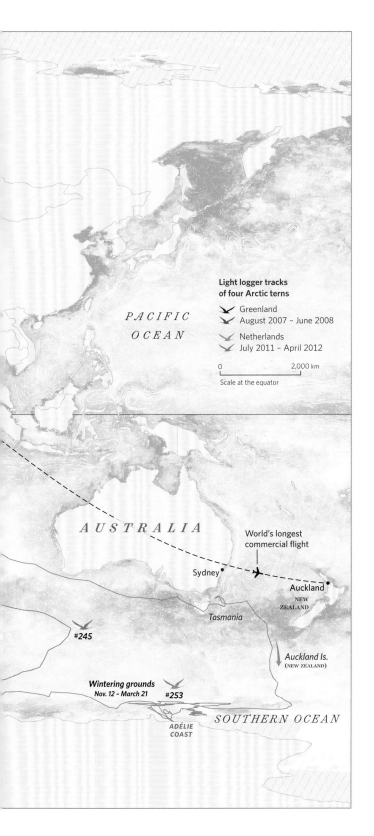

Light logger tracks
of four Arctic terns

⌄ Greenland
⌄ August 2007 – June 2008

⌄ Netherlands
⌄ July 2011 – April 2012

0   2,000 km

Scale at the equator

PACIFIC
OCEAN

AUSTRALIA

World's longest
commercial flight

Sydney•
Auckland•
NEW
ZEALAND

Tasmania

Auckland Is.
(NEW ZEALAND)

#245

Wintering grounds
Nov. 12 – March 21   #253

SOUTHERN OCEAN

ADÉLIE
COAST

The Terns' World Record

IN JULY 2007, Arctic biologist Carsten Egevang attached light loggers—sunlight-sensing geo-locators the weight of a paperclip—to the legs of 50 Arctic terns before they left their breeding grounds in Greenland. Of these, only ten came back intact the following summer, but those ten contained record-breaking data. On average, the terns had flown 70,900 kilometers from an island in the Arctic to sea ice off Antarctica and back. (For comparison, the longest nonstop commercial flight in the world is 14,200 kilometers from Dubai to Auckland.) It was the longest animal migration ever recorded, nearly doubling previous estimates for the species. The record stood for four years until five terns—tagged by Ruben Fijn and Jan van der Winden in the Netherlands—traveled an average distance of 90,000 kilo-meters. It's not yet clear why the Dutch terns went farther, but Fijn believes it's only a matter of time before that record falls too. If terns from Norway or northern Russia go as far as Australia, their odometers will hit six digits.

SOURCES: CARSTEN EGEVANG, GREENLAND INSTITUTE OF NATURAL RESOURCES;
RUBEN FIJN AND JAN VAN DER WINDEN, BUREAU WAARDENBURG; NPP; SODA; NE; GADM

Campbell Glacier

Cape
Washington

Zuchelli
Research Station
(ITALY)

S E A   I C E

AREA
ENLARGED

Cape Washington
juts ten kilometers into
Terra Nova Bay. At the
tip of this fang of rock
and ice, Fretwell spotted
a 500m² guano stain,
evidence of emperor
penguins. Sea ice fastens
to the cape from March
to December, making it
a perfect place for
emperors to lay eggs
and raise their chicks.
So Fretwell sent another
satellite to photograph
the stains in higher detail
on October 16, 2009.
He then used image-
recognition software to
isolate penguin areas
(red) from other pixels.
Using an area-to-number
conversion, he determined
these areas represented
11,808 penguins.

0   5 km

T E R R A
N O V A
B A Y

Satellite
image after
pansharpening

■ Penguin
□ Snow
■ Shadow
▨ Guano

The Penguins Seen from Space

SATELLITE IMAGES help us answer questions: Which route should I take? Or, is that restaurant near public transportation? In 2008, Peter Fretwell, a Geographic Information Officer at the British Antarctic Survey, began wondering if those eyes in the sky could help with another: how many emperor penguins exist? In the age of Google, it may seem like an easy question to answer. The problem was no one had ever counted.

To be fair, people had tried. In 1992, the authors of *Handbook of the Birds of the World* summed up decades of studies and put the population between 270,000 and 350,000 penguins. Sixteen years on, those counts were old, not to mention incomplete. Because Antarctica is so cold, remote and vast, it's impossible for researchers to observe every penguin colony in a single breeding season. For most of the areas thought to be inhabited by penguins, there were no data. What's a scientist to do?

To get population figures, elephant researchers will fly over a small area and count every individual they see. Then they scale that number for an entire region. It's called an aerial census. From his office in Cambridge, UK, Fretwell decided to try something similar for penguins—only from much higher up.

He started his satellite search in September 2009 along the Antarctic coastline. At that time, both males and females were tending newly hatched chicks. On this first pass, he used coarse imagery across broad swathes. An individual penguin didn't show up at this resolution, but on the white ice, the brown stain of an entire colony's guano certainly did. Fretwell found 46 such stains. So he sent very-high-resolution satellites to photograph them in detail.

"The great thing about emps," he says, "is that they offer crisp black silhouettes against the bright white snow." That contrast—plus the fact that emperors huddle in clusters—allowed Fretwell to isolate the penguin pixels through a process he calls "pansharpening" (see inset). His software works like facial-recognition on Facebook. Whenever you tag your face in a photo, you

0   500 km

Emperor penguin colonies
2015

Known
before 2009

Found or confirmed
by satellite since

Satellite images helped Fretwell raise the number of known colonies from 31 to 53. Climate change will not affect them evenly; areas north of 70° South are at highest risk for sea ice loss. By his count, 26 colonies breed north of that latitude. That's 200,000 birds.

SOURCES: PETER FRETWELL, BRITISH ANTARCTIC SURVEY; LANDSAT; GSHHG

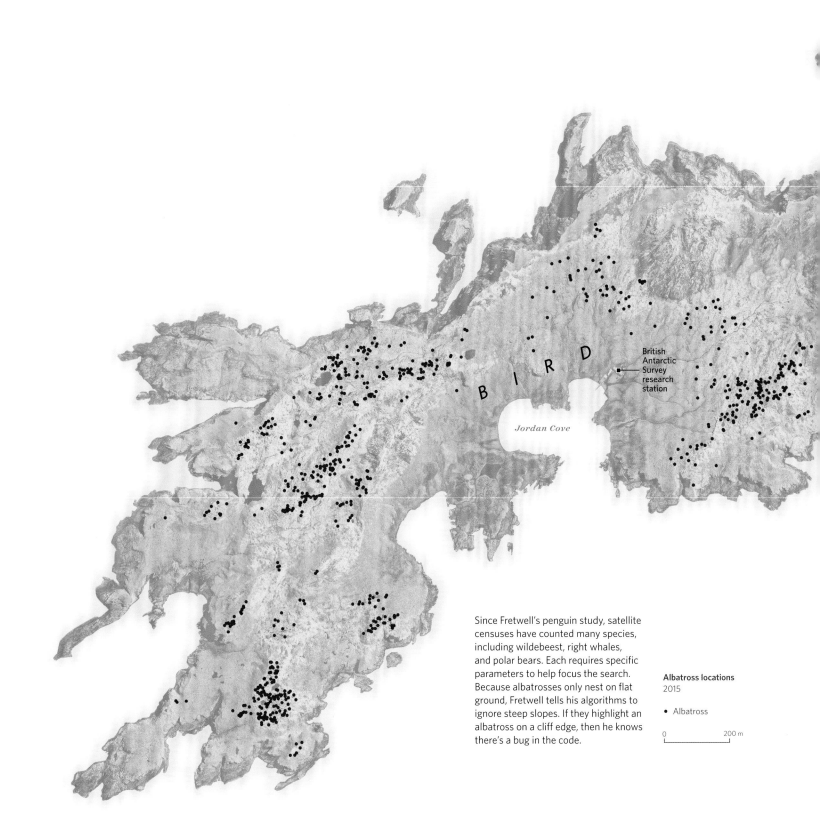

Jordan Cove

B I R D

British
Antarctic
Survey
research
station

Since Fretwell's penguin study, satellite censuses have counted many species, including wildebeest, right whales, and polar bears. Each requires specific parameters to help focus the search. Because albatrosses only nest on flat ground, Fretwell tells his algorithms to ignore steep slopes. If they highlight an albatross on a cliff edge, then he knows there's a bug in the code.

Albatross locations
2015

• Albatross

0   200 m

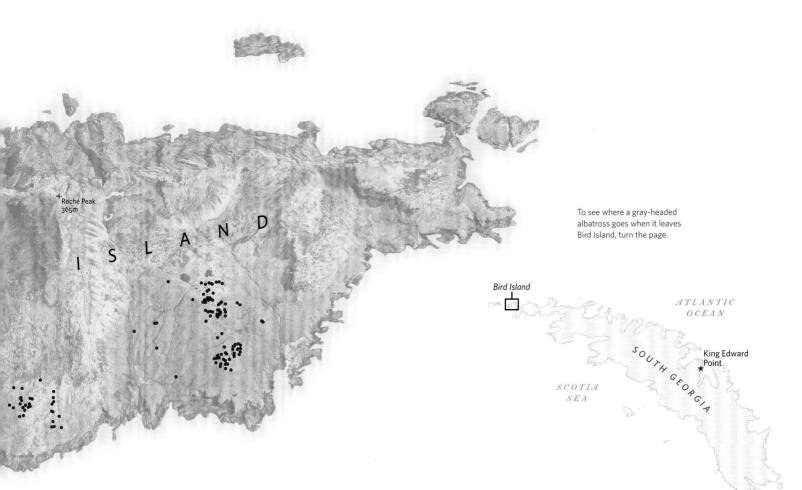

Roché Peak
365m

I S L A N D

To see where a gray-headed
albatross goes when it leaves
Bird Island, turn the page.

Bird Island

ATLANTIC
OCEAN

King Edward
Point

SCOTIA
SEA

SOUTH GEORGIA

SOUTH
AMERICA

ATLANTIC
OCEAN

South Georgia

teach its algorithms to recognize your features in an array of pixels. In much the same way, Fretwell tweaked his algorithms until they learned the difference between pixels that were penguins and those that were snow, shadow, and guano.

Here's where it becomes fascinating. From on-the-ground observations and aerial photography, he knew how closely penguins stand: roughly one adult per square meter. With this area-to-number conversion, he could now get a count for the continent. All he had to do was find how much space penguins occupied in each image. Take the Cape Washington colony (p. 128). Penguin pixels (red) took up 12,000 square meters. Translation:

12,000 penguins. Pansharpening all 46 guano stains yielded 595,000 penguins, twice the previous estimate. To verify these numbers, Fretwell ran his code *ten thousand times*.

It was the first census of any species using satellite imagery. Once again, technology saved time and resources; it may save birds, too. Without a baseline, it had been impossible to tell if and where emperors were dying as the climate warms and sea ice thins. Now Fretwell had the complete picture and the means to update it. He has not done another count, but he keeps an eye on the colonies. Since 2012, his team has found a few small colonies, bringing the world total to 53.

SOURCES: PETER FRETWELL, BRITISH ANTARCTIC SURVEY; LANDSAT; GSHHG

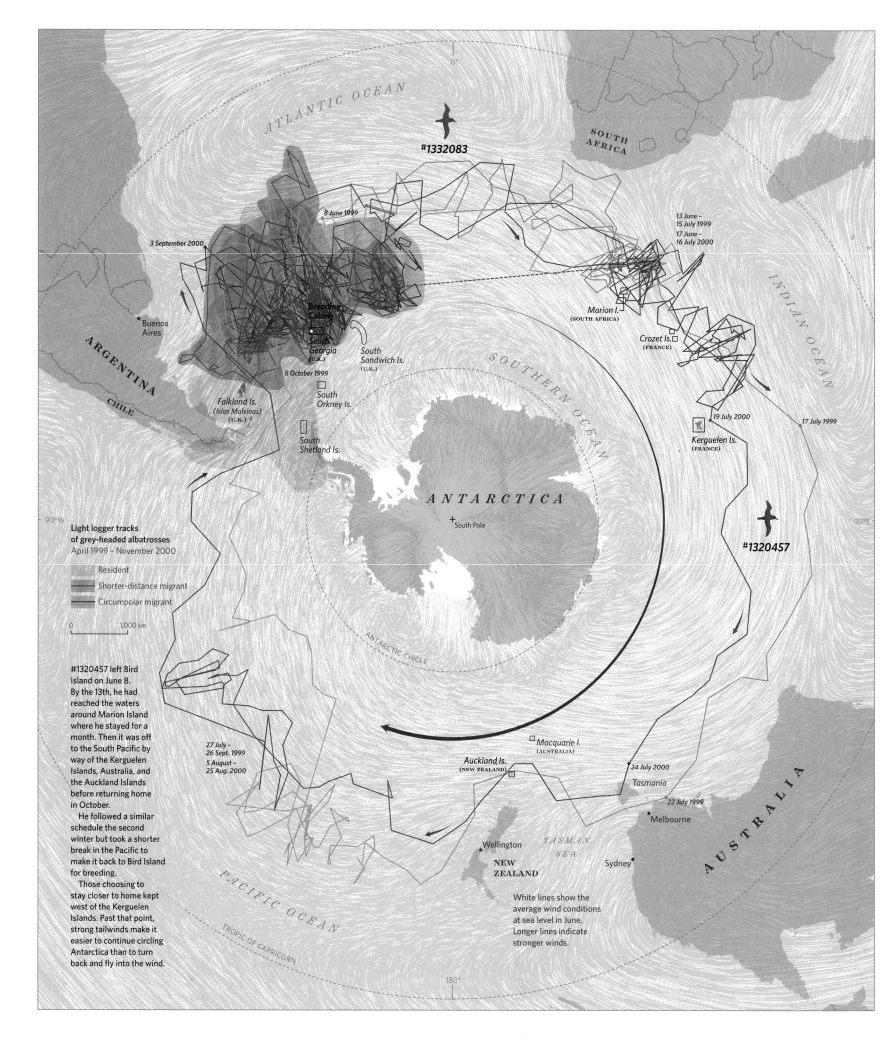

#1332083

13 June –
15 July 1999

17 June –
16 July 2000

SOUTH
AFRICA

ATLANTIC OCEAN

8 June 1999

3 September 2000

Buenos
Aires

ARGENTINA

CHILE

Breeding
Colony

South
Georgia
(U.K.)

South
Sandwich Is.
(U.K.)

8 October 1999

Falkland Is.
(Islas Malvinas)
(U.K.)

South
Orkney Is.

South
Shetland Is.

Marion I.
(SOUTH AFRICA)

Crozet Is.
(FRANCE)

INDIAN OCEAN

19 July 2000

17 July 1999

Kerguelen Is.
(FRANCE)

SOUTHERN OCEAN

ANTARCTICA

South Pole

90°W

90°E

ANTARCTIC CIRCLE

**Light logger tracks
of grey-headed albatrosses**
April 1999 – November 2000

Resident

Shorter-distance migrant

Circumpolar migrant

0   1,000 km

#1320457 left Bird
Island on June 8.
By the 13th, he had
reached the waters
around Marion Island
where he stayed for a
month. Then it was off
to the South Pacific by
way of the Kerguelen
Islands, Australia, and
the Auckland Islands
before returning home
in October.
    He followed a similar
schedule the second
winter but took a shorter
break in the Pacific to
make it back to Bird Island
for breeding.
    Those choosing to
stay closer to home kept
west of the Kerguelen
Islands. Past that point,
strong tailwinds make it
easier to continue circling
Antarctica than to turn
back and fly into the wind.

#1320457

27 July –
26 Sept. 1999

5 August –
25 Aug. 2000

Macquarie I.
(AUSTRALIA)

Auckland Is.
(NEW ZEALAND)

24 July 2000

Tasmania

22 July 1999

Melbourne

PACIFIC OCEAN

TASMAN
SEA

Wellington

NEW
ZEALAND

Sydney

AUSTRALIA

White lines show the
average wind conditions
at sea level in June.
Longer lines indicate
stronger winds.

TROPIC OF CAPRICORN

180°

The Albatrosses Circling Antarctica

VISIT THE BRITISH ANTARCTIC SURVEY's headquarters on the outskirts of Cambridge, UK, and you might encounter a stuffed albatross and her chick. Their 15,000-kilometer journey from Bird Island in South Georgia was a short hop compared to the 25,000-kilometer circumpolar migrations some albatrosses make. With wingspans of up to 3.5 meters, these birds can cover huge distances with only a few flaps of their wings. On this map, we show eighteen months of a study that has been tracking such journeys for more than a decade.

In April 1999, light loggers were attached to the legs of 47 gray-headed albatrosses at the end of a successful breeding season. The data they recorded revealed three distinct behaviors: seven birds stayed near their breeding area in the southwest Atlantic; three made trips to the Indian Ocean and back; and twelve males flew round the entire Southern Ocean. Three even managed a double loop.

A circumpolar migration has three stages. The first—from South Georgia to the Indian Ocean—they completed in six days, on average, at a pace of 950 kilometers per day. That's like flying the length of Italy every day. After a month-long food stop in the seas near Marion Island and the Crozet archipelago, they resumed that pace for thirteen days to New Zealand before slowing to 750 kilometers per day on the homestretch as polar winds dissipated over the open Pacific Ocean. The fastest completed his circle in 46 days.

This study revealed critical feeding areas in the southern Indian and Pacific Oceans, where migrants stop to rest and enjoy a rich food supply. However, these waters also attract longline fishing boats, which set lines up to 130 kilometers long on the ocean surface. Albatrosses bite the baited hooks, get dragged under and drown at a rate of 100,000 a year. Protective measures exist (e.g. lines can be set at night or deeper underwater), but their use is rarely enforced. Although it is unlikely to happen, keeping longliners out of stopover areas is probably the only true way to ensure the world's most threatened family of birds continues to soar.

SOURCES: RICHARD PHILLIPS, BRITISH ANTARCTIC SURVEY; TCR; GSHHG; SCAR

The Geese
of the Himalayas

On an April night from a camp at 4,500 meters on Barun Glacier, I myself have heard the distant honking of these birds flying miles above me unseen against the stars over Makalu . . . one can only speculate on what adaptations permit them to accomplish this feat.

WHEN BIOLOGIST LAWRENCE W. SWAN wrote these words in 1961, he established what became the prevailing view that bar-headed geese were high-altitude specialists. This remained untested for half a century until a team led by Charles Bishop from Bangor University strapped GPS-enabled backpacks to 91 birds before their biannual migration across the Himalayas—a journey thought to be older than the mountains themselves.

After sifting through 150,000 GPS locations from India to Mongolia, Lucy Hawkes, the project's analyst, found two surprises: no goose topped 7,290 meters above sea level and 98% of their tracks were below 5,500 meters. Mapping revealed routes along valleys and wetlands rather than over mountains, leading her team to conclude that "geese tended to minimize their altitude wherever possible." In other words, the honks Swan heard were more likely echoing from a valley *below* him.

This in no way undermines the flying capabilities of the geese. Oxygen levels are extremely low at these altitudes. Biosensors in the backpacks showed that bar-heads can keep their wings flapping in the thin air because their hearts have evolved to beat at up to 500 times per minute—7.2 times faster than at sea level. As Hawkes says, "They're like metronomes. They just keep going."

Shortest possible route

On average, the geese traveled a route that was 112 kilometers longer than the shortest possible route.

Lake Baikal

Yellow

Ulaanbaatar ★

Hovsgol Lake

May 17

August 23, 2009

Terhiyn Tsagaan Lake

Aug. 29

May 9

September 20–27

Qinghai Lake

Apr. 26

R U S S I A

M O N G O L I A

C H I N A

A L T A Y

M T S.

K U N L U N   M T S.

PAK.

Boundary claimed by India

Boundary claimed by Pakistan

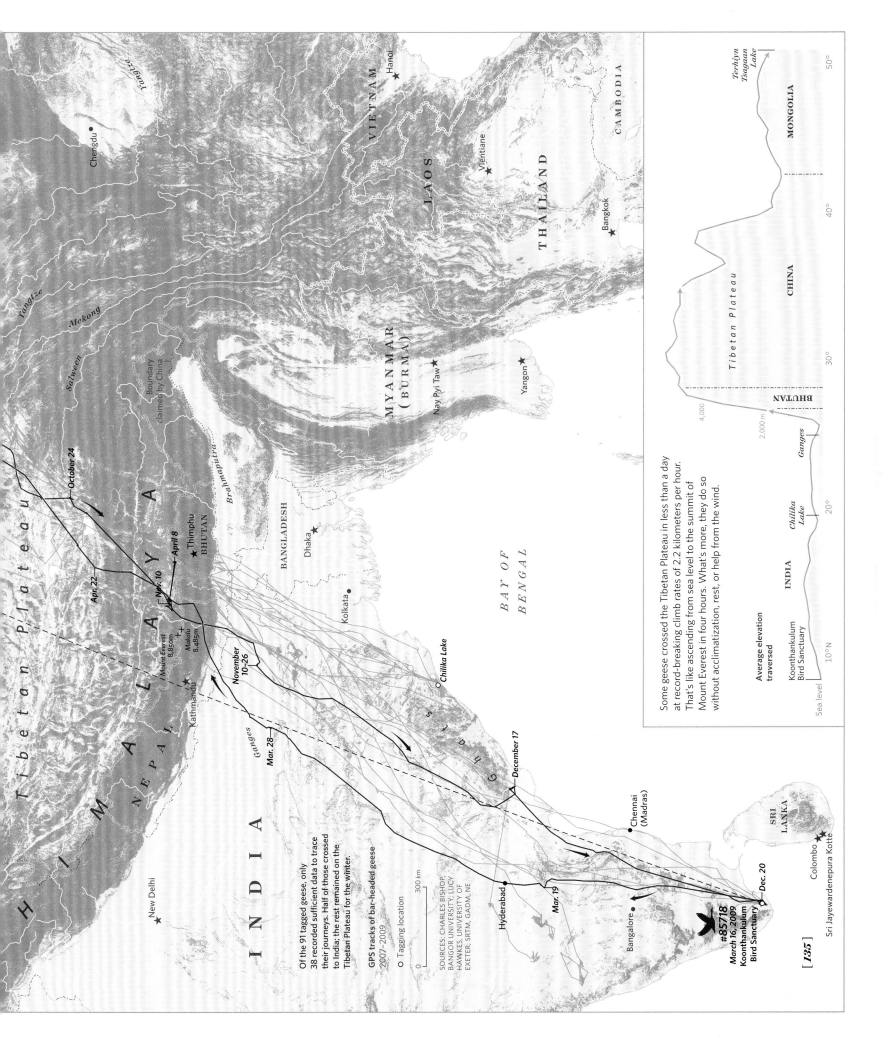

Tibetan Plateau

Yangtze

Mekong

Salween

Yangtze

Chengdu •

Boundary
claimed by China

Brahmaputra

VIETNAM   Hanoi ★

L A O S

Vientiane ★

October 24

Thimphu
★ BHUTAN

April 8

Apr. 22

Nov. 10

MYANMAR
(B U R M A)

Nay Pyi Taw ★

THAILAND

Bangkok ★

H   I   M   A   L   A   Y   A

I Mount Everest
8,850m
+
Makalu
8,485m

NEPAL

Kathmandu ★

November
10–26

Yangon ★

BANGLADESH

Dhaka ★

Kolkata •

BAY   OF

BENGAL

Mar. 28

Ganges

G   h   a   t   s

Chilika Lake

December 17

I   N   D   I   A

New Delhi ★

Of the 91 tagged geese, only
38 recorded sufficient data to trace
their journeys. Half of those crossed
to India; the rest remained on the
Tibetan Plateau for the winter.

GPS tracks of bar-headed geese
2007–2009

○ Tagging location

0   300 km

SOURCES: CHARLES BISHOP,
BANGOR UNIVERSITY; LUCY
HAWKES, UNIVERSITY OF
EXETER; SRTM, GADM, NE

Hyderabad •

Mar. 19

Bangalore •

Chennai
(Madras) •

SRI
LANKA

Colombo •

#85718
March 16, 2009
Koonthankulum
Bird Sanctuary

Dec. 20

[*135*]

Sri Jayewardenepura Kotte

Some geese crossed the Tibetan Plateau in less than a day
at record-breaking climb rates of 2.2 kilometers per hour.
That's like ascending from sea level to the summit of
Mount Everest in four hours. What's more, they do so
without acclimatization, rest, or help from the wind.

Average elevation
traversed

Sea level

Koonthankulum
Bird Sanctuary

INDIA

10°N

Chilika
Lake

Ganges

20°

2,000 m

BHUTAN

Tibetan Plateau

4,000

CHINA

30°

MONGOLIA

40°

Terhiyn
Tsagaan
Lake

50°

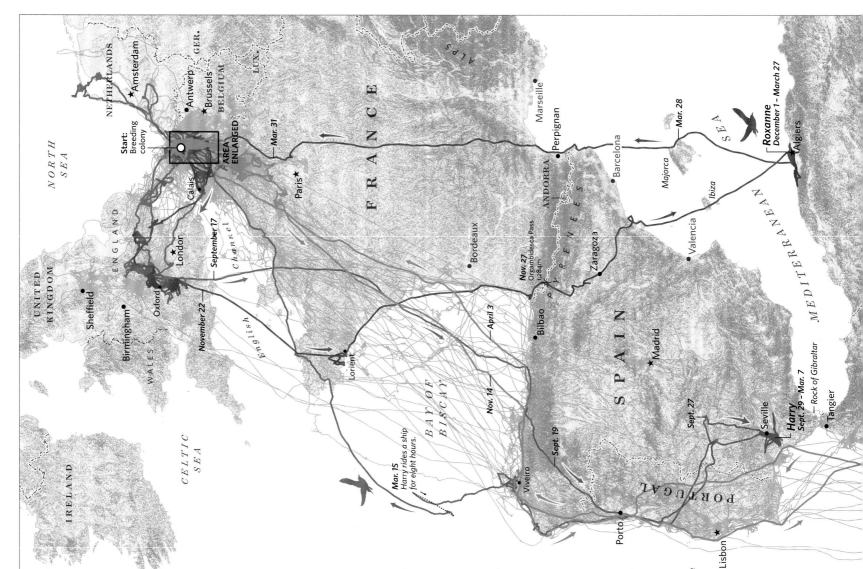

The Gulls Who Crave Chips

WITH TITLES LIKE "DATA SCIENTIST" and "Open Data Publisher," the LifeWatch team at Belgium's Research Institute for Nature and Forest sounds more like a tech startup than a science lab. Don't be fooled. These coders are next-generation biologists. In three years, their system has gathered 2.5 million GPS fixes from 101 gulls, some of which migrate as far as Gambia and back.

When tagged gulls return to the colony, they transmit their data to a base station. From there the last four days of locations feed into maps on the LifeWatch website while another program automatically cleans and stores the full journey on a database at the University of Antwerp. Those steps alone are novel, but what LifeWatch does next with the data is revolutionary: they share them.

Scientists often squirrel away their findings to keep someone else from publishing them before they can. LifeWatch doesn't think that way. In the spring of 2016, they lent their data to a hackathon in Helsinki, Finland. The organizers challenged their attendees to find and visualize patterns in the gulls' migration and foraging behavior. For instance, do different gulls of the same species go to different places? Do they balance energy use with food availability? Consider this map our entry. To the first question, we invite you to compare the tracks of three lesser black-backed gulls named Harry, Eric, and Roxanne. To the second, see the area enlarged. When you give gulls easy access to a giant pile of potato scraps, they take it.

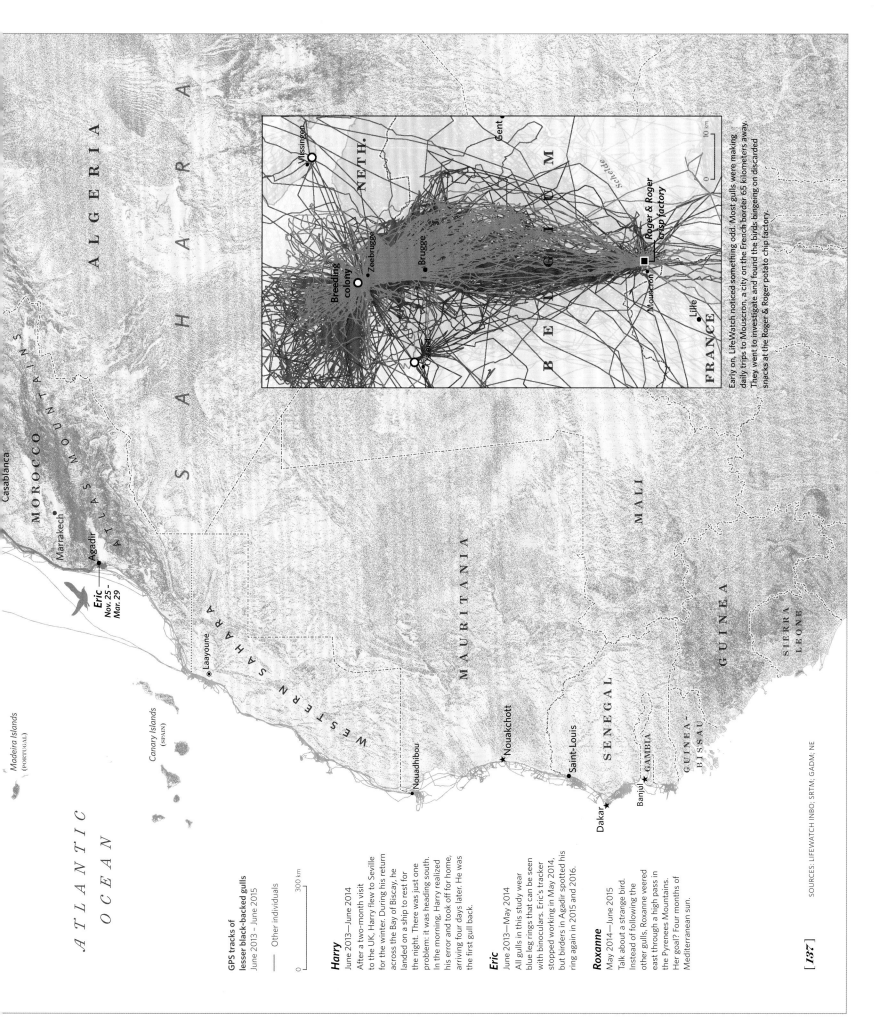

ATLANTIC

OCEAN

Madeira Islands
(PORTUGAL)

Canary Islands
(SPAIN)

Casablanca

MOROCCO

Marrakech

Agadir

ATLAS MOUNTAINS

Eric
Nov. 25 –
Mar. 29

Laayoune

WESTERN SAHARA

Nouadhibou

Nouakchott

MAURITANIA

Saint-Louis

Dakar

Banjul
GAMBIA

SENEGAL

GUINEA-BISSAU

GUINEA

SIERRA
LEONE

S A H A R A

ALGERIA

MALI

**GPS tracks of
lesser black-backed gulls**
June 2013 – June 2015

—— Other individuals

0 ____ 300 km

Harry

June 2013—June 2014

After a two-month visit
to the UK, Harry flew to Seville
for the winter. During his return
across the Bay of Biscay, he
landed on a ship to rest for
the night. There was just one
problem: it was heading south.
In the morning, Harry realized
his error and took off for home,
arriving four days later. He was
the first gull back.

Eric

June 2013—May 2014

All gulls in this study wear
blue leg rings that can be seen
with binoculars. Eric's tracker
stopped working in May 2014,
but birders in Agadir spotted his
ring again in 2015 and 2016.

Roxanne

May 2014—June 2015

Talk about a strange bird.
Instead of following the
other gulls, Roxanne veered
east through a high pass in
the Pyrenees Mountains.
Her goal? Four months of
Mediterranean sun.

Vlissingen

NETH.

Gent

Breeding
colony

Zeebrugge

Brugge

BELGIUM

Schelde

Mouscron

**Roger & Roger
crisp factory**

Lille

FRANCE

0 ____ 10 km

Early on, LifeWatch noticed something odd: Most gulls were making
daily trips to Mouscron, a city on the French border 65 kilometers away.
They went to investigate and found the birds bingeing on discarded
snacks at the Roger & Roger potato chip factory.

SOURCES: LIFEWATCH INBO; SRTM; GADM; NE

The Vultures
Spiraling Overhead

EUROPE

FRANCE

ON AN ENORMOUS MOSAIC of flat screens, millions of data points form swirls, orbs, and webs, revealing the movements of soaring vultures, diving cormorants, and digging badgers. This is Swansea University's "Simultaneous Localization and Mapping Visualization Suite" in the Department of Biosciences. In short, it's Mission Control for animal movement. The facility is the vision of animal-tracking legend Rory Wilson, who believes visualization is vital to understanding airborne animals. As Wilson's colleague Emily Shepard says, "air is massively fickle. It can be fantastically energy-giving or energy-sapping." So if their team can quantify how a bird conserves energy, millisecond by millisecond, it will help them understand not only where it goes but also *why*.

Over the past forty years, Wilson has invented many "spy technologies" to follow the lives of animals. His masterpiece is a suite of sensors dubbed the "Daily Diary." It acts as an in-flight recorder for birds, though he has deployed them on marine and land animals too. In addition to collecting GPS locations, Daily Diaries record pressure, humidity, temperature, light level, speed, and acceleration all while tri-axial magnetometers use the Earth's magnetic field to detail the direction and posture of the animals to which they're attached.

Take griffon vultures. Like many larger birds, these bare-headed carcass-eaters stay aloft by riding plumes of hot air—or thermals—rising off the Earth. Using the Diaries, Wilson's team hopes to discover how the birds locate these updrafts and how they modulate their behavior within them. "It's an interesting balancing act," says Shepard. "They must stay within the part of the thermal where the air is rising faster than the birds are sinking."

One of Shepard's colleagues loads a vulture's Diary on the big screen—over 8,000 readings of direction and air temperature collected from just 3.5 minutes of flight above Rocamadour, a hilltop village in Southern France. As the track spirals up, Shepard narrates how a vulture pulls potential energy out of thin air. We do the same here.

SOURCES: EMILY SHEPARD, SWANSEA UNIVERSITY; OLIVIER DURIEZ, UNIVERSITY OF MONTPELLIER; LE ROCHER DES AIGLES FALCONRY CENTER

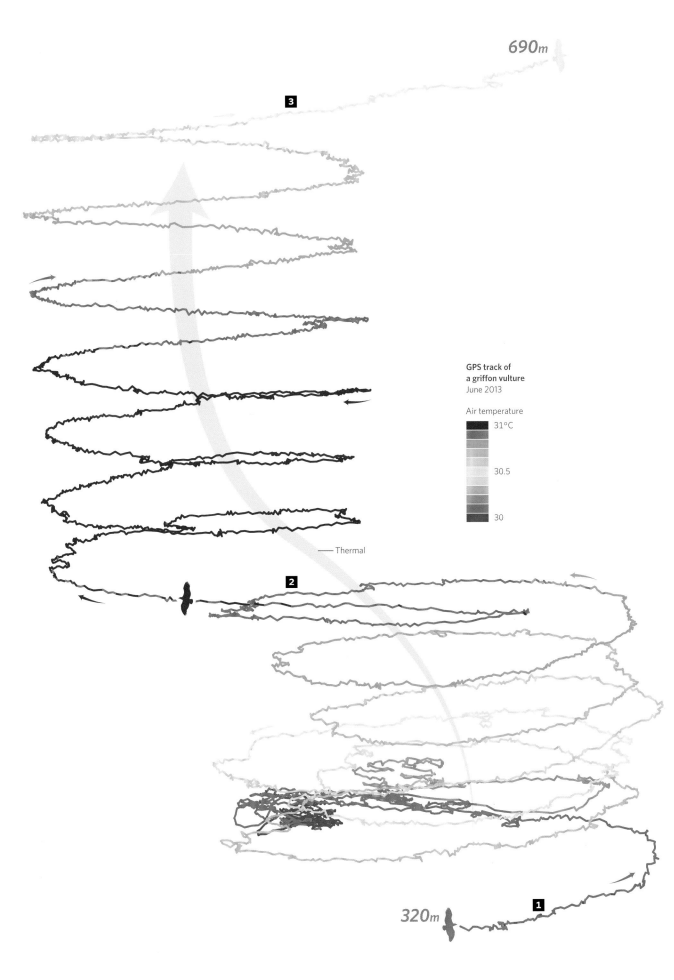

690m

3

GPS track of
a griffon vulture
June 2013

Air temperature

31°C

30.5

30

— Thermal

2

1

320m

ANATOMY OF
AN UPDRAFT

Vultures are scaven-
gers. They fly during
daylight to look for dead
things to eat. Because
large birds are less
able to sustain flapping
flight, vultures must
find sources of warm,
rising air to make their
extended daily searches.
"Predicting where the
thermals form at fine
scales is beyond the
scope of most computer
models," says Shepard.
"The birds show us
where they are."

3 Top
Once the vulture has
gained enough potential
energy in terms of altitude
to glide across the land-
scape, it exits the thermal
in search of food and
the next updraft.

2 Middle
As the thermal rises, it
expands and becomes
stronger. The birds can
now make larger turns
and ascend faster.

1 Bottom
Near the ground, thermals
tend to be narrower and
weaker. Vultures must
make tight turns in the
thermal's "core" in order
to ascend within it. The
bird gains altitude slowly.

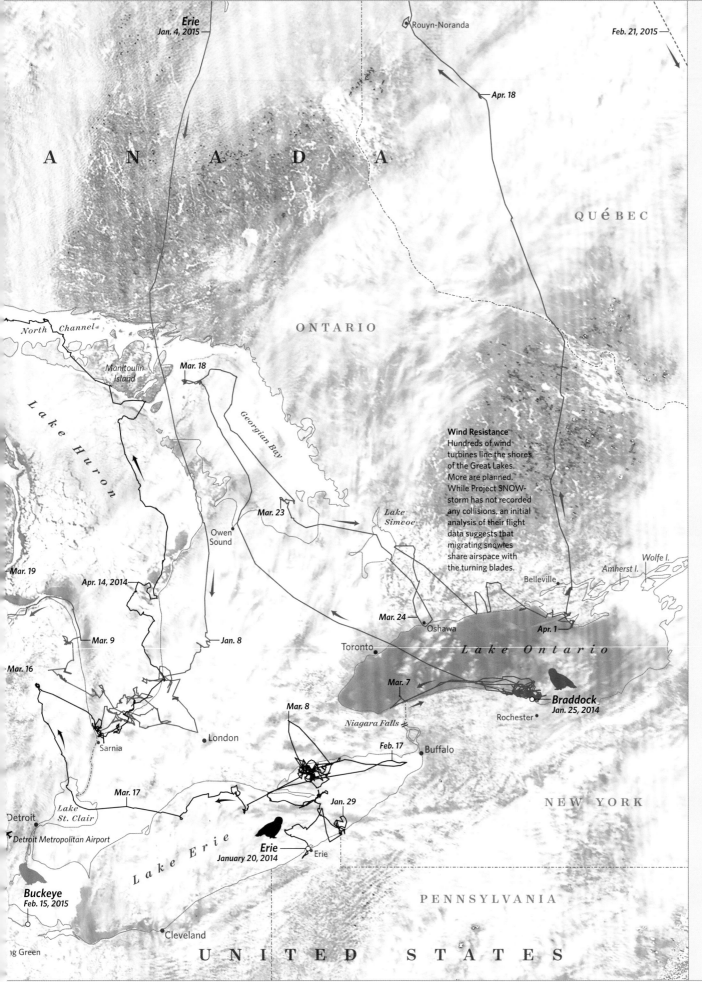

Erie
Jan. 4, 2015

Feb. 21, 2015

Rouyn-Noranda

Apr. 18

C A N A D A

QUÉBEC

ONTARIO

North Channel

Manitoulin Island

Mar. 18

Georgian Bay

Lake Simcoe

Lake Huron

Mar. 23

Owen Sound

Apr. 14, 2014

Mar. 19

Mar. 9

Jan. 8

Mar. 16

Belleville

Amherst I.

Wolfe I.

Wind Resistance
Hundreds of wind turbines line the shores of the Great Lakes. More are planned. While Project SNOWstorm has not recorded any collisions, an initial analysis of their flight data suggests that migrating snowies share airspace with the turning blades.

Apr. 1

Mar. 24

Oshawa

Toronto

Lake Ontario

Braddock
Jan. 25, 2014

Rochester

Mar. 7

Mar. 8

Niagara Falls

Feb. 17

Buffalo

London

Sarnia

Mar. 17

Detroit

Lake St. Clair

Detroit Metropolitan Airport

Jan. 29

NEW YORK

Lake Erie

Erie
January 20, 2014

Erie

Buckeye
Feb. 15, 2015

PENNSYLVANIA

ng Green

Cleveland

U N I T E D   S T A T E S

GPS tracks of snowy owls
2014–2015

○ Tagging location

0 ———— 50 km

Satellite image is from February 19, 2014

Erie
Jan. 2014—May 2015

Tagged near Erie, Pennsylvania, in 2014, this young male was one of the few "returners" a year later. He spent much of his second winter (light purple) along Lake Huron before heading north to a frozen Lake Superior.

Braddock
Jan. 2014—Feb. 2015

This male wintered on the shores of Lake Ontario. Following a brief visit to Georgian Bay in March, he left for the Arctic in April.

Kewaunee
Feb.—May 2014

This male spent the winter hunting over Wisconsin farmland before heading north to Green Bay and Michigan's Upper Peninsula.

Buckeye
Feb.—Apr. 2015

Captured near Detroit's airport, this female was relocated to Ohio. Less than a month later, she returned to Michigan.

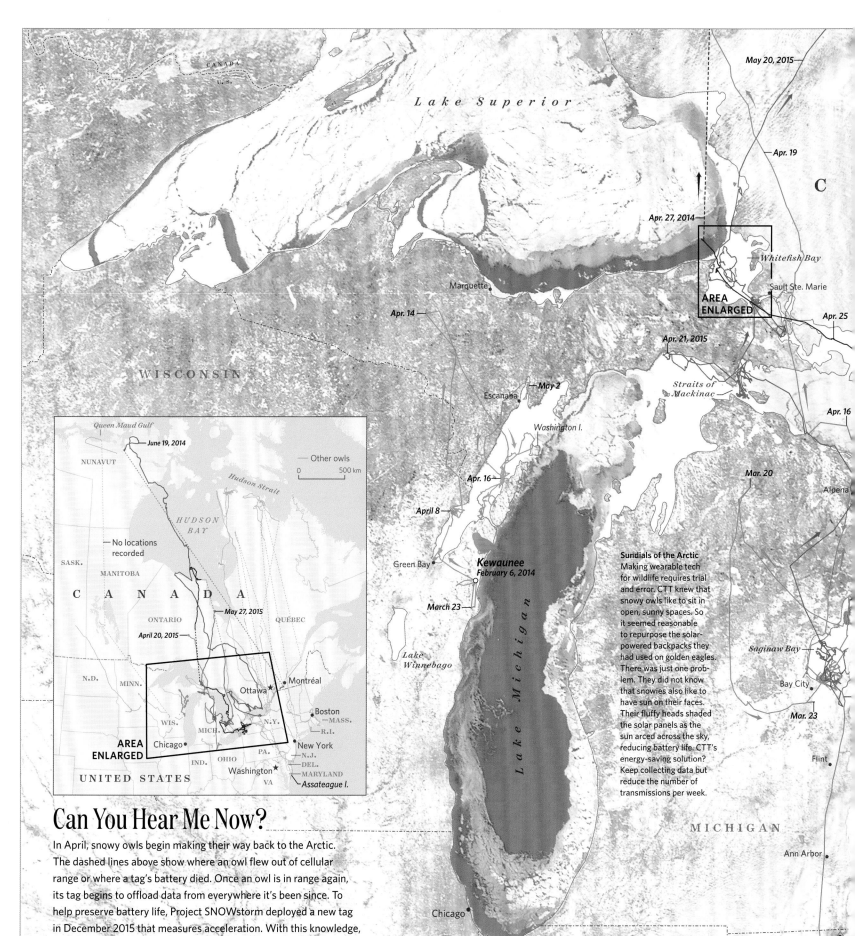

Lake Superior

CANADA
U.S.

May 20, 2015

Apr. 19

C

Apr. 27, 2014 — Whitefish Bay

AREA ENLARGED

Sault Ste. Marie

Apr. 25

Marquette

Apr. 14

Apr. 21, 2015

WISCONSIN

May 2

Straits of Mackinac

Apr. 16

Escanaba

Washington I.

Mar. 20

Alpena

Apr. 16

April 8

Sundials of the Arctic
Making wearable tech for wildlife requires trial and error. CTT knew that snowy owls like to sit in open, sunny spaces. So it seemed reasonable to repurpose the solar-powered backpacks they had used on golden eagles. There was just one problem. They did not know that snowies also like to have sun on their faces. Their fluffy heads shaded the solar panels as the sun arced across the sky, reducing battery life. CTT's energy-saving solution? Keep collecting data but reduce the number of transmissions per week.

Green Bay

Kewaunee
February 6, 2014

March 23

Lake Winnebago

Lake Michigan

Saginaw Bay

Bay City

Mar. 23

Flint

MICHIGAN

Ann Arbor

Chicago

Toledo

OHIO

Bow...

Queen Maud Gulf

June 19, 2014

NUNAVUT

Hudson Strait

Other owls

0   500 km

No locations recorded

HUDSON BAY

SASK.

MANITOBA

CANADA

ONTARIO

QUÉBEC

May 27, 2015

April 20, 2015

N.D.

MINN.

WIS.

MICH.

Ottawa ★

Montréal

Boston
MASS.
R.I.

AREA ENLARGED

Chicago

IND.   OHIO

PA.

N.J.

New York

DEL.

MARYLAND

UNITED STATES

Washington ★

VA.

Assateague I.

Can You Hear Me Now?

In April, snowy owls begin making their way back to the Arctic. The dashed lines above show where an owl flew out of cellular range or where a tag's battery died. Once an owl is in range again, its tag begins to offload data from everywhere it's been since. To help preserve battery life, Project SNOWstorm deployed a new tag in December 2015 that measures acceleration. With this knowledge, the researchers hope to program tags to collect data when the owls are flying and to go to sleep when they're not.

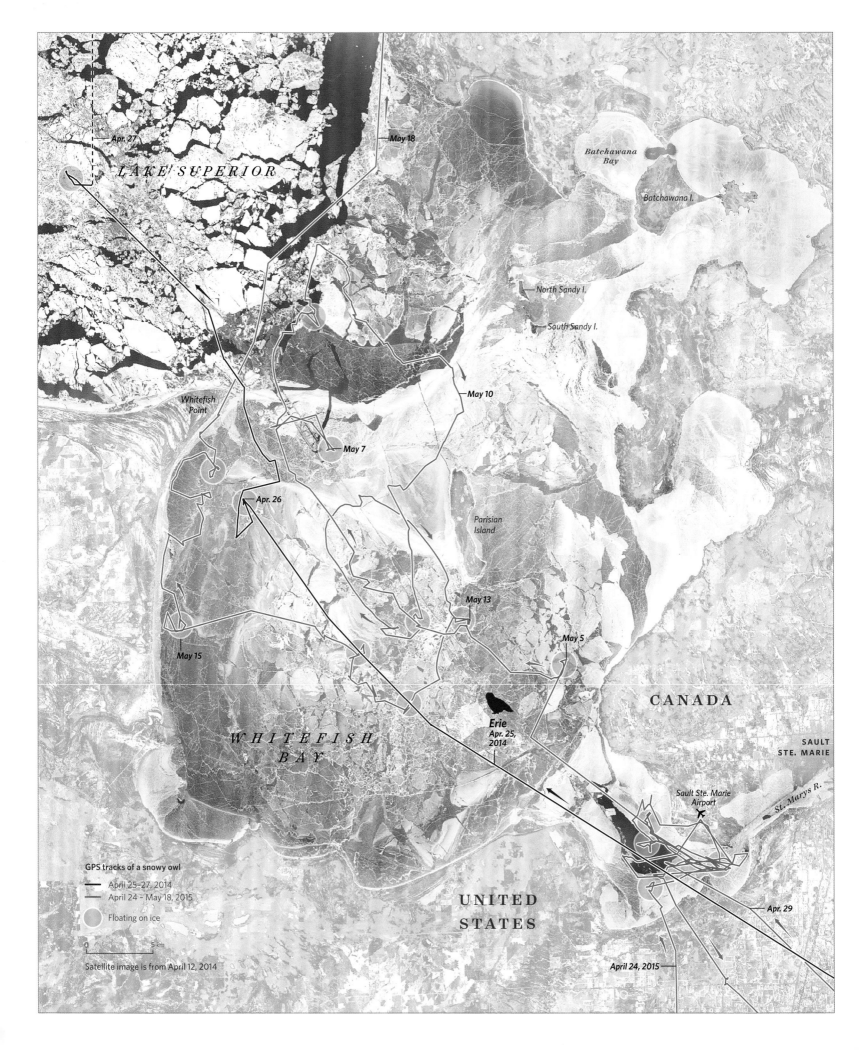

LAKE SUPERIOR

Apr. 27

May 18

Batchawana
Bay

Batchawana I.

North Sandy I.

South Sandy I.

May 10

Whitefish
Point

May 7

Parisian
Island

Apr. 26

May 13

May 15

May 5

CANADA

W H I T E F I S H
B A Y

Erie
Apr. 25,
2014

SAULT
STE. MARIE

Sault Ste. Marie
Airport

St. Marys R.

GPS tracks of a snowy owl

April 25–27, 2014

April 24 – May 18, 2015

Floating on ice

UNITED
STATES

Apr. 29

0   5 km

Satellite image is from April 12, 2014

April 24, 2015

The Owls of the Frozen Lakes

YOU DON'T NEED AN ACADEMIC GRANT to join the tracking revolution. Just ask the founders of Project SNOWstorm. In December 2013, Dave Brinker, a biologist for the State of Maryland, was banding saw-whet owls on Assateague Island when he began to see snowy owls too. Typically, snowies do not winter that far south. But 2013 wasn't a typical year. Up in the owls' Arctic breeding grounds, there had been a boom in the lemming population that summer. More prey meant more breeding and soon far more owlets than usual. By December, thousands of young owls were flying south in what would become the largest snowy owl "irruption" in the East since the 1920s. Brinker thought it'd be neat to track some.

He called Scott Weidensaul, a fellow birder, who then got a call from a friend at Cellular Tracking Technologies (CTT). CTT had recently developed a GPS tag that could transmit via cellphone networks. As birders themselves, they were also keen to track snowy owls and offered to provide the devices at cost. Weidensaul set up a funding page with a goal of $20,000. In three months, the team raised more than $72,000, enough for 22 tags.

Cellular tags can send more data, more quickly, more cheaply, and with less energy than a traditional satellite tag. This changes the questions you can ask. "If you collect enough data, you might be able to figure out at what point an animal made a decision that changes its trajectory," says CTT rep Andy McGann. For example, why would an owl fly to the middle of a frozen lake? Before Project SNOWstorm began, most birders thought snowy owls fed mostly on rodents in winter. With location data down to the meter, every 30 minutes, SNOWstorm biologists could now see owls such as Erie (purple) spending weeks on the ice, hunting waterfowl. And that's just one of their findings.

Since that first winter, Project SNOWstorm has tagged more than 40 owls in collaboration with scientists, veterinarians, and volunteers in ten states. "We're very lucky because snowy owls are big and beautiful and charismatic," says Weidensaul. "Everyone wants to help."

After spending much of the winter on Lake Huron, a young male owl named Erie takes to Whitefish Bay to hunt ducks and gulls along cracks in the ice. Other studies have shown that, as adults, some snowy owls deploy a similar strategy in the high Arctic.

SOURCES: DAVID F. BRINKER, STEVE HUY, NORMAN SMITH, AND SCOTT WEIDENSAUL, PROJECT SNOWSTORM; MODIS; USGS; NE

The Storks with Unhealthy Tastes

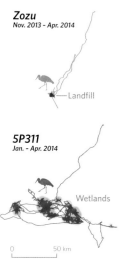

Zozu
Nov. 2013 - Apr. 2014

—Landfill

5P311
Jan. - Apr. 2014

Wetlands

0   50 km

These two storks chose
very different ways to
spend the winter.

WHAT SEEMS OBVIOUS TODAY wasn't always so. Aristotle believed birds hibernated; a 1703 essay on the subject said they wintered on the moon. So it was a pretty big deal on May 21, 1822, when a white stork returned to Northern Germany with an 80-centimeter spear through its neck. The spear was from Central Africa, offering the first definitive proof of long-distance migrations.

Fortunately for storks, we no longer need spears to prove their movements. Scientists can attach GPS loggers instead. However, a recent study led by Andrea Flack at Germany's Max Planck Institute for Ornithology illustrates a sad irony. Now that we have the technology to follow these epic journeys, it seems the storks are less keen to make them. The reason? There's faster food closer to home. With an almost limitless supply of treats, garbage dumps and landfill sites are hard to resist. Storks, such as Zozu (from Germany), see less need to make the grueling flight to wintering grounds south of the Sahara. In fact, they don't seem to fly much at all. Flack says those

wintering near landfills just "get up, fly to the dump, stay there, and then fly back in the evening." Other storks, such as 5P311 (Poland), still make an 8,000-kilometer trip and forage actively on arrival.

Of the 70 storks tagged by Flack, only 21 survived another year. The physical drain of migration felled many; perching on power lines killed the most. For the likes of Zozu, life in the dumps is good so long as they scavenge carefully. A poor choice of snack could also prove fatal. We plotted the survivors here alongside a remarkable stork named Prinzesschen, who was tracked for 125,000 kilometers by Max Planck's Peter Berthold. He logged the first data points of any stork in 1994 and continued to do so until December 23, 2006, when Prinzesschen died of natural causes on a farm in South Africa. A headstone marks her grave with this inscription:

A WONDERFUL JOURNEY FINDS ITS END HERE

SOURCES: ANDREA FLACK, MAX PLANCK INSTITUTE FOR ORNITHOLOGY; WOLFGANG FIEDLER; MICHAEL KAATZ; RAN NATHAN; IVAN POKROVSKY; NE; GELU

Prinzesschen tagged
August 1994

Moscow

RUSSIA

Berlin
POLAND
Aug. 2013

EUROPE

GERMANY
FRANCE

KAZAKHSTAN

Lyon
ALPS
Aug. 2013
SWITZERLAND

SLOVAKIA
HUNGARY
MOLDOVA
UKRAINE

Odesa

UZBEKISTAN
Tashkent

June 2014
PYRENEES

Madrid

PORTUGAL
SPAIN

Strait of
Gibraltar

BULGARIA
ROMANIA

BLACK SEA

Istanbul

ARMENIA
Yerevan

CASPIAN SEA

TAJIKISTAN

ASIA

GREECE

TURKEY

Iskenderun

Lake
Urmia

Zozu
November 2013 –
April 2014

Rabat
AREA
ENLARGED

Tunis

SYRIA

Baghdad

IRAN

None of the storks tagged in
Uzbekistan chose to escape
its harsh winters. Flack thinks
they found fish farms nearby
and saw no need to fly to
their usual wintering grounds
in China or India.

Agadir
ATLAS MTS.

TUNISIA

MEDITERRANEAN SEA

Tripoli

Damascus

LEBANON
ISRAEL

Jerusalem
JORDAN

Benghazi

Cairo
Sinai

IRAQ

PERSIAN GULF

ALGERIA

LIBYA

EGYPT

Nile

RED SEA

S A H A R A

MAURITANIA

Niger

NIGER

CHAD

Dakar
SENEGAL
GAMBIA
MALI

Niamey

N'Djamena

September 2013

Khartoum
SUDAN

ERITREA

Lake
Tana

ETHIOPIAN

Addis Ababa

HIGHLANDS

ETHIOPIA

CENTRAL AFRICAN
REPUBLIC

SOUTH
SUDAN

SOMALIA

A F R I C A

White stork tracks
from eight populations

○ Tagging location

Population
— Armenia
— Germany
— Greece
— Poland
— Russia
— Spain
— Tunisia
— Uzbekistan

Scale varies in this projection

Straight-line distance from Addis
Ababa to Nairobi is about 1160 km

UGANDA

Lake
Victoria

Dec. 2013

KENYA

Kisumu

Nairobi

Killimanjaro
5,895m

EQUATOR

INDIAN

OCEAN

Lake
Tanganika

Dodoma

Dar es Salaam

TANZANIA

Luangwa R.

Lake
Malawi

MALAWI

ATLANTIC

OCEAN

SP311
January –
April 2014

AREA
ENLARGED

ZAMBIA

Makgadikgadi
Pans

Zambezi

ZIMBABWE

Bulawayo

MOZAMBIQUE

BOTSWANA

Gaborone

Johannesburg

SOUTH
AFRICA

Prinzesschen dies
December 23, 2006

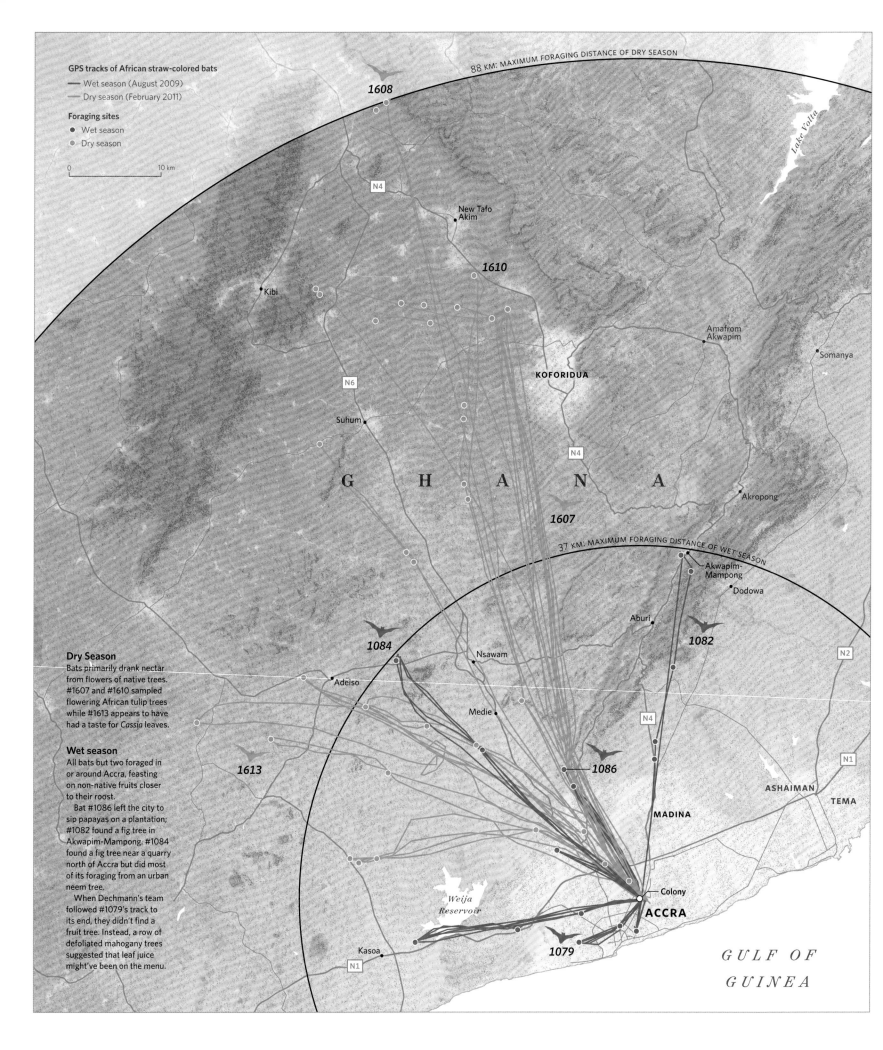

GPS tracks of African straw-colored bats
— Wet season (August 2009)
— Dry season (February 2011)

Foraging sites
● Wet season
○ Dry season

0 |⎯⎯⎯⎯⎯| 10 km

88 KM: MAXIMUM FORAGING DISTANCE OF DRY SEASON

Lake Volta

1608

New Tafo
Akim

1610

Kibi

Amafrom
Akwapim

Somanya

KOFORIDUA

N4

N6

Suhum

G   H   A   N   A

Akropong

1607

37 KM: MAXIMUM FORAGING DISTANCE OF WET SEASON

Akwapim-
Mampong

Dodowa

N2

Aburi

Dry Season
Bats primarily drank nectar
from flowers of native trees.
#1607 and #1610 sampled
flowering African tulip trees
while #1613 appears to have
had a taste for *Cassia* leaves.

Adeiso

Nsawam

1084

1082

Medie

Wet season
All bats but two foraged in
or around Accra, feasting
on non-native fruits closer
to their roost.
   Bat #1086 left the city to
sip papayas on a plantation;
#1082 found a fig tree in
Akwapim-Mampong. #1084
found a fig tree near a quarry
north of Accra but did most
of its foraging from an urban
neem tree.
   When Dechmann's team
followed #1079's track to
its end, they didn't find a
fruit tree. Instead, a row of
defoliated mahogany trees
suggested that leaf juice
might've been on the menu.

1613

1086

N4

ASHAIMAN

MADINA

TEMA

N1

*Weija
Reservoir*

Colony

ACCRA

Kasoa

1079

N1

GULF OF

GUINEA

The Fruit Bats
with Plenty of Juice

WHEN WE WROTE to Dina Dechmann at the Smithsonian Tropical Research Institute, her out-of-office response read: "I am in the field until 11 March and will only have sporadic and sleep-deprived email access." The words of a true chiropterologist.

Her team made headlines when they discovered that African straw-colored bats fly farther for food than any other bat species. They were studying a colony in Accra, Ghana that spends its days in old mahogany trees beside a military hospital. At sundown, up to 150,000 sets of wings take to the skies in a dark, chirping cloud. Where do they go? To find out, the team fitted 30 bats with GPS loggers (10 in the wet season, 20 in the dry) plus accelerometers to note when the bats were resting, commuting, or foraging in a tree. Each held enough battery life for seven days. Bat #1608 needed only one day to fly 88 kilometers north. Dechmann couldn't believe his endurance.

"Imagine a fruit-eating bat. They don't eat all day, and then they have to power a long-distance flight on an empty stomach." Once they find fruit, they don't even eat the whole thing. As Dechmann explains, "they chew it, press out the juice, and then spit out a pellet," making them key gardeners of Africa's forests. Basically, these bats survive solely on juice. No one knows how they do it.

One thing is clear: the bats' tastes are seasonal. During rainy months (April–September), they stayed near the coast, bingeing on the olive-shaped fruits of neem trees as well as mangos, figs, and papayas. Two bats even raided gardens, possibly in search of bananas. During the dry season (October–March), they flew nearly three times farther, often bypassing favorite fruits to drink nectar from the flowers of kapok trees.

Dechmann acknowledges that these findings are snapshots. A year's worth of tracks will be necessary to confirm whether seasonal shifts in colony size or food availability (or both) motivate the bats' record-breaking commutes. But that length of study requires two things: longer-lasting tags and a researcher willing to lose sleep for a year.

AFRICA
GHANA
★Accra

In the wet season, 97% of the Accra colony migrates to northern savannas, making it easier for bats that stay behind to find fruit. When the migrants return, competition may force some bats to forage farther afield.

SOURCES: DINA DECHMANN, JAKOB FAHR, AND MICHAEL ABEDI-LARTEY, MAX PLANCK INSTITUTE FOR ORNITHOLOGY; GLCF; OSM; NE; GSHHG

The Birds Who "Never See Sunlight"

OILBIRDS—or *guácharos* as they are known onomatopoeically in Spanish—intrigued the 18th-century naturalist Alexander von Humboldt after his first encounter with them, deep in a Venezuelan cave: *Where the light began to fail, we heard from afar the hoarse sounds of the nocturnal birds; sounds which the natives think belong exclusively to those subterraneous places.* From what he could tell, these birds "quit the cavern at nightfall" to forage on fruit and returned to their caves before dawn. For more than 200 years, his observations stood the test of time. Then along came GPS.

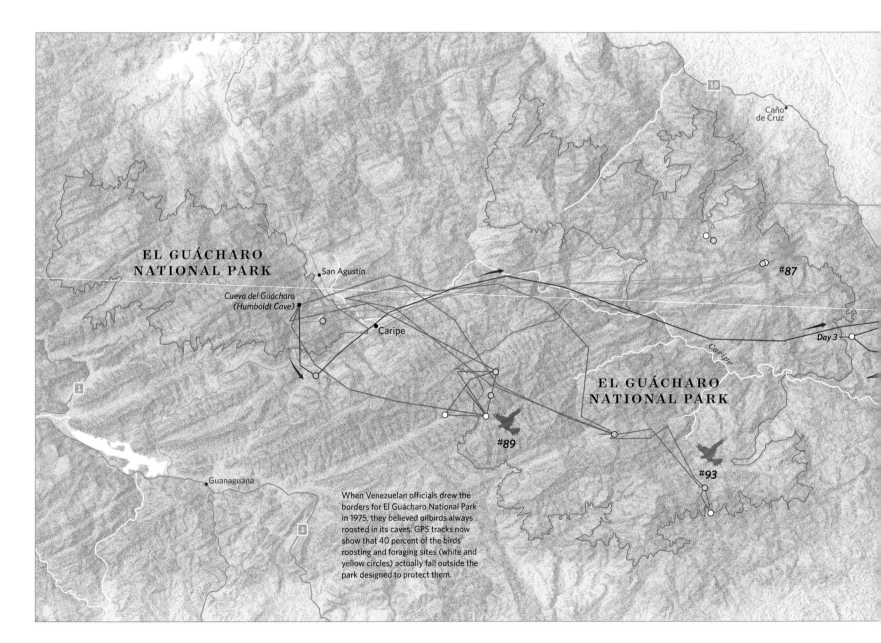

EL GUÁCHARO NATIONAL PARK

San Agustín

Cueva del Guácharo
(Humboldt Cave)

Caripe

EL GUÁCHARO NATIONAL PARK

Caño de Cruz

#87

Day 3

#89

#93

Guanaguana

When Venezuelan officials drew the borders for El Guácharo National Park in 1975, they believed oilbirds always roosted in its caves. GPS tracks now show that 40 percent of the birds' roosting and foraging sites (white and yellow circles) actually fall outside the park designed to protect them.

Bio-logging technologies have led to findings that would have thrilled Humboldt. For example, the "hoarse sounds" he described are now known to be a form of echolocation similar to that used by bats. We can also be sure that oilbirds spend much less time in caves than previously thought.

In 2007, an international team led by Richard Holland from the Max Planck Institute for Ornithology attached GPS loggers to twelve oilbirds. They wanted to better understand their role in seed dispersal. Holland's colleague Martin Wikelski recalls that before their study, the consensus was that "oilbirds fly out in the forest, grab seeds, bring them back to the cave, drop them there, and that's it—parasites of the forest." The data retrieved from the birds, however, told a different story. "Exactly the opposite of what Humboldt thought," says Wikelski. Instead of returning to the cave each night, oilbirds stayed out for three nights and roosted in trees during the day. In fact, during the study, they spent most of their roosting time *outside* the cave. With data, oilbirds went from "parasites" to the main seed dispersers of the rainforest, overnight.

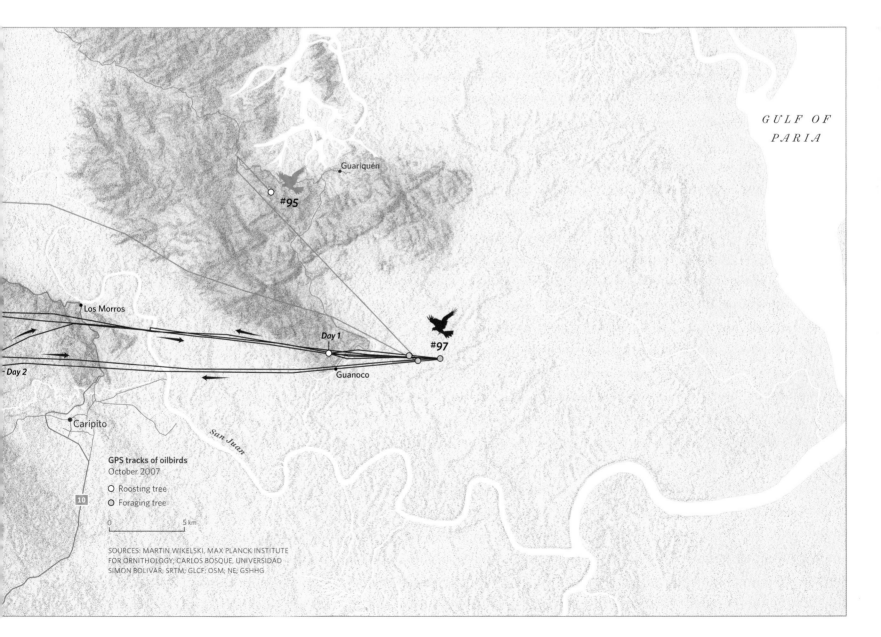

Caracas

AREA ENLARGED

VENEZUELA

SOUTH AMERICA

GULF OF PARIA

Guariquén

#95

Los Morros

Day 1

#97

Day 2

Guanoco

Caripito

San Juan

GPS tracks of oilbirds
October 2007

O Roosting tree
O Foraging tree

10

0   5 km

SOURCES: MARTIN WIKELSKI, MAX PLANCK INSTITUTE FOR ORNITHOLOGY; CARLOS BOSQUE, UNIVERSIDAD SIMON BOLIVAR; SRTM; GLCF; OSM; NE; GSHHG

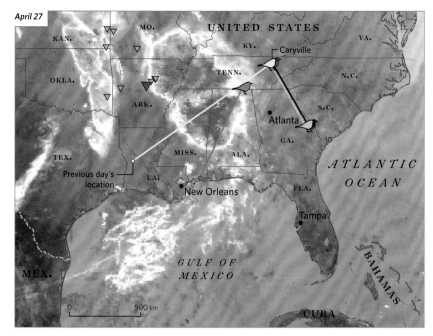

April 27

UNITED STATES

MO.
KAN.
OKLA.
ARK.
TEX.
MEX.
TENN.
KY.
VA.
N.C.
S.C.
Caryville
Atlanta
GA.
ALA.
MISS.
LA.
New Orleans
FLA.
Tampa
ATLANTIC OCEAN
GULF OF MEXICO
CUBA
BAHAMAS
Previous day's location
500 km

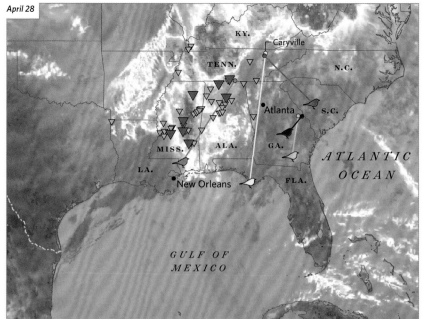

April 28

KY.
TENN.
N.C.
Caryville
Atlanta
S.C.
GA.
ALA.
MISS.
LA.
New Orleans
FLA.
ATLANTIC OCEAN
GULF OF MEXICO

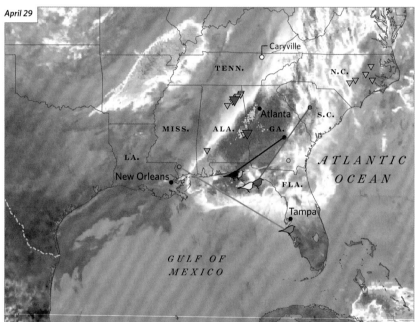

April 29

TENN.
N.C.
Caryville
Atlanta
S.C.
GA.
ALA.
MISS.
LA.
New Orleans
FLA.
Tampa
ATLANTIC OCEAN
GULF OF MEXICO

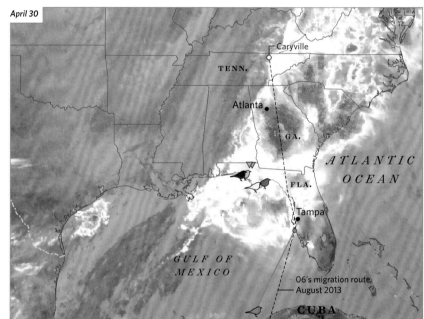

April 30

Caryville
TENN.
Atlanta
GA.
FLA.
Tampa
ATLANTIC OCEAN
GULF OF MEXICO
CUBA
06's migration route,
August 2013

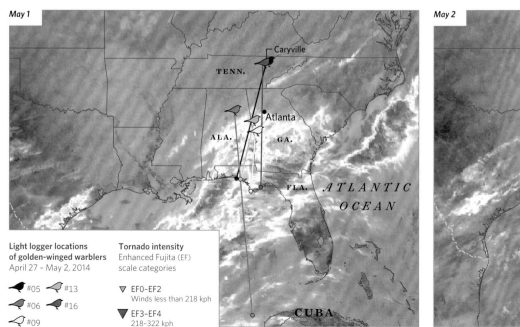

May 1

Caryville
TENN.
Atlanta
ALA.
GA.
FLA.
ATLANTIC OCEAN
CUBA

Light logger locations of golden-winged warblers
April 27 – May 2, 2014

#05   #13
#06   #16
#09

Tornado intensity
Enhanced Fujita (EF) scale categories

▽ EF0–EF2
Winds less than 218 kph

▼ EF3–EF4
218–322 kph

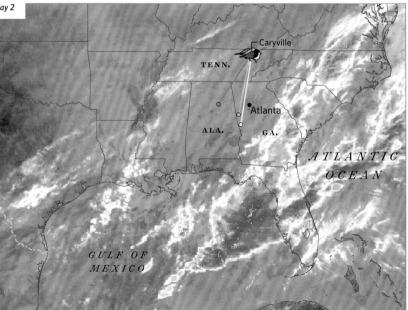

May 2

Caryville
TENN.
Atlanta
ALA.
GA.
ATLANTIC OCEAN
GULF OF MEXICO

The Warblers
Who Dodged Tornadoes

HENRY STREBY HUNKERED DOWN in a hotel and waited for the storm to pass. His birds had taken a different tack. Of course, he didn't know that yet.

It was April 29, 2014, and Streby, a postdoctoral fellow with the University of Tennessee, was investigating the decline of golden-winged warblers in the eastern US. A year earlier, he'd fitted 20 of them with light loggers in the hopes of discovering where they wintered. Now he anxiously awaited their return. To continue his research, he had to prove that the warblers could still migrate while wearing his tags. So far, only one had come back. Meanwhile, a tornado outbreak was obliterating buildings from Oklahoma to North Carolina. As of that evening, 35 people were dead. How would songbirds the weight of small strawberries survive?

On the first of May, the weather cleared. Streby soon found five of his birds and downloaded their data. All had gone to Colombia. End of story. Then Streby began analyzing the tracks in more detail. On April 27, all but one had arrived at their breeding grounds near Caryville, Tennessee. Two days later, the birds appeared in Florida. At first, he assumed trees had shaded the tags' sensors to think day lengths were shorter (and thus farther south) than they actually were. But the offsets were greater than any "shading error" he'd seen. He couldn't make sense of it. Then he remembered the storms. Had the birds reacted to changes in air pressure, temperature, or wind speed? Streby doubts it. "All these things happen within a few hours before a storm. The warblers moved two *days* before the storm." Something else had warned them. It may have been sound.

Tornadoes emit rumbles below our range of hearing. Birds, however, can hear these hundreds of kilometers away; they can also sense whether sounds are moving toward them. If the warblers did detect the storms, imagine yourself in their feathers. Would you (a) stay put; (b) fly north into the grip of winter; (c) go east or west along the storm's path; or (d) head south to familiar places from your migration routes?

Perfect habitat management in the US or Colombia won't stop the warblers' decline if a key stopover site in Central America has been deforested. Streby is now tracking 430 warblers to connect more dots along their routes. "If you want to study birds," he says, "you have to study the whole system."

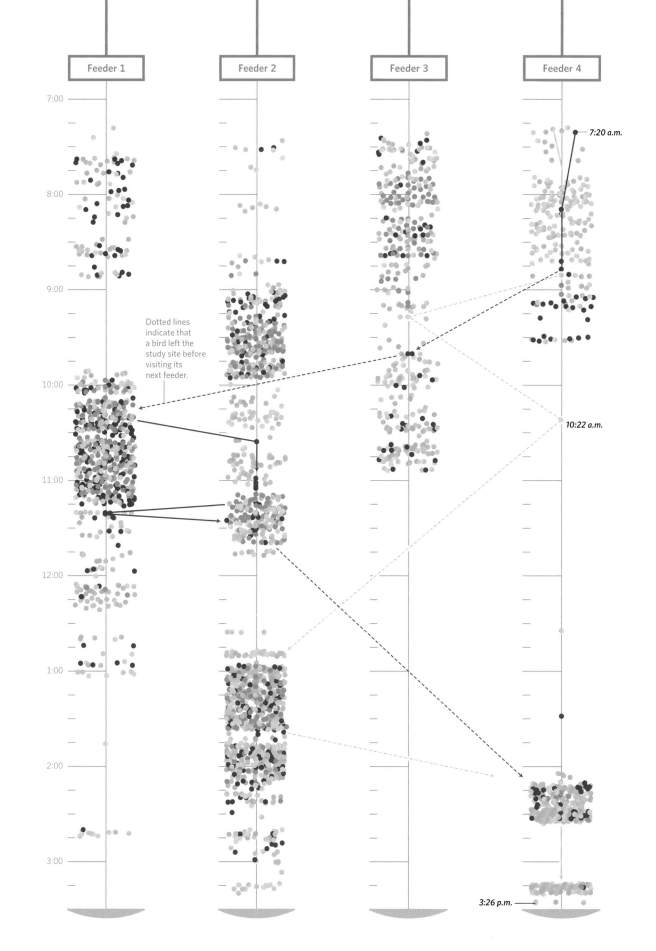

Songbird movements between feeders
7:00 a.m. – 3:30 p.m.
February 7, 2012

- Blue tit
- Coal tit
- Great tit
- Marsh tit
- Eurasian nuthatch

The black arrows follow the movements of a single coal tit. At 7:20 a.m., it arrived at feeder 4 and joined the blue, marsh, and great tits feeding there for over an hour. It then flew to feeder 1, via feeder 3, for a mid-morning snack. After ping-ponging between feeders 1 and 2, it took wing to the woods until its last feed of the day at feeder 4 around 2:15 p.m.

Our chosen great tit (yellow arrows) started the day in a similar way but is noteworthy for a solo excursion to feeder 4 at 10:22 a.m. It then rejoined the flock around one o'clock before ending the day at feeder 4.

Dotted lines indicate that a bird left the study site before visiting its next feeder.

Feeder 1
Feeder 2
Feeder 3
Feeder 4

7:00
8:00
9:00
10:00
11:00
12:00
1:00
2:00
3:00

7:20 a.m.

10:22 a.m.

3:26 p.m.

How Songbirds Flock Together

FOR MORE THAN SIXTY YEARS, pioneering scientists have treated the University of Oxford's Wytham Woods as their outdoor laboratory and its many occupants as their unwitting subjects. Eminent zoologist Robert Hinde (and Jane Goodall's PhD advisor) has written that, for his early research, he "wandered around Wytham Woods with a notebook and pencil and wrote down what [he] saw—a piece of cake really." How times have changed. Researchers are now finding that even a walk in the woods is an exercise in complexity.

As a principal investigator in the Department of Collective Behaviour at the Max Planck Institute for Ornithology, Damien Farine wants to understand the social components of animal movement. So a few years ago, he and colleagues attached radio-identification tags to 3,000 of Wytham's songbirds. They then set up a grid of 65 automated monitoring stations to track their flights from tree to tree. With that proof of concept, Farine attached the same technology to four bird feeders spaced 50 meters apart in order to see the ways species interact when feeding. For example, why would a tit opt to jostle around a busy feeder when it could have one to itself? Farine thinks the birds judge how much food is available and its quality by a feeder's popularity. Are humans so different? We'll queue for an hour outside a packed restaurant before taking a risk on its empty neighbor.

The complete study recorded 91,576 feeding events by 1,904 birds across four consecutive winter days. Here we show eight hours of interactions between five species on February 7, 2012. Whenever a feeder detected a bird, it recorded a point. Great tits (yellow dots) preferred feeders frequented by other great tits, while blue tits (blue) seemed to prefer a more diverse crowd; at least half the birds needed to be of a different species for them to feed there. Farine has built these rules into a computer simulation that he can set to test how the birds might react to events such as a nearby predator. In that case, he predicts the tits will become even less fussy about their dining companions and choose safety in numbers instead.

UNITED KINGDOM

Wytham Woods

London

SOURCE: DAMIEN FARINE, MAX PLANCK INSTITUTE FOR ORNITHOLOGY AND UNIVERSITY OF OXFORD

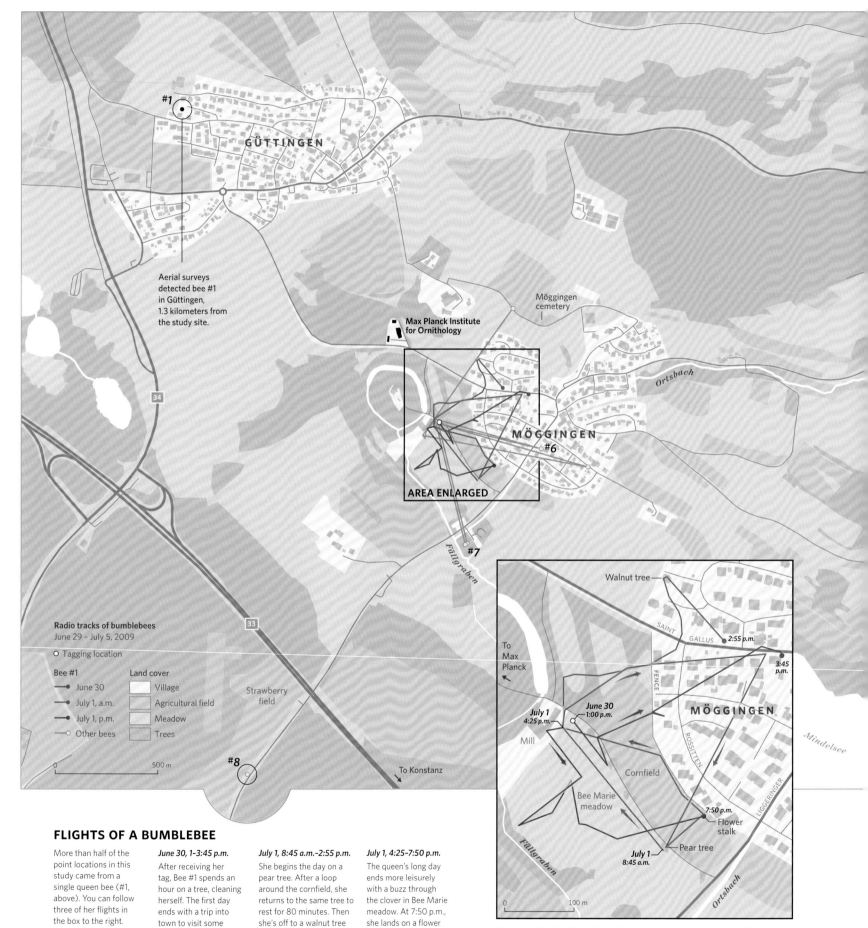

#1

GÜTTINGEN

Aerial surveys
detected bee #1
in Güttingen,
1.3 kilometers from
the study site.

Möggingen
cemetery

Max Planck Institute
for Ornithology

Ortsbach

MÖGGINGEN
#6

AREA ENLARGED

#7

Fällgraben

Radio tracks of bumblebees
June 29 – July 5, 2009

○ Tagging location

Bee #1   Land cover
●— June 30   ☐ Village
●— July 1, a.m.   ☐ Agricultural field
●— July 1, p.m.   ☐ Meadow
○— Other bees   ☐ Trees

Strawberry
field

0 ————— 500 m

#8

To Konstanz

Walnut tree

SAINT GALLUS   2:55 p.m.

3:45
p.m.

To
Max
Planck

July 1
4:25 p.m.

June 30
1:00 p.m.

FENCE

MÖGGINGEN

Mill

Cornfield

ROSSTTEN

Mindelsee

Bee Marie
meadow

LIGGERINGER

Fällgraben

July 1
8:45 a.m.

7:50 p.m.

Flower
stalk

July 1
8:45 a.m.

Pear tree

Ortsbach

0 ————— 100 m

FLIGHTS OF A BUMBLEBEE

More than half of the
point locations in this
study came from a
single queen bee (#1,
above). You can follow
three of her flights in
the box to the right.

June 30, 1–3:45 p.m.
After receiving her
tag, Bee #1 spends an
hour on a tree, cleaning
herself. The first day
ends with a trip into
town to visit some
lavender, linden, and a
blossoming tree.

July 1, 8:45 a.m.–2:55 p.m.
She begins the day on a
pear tree. After a loop
around the cornfield, she
returns to the same tree to
rest for 80 minutes. Then
she's off to a walnut tree
in west Möggingen for
another long break.

July 1, 4:25–7:50 p.m.
The queen's long day
ends more leisurely
with a buzz through
the clover in Bee Marie
meadow. At 7:50 p.m.,
she lands on a flower
stalk in a garden and
stays there overnight.

Hagen and Kissling followed bee #1 on foot for twelve hours on June 30 and July 1.
To their surprise, the young queen spent half her time inside the village.

LIGGERINGEN

#2

#3
Dürrenhof
farm

The Bees in Back Gardens

THERE'S A STUBBORN MYTH that bumblebees should be too heavy to fly. That thinking assumes bees behave like airplanes. Bees behave like bees— their wings flap in figures of eight and generate tiny vortices of lift—so perhaps we should set aside assumptions and study how they behave?

In July 2009, Melanie Hagen, Daniel Kissling, and Martin Wikelski glued minuscule radio transmitters to bumblebees from three species in Möggingen, Germany, in order to follow their movements for the first time. They took four *Bombus terrestris* from a local nest and found three *B. horturum* and one *B. ruderatus* in the wild. Once tagged, each rested on a nearby plant and spent up to two hours trying to rid itself of the new appendage. Eventually, all took to the air. The scientists weren't far behind.

Hagen and Kissling combed the village's fields and gardens while Wikelski tracked long-distance fliers from a small plane. The 200-milligram tags weighed as much as some worker bees. Even

under that burden, at least one from each species traveled farther than a kilometer. Bee #2 (*B. terrestris*) flew 2.5 kilometers to the village of Liggeringen; #3 (*B. ruderatus*) stopped by Möggingen cemetery en route to a farm 1.9 kilometers away; and one young queen (*B. horturum*) ventured 1.3 kilometers to Güttingen.

The bees showed little interest in crops at this time of year. More often, the pollinators patrolled Möggingen's meadows and back gardens, frequently returning to feed or rest on the same tree, fence, or flower.

Back in the meadow, the researchers watched tagged and untagged bees forage in a patch of wildflowers. Those with tags visited fewer flower heads than their unencumbered kin, a sign that the tiny tech should be tinier still. But let's keep some perspective. The Wright Brothers managed four flights on their first day at Kitty Hawk. The longest lasted 59 seconds and they deemed it "a grand success." After all, humans weren't supposed to be able to fly either.

EUROPE

★Berlin

AREA
ENLARGED   GERMANY

SOURCES: MELANIE HAGEN, UNIVERSITY OF BIELEFELD; DANIEL KISSLING, AARHUS UNIVERSITY; MARTIN WIKELSKI, MAX PLANCK INSTITUTE FOR ORNITHOLOGY; OSM

We shall not cease from exploration
And the end of all our exploring
Will be to arrive where we started
And know the place for the first time.

—T. S. ELIOT

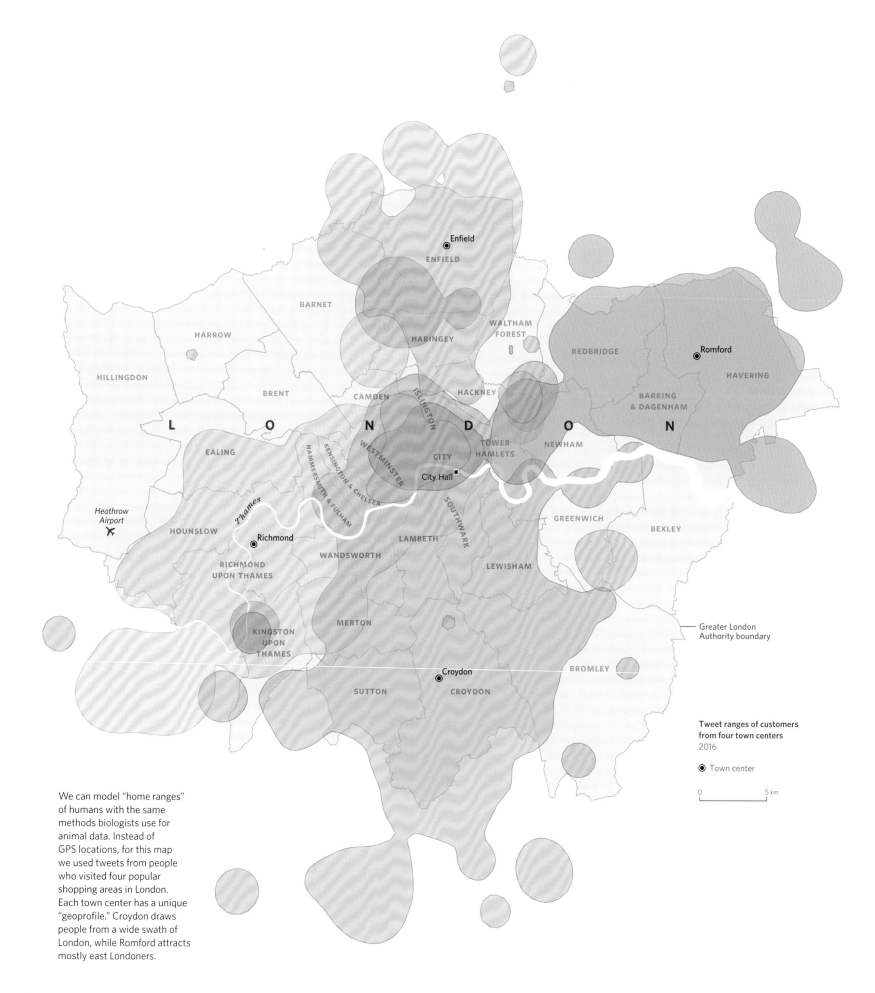

Enfield

ENFIELD

BARNET

HARROW

WALTHAM
FOREST

REDBRIDGE

Romford

HILLINGDON

BRENT

CAMDEN

HARINGEY

HACKNEY

ISLINGTON

HAVERING

BARKING
& DAGENHAM

L   O   N   D   O   N

EALING

Heathrow
Airport

HOUNSLOW

Thames

Richmond

RICHMOND
UPON THAMES

HAMMERSMITH & FULHAM

KENSINGTON & CHELSEA

WESTMINSTER

CITY

City Hall

TOWER
HAMLETS

NEWHAM

SOUTHWARK

GREENWICH

BEXLEY

LAMBETH

WANDSWORTH

LEWISHAM

KINGSTON
UPON
THAMES

MERTON

Greater London
Authority boundary

Croydon

BROMLEY

SUTTON

CROYDON

**Tweet ranges of customers
from four town centers**
2016

◉ Town center

0   5 km

We can model "home ranges"
of humans with the same
methods biologists use for
animal data. Instead of
GPS locations, for this map
we used tweets from people
who visited four popular
shopping areas in London.
Each town center has a unique
"geoprofile." Croydon draws
people from a wide swath of
London, while Romford attracts
mostly east Londoners.

Where the Humans Go

by James Cheshire

Look at the baiji, the river dolphin in China. There were just a couple of papers on the vocalizations they were making and then the bugger went extinct. That was it. Those papers suddenly went from being the first pilot study of an interesting animal to the last word on the topic.

—Mark Johnson, Sea Mammal Research Unit, University of St Andrews

GEOGRAPHY IS A HUGELY BROAD SUBJECT. My colleagues at University College London research everything from how far people travel to do their weekly shop to the impacts of climate change on groundwater in Africa. To help distinguish between such diverse interests, the discipline splits into "human" geographers who study people and "physical" geographers who study the Earth's processes and environment. I specialize in human geography and spend much of my time working with data collected in the Census, by transport providers, or by the government. So at first, a book on animal behavior felt like a departure. Yet once I began working with the tracking data, it all felt oddly familiar. I came to see parallels between what biologists were trying to learn from animals and what my research has tried to learn about humans. Many of the biologists we worked with

SOURCES: ALYSON LLOYD, UNIVERSITY COLLEGE LONDON;
CROWN COPYRIGHT ORDNANCE SURVEY 2016

saw the parallels too. What unites us is the appreciation that in order to fully understand *why* something happens we often need to know *where* it happens. Location is everything. And the way we study this is the same whether it relates to an ant, a diving whale, or a person with a smartphone. Two coordinates, x and y, will describe any position on the planet. To specify elevation, altitude, or depth in the sea, we can add a third coordinate—z. We are all always somewhere: x, y, and z.

Researchers are now collecting x, y, and z for hundreds of species—including humans. There may even be a tracking device in your pocket right now. The sensors that Scott LaPoint used to track Albany's fishers (see pp. 60–61) are the same sensors we voluntarily activate in the guise of fitness apps on our phones. When fitted to cars, the same technology that Emily Shepard used to show the detail of a vulture's spiral (see pp. 138–9) can alert your insurance company to an accident as soon as it happens. Or take the text message that Kulling's collar sent out after she was shot (see p. 38). The algorithms that triggered that alert could also be used to notify you that a grandparent has become lost or confused on the way back from the store.

For these applications to work, software needs to know what is and isn't "normal" behavior. For example, Google's mapping app expects cars on a motorway to move at 70 miles per hour. When your car—together with you and your cell phone—slows to half that speed, the app knows that stretch of road is congested. Similarly, researchers studying both people and animals

are now using sensors to define a universal set of rules for movement. What velocities, sequences, and postures distinguish foraging behavior from resting, or riding a bus from riding a bike?

Soon data may also be able to detect states of mind. Mirco Musolesi, a colleague of mine at University College London, has shown how smartphones can be used to monitor depression. He and Luca Canzian (University of Birmingham) developed an app that allowed the study's participants to monitor their own movements. From these tracks, they found that how far people move in a day, the number of places they visit, and how frequently they visit them could indicate a depressive state if a person's movements vary from his or her routine. The hope is that such early warning systems could trigger a call from a healthcare officer if there's enough data to indicate a problem.

In turn, these advances will enable more sophisticated monitoring of animals. And so it goes, biologists and software engineers in symbiosis.

MY OWN PHD RESEARCH into the geographic spread of surnames borrowed heavily from zoology. I was looking at ways we could use names to shed light on historic and contemporary cultural groupings across Europe. In the process, I identified areas where a surname (e.g. Uberti) was most likely to be found (northern Italy), the thinking being that such areas mark the likely origin of that name or at least the first place it appeared in a country. Scientists use a similar method to study the lives of the many animals in this book. They take a collection of "sightings" and draw a line around areas of highest concentration. I called this a "core" region in relation to surnames; a zoologist would call it an animal's "home range."

This process is known as "geoprofiling" and we're only beginning to discover its potential. Steve Le Comber from Queen Mary University of London and Canadian criminologist Kim Rossmo used it to open the cold-case investigation of Jack the Ripper. By plugging each murder location into their model, they surmised that the legendary serial killer lived on Flower and Dean Street in London's East End. Le Comber has even leveraged the locations of 140 of Banksy's artworks to guess the elusive artist's identity.

Meanwhile, one of my doctoral students and I have been investigating ways to examine the vibrancy of town centers in London. Successful shopkeepers know their customers, and many use social media to reach them. With this in mind, Alyson Lloyd has mined millions of tweets to find ones sent in the vicinity of a town center. She then mapped where else those same people tweeted in London. On the previous page, we show four of these tweet ranges to demonstrate their differences in size and shape—information that helps businesses better understand who's visiting their stores. This approach is much like the way Andrea Flack could spot whether a stork was feeding at wetlands or a garbage dump (see pp. 144–5).

The skills used are so similar that it's possible for data scientists to determine where a new school is most needed and then change a couple of lines of code to identify a favorite feeding spot for Arctic terns. Perhaps we can now ask criminologists to predict where a burglar might strike next in the same way that scientists can guess which cluster of flowers a bumblebee will visit. Both examples gloss over the challenge of collecting the required data, but once we have them, the lines between human and animal behavior blur.

Having spent hundreds of hours working with this book's bio-logging data and talking to the researchers who collected them, I am convinced that nestled away in the tangles, dives, and clusters of many animal tracks could be clues to solving some of humanity's more persistent problems. The importance of data for conservation cannot be overstated, but the converse is also true. Without conservation, many species will perish before we can collect and decipher their data.

Location is everything. And the way we study this is the same whether it relates to an ant, a diving whale, or a person with a smartphone.

Back in 1976, Torsten Hägerstrand, a pioneer of tracking and movement analysis, wrote an article about the "interaction between Nature and Society" in the face of scientific and technological revolution. He urged geographers to consider "how to make the individual human life into a rich experience and still . . . be able to let fellow animals and plants live their lives in peace." The twenty-first century presents us with a tremendous opportunity to fulfil Hägerstrand's vision. The human need to innovate will not subside, but we can use technology to support rather than threaten the natural world. In doing so, we just might come to better understand our own behavior along the way.

ON ANIMALS

No book makes the case for the sentience and individuality of animals better than Carl Safina's *Beyond Words* (2015). It's a must read. *Among the Elephants* (1975) and *Battle for the Elephants* (1992) by Iain and Oria Douglas-Hamilton are riveting accounts of their research beside Lake Manyara and then their struggle to alert the world to the devastation of the ivory trade. Philip Hoare's *Leviathan, or the Whale* (2009) informed our foray into cetology while *Ten Thousand Birds* (Birkhead, T., Wimpenny, J., Montgomerie, B., 2014) and Horatio Clare's *A Single Swallow* (2010) got us thinking like migratory birds.

For more on the early days of tracking technologies, Etienne Benson's *Wired Wilderness* (2010) provides incredible detail. Peter Miller's *The Smart Swarm* (2010) reveals how humans have benefited from mimicking the habits of birds and insects.

For a jolt of optimism, Jane Goodall has dozens of stories of species recovering from the brink in *Hope for Animals and Their World* (2009). In *Feral* (2014), George Monbiot describes how landscapes can be "rewilded." And E. O. Wilson's *A Window on Eternity* (2014) proves it.

ON MAPS

The principles outlined in Edward Tufte's classic trio—*Envisioning Information* (1990), *Visual Explanations* (1997), and *The Visual Display of Quantitative Information* (2001)—guided our thinking throughout the book. Hebert Bayer's *World Geographic Atlas* (1953) remains the benchmark for cartographic design, while *Maps of the Imagination* (Turchi, P., 2004) demonstrates the similarities between cartographers and writers; *Semiology of Graphics* (Bertin, J., 2011 ed.) and *Cartographic Relief Presentation* (Imhof, E., 2007 ed.) are timeless classics. Finally, Judith Schalansky's *Atlas of Remote Islands* (2010) deserves special mention. Her hand-stippled maps inspired us to write software to generate that look on a continental scale.

ON DATA

If you have been inspired to create your own graphics and are looking for animal data, Movebank (*movebank.org*), zoaTrack (*zoatrack.org*) and Dryad (*datadryad.org*) are the places to start.

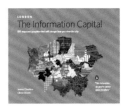

London has a long history of innovative maps and data visualization. James and Oliver's first book, *London: The Information Capital* (2014), continues that legacy with 100 maps and graphics that will change the way you view the city.

[NOTES]

Best Beloved: Kipling, Rudyard. (1902) *Just So Stories*. London: Macmillan and Co., 225.

PREFACE

Population figures, details of the collaring expedition, Fay's quote, and the map of Annie's tracks: Fay, J. Michael. "Ivory Wars: Last Stand in Zakouma." *National Geographic*, March 2007.

If you can put yourself: Ibid., video. ngm.nationalgeographic.com/2007/03/ivory-wars/zakouma-video-interactive

It's much, much easier: Douglas-Hamilton, Iain. Interview. March 17, 2016.

In 2008, the Wildlife Conservation Society: Christy, Bryan. "Tracking Ivory." *National Geographic*, September 2015, 53.

Nearly 90 percent: Ibid., 41.

Two kills in 2015: Neme, Laurel. "Elephant Killings in Chad's Signature Park Cause Alarm." *National Geographic*, September 1, 2015. news.nationalgeographic.com/2015/09/150901-elephants-poaching-chad-zakouma-national-park-ivory

INTRODUCTION

It seems that people: Benson, Etienne. (2010) *Wired Wilderness*. Baltimore: The Johns Hopkins University Press, 23.

Audubon was tying threads: Callahan, D. *A History of Birdwatching in 100 Objects*. London: Bloomsbury, 2014.

Pigeons with automatic cameras: en.wikipedia.org/wiki/Pigeon_photography

Radio transmitter: Lord, Jr., Rexford D. et al. (1962) Radiotelemetry of the Respiration of a Flying Duck. *Science* 137: 39–40.

GPS collars: Douglas-Hamilton, Iain. (1998) "Tracking African Elephants with a Global Positioning System (GPS) Radio Collar." *Pachyderm* 25: 81–92.

Non-invasive observation: Owen, Megan. Interview. October 20, 2015.

For more on bio-logging:
Hays, G. et al. (2016) Key questions in marine megafauna movement ecology. *Trends in Ecology & Evolution* 31: 463–75.

Kays, R. et al. (2015) Terrestrial animal tracking as an eye on life and planet. *Science* 348: 1255642.

Hussey, N. et al. (2015) Aquatic animal telemetry: a panoramic window into the underwater world. *Science* 348: 1–10.

Naito, Y. (2003) New steps in bio-logging science. *Memoirs of National Institute of Polar Research* 58: 50–57.

Starting in February: NOAA. www.fisheries.noaa.gov/pr/species/mammals/seals/northern-fur-seal.html

Where we are with giraffe: O'Connor, David. Presentation at San Diego Zoo Global. May 15, 2015.

Fennessy quotes, giraffe population figures, and collaring stories: Fennessy, Julian. Interview. January 12, 2016.

OJ1: Flanagan, S. et al. (2016) Use of home range behavior to assess establishment in translocated giraffes. *African Journal of Ecology* 54 (3): 365–74.

He equipped each badger: Noonan, M. J. et al. (2015) A new magneto-inductive tracking technique to uncover subterranean activity: what do animals do underground? *Methods in Ecology and Evolution* 6: 510–520.

Wilson anecdotes and quotes: Wilson, Rory. Interview. April 19, 2016

Hebert anecdotes, quotes, and biodiversity figures: Hebert, Paul. Interview. April 5, 2016.

5 million specimens: Barcode of Life Data System. boldsystems.org

DNA of seized ivory: Wasser, Samuel K. et al. "The Ivory Trail." *Scientific American*, July 2009, 68–76.

Dung of two zebra: Kartzinel, Tyler R. et al. (2015) DNA metabarcoding illuminates dietary niche partitioning by African large herbivores. *PNAS* 112 (26): 8019–24.

DNA in the leeches: Ji, Yinqiu et al. (2013) Reliable, verifiable, and efficient monitoring of biodiversity via metabarcoding. *Ecology Letters* 16: 1245–57.

Due to human impact: Williams, M. et al. (2015) The Anthropocene biosphere. *The Anthropocene Review* 2 (3): 196–219.

We all use data differently: Franklin, Craig. Interview. March 15, 2016.

They're sitting on: Dwyer, Ross. Interview. March 2016.

For more on zooTrack, see: Dwyer, R. et al. (2015) An open Web-based system for the analysis and sharing of animal tracking data. *Animal Biotelemetry* 3 (1): s40317-014-0021-8.

As soon as we tag: Johnson, Mark. Interview. April 14, 2016.

Collaring is a stress: Douglas-Hamilton, Iain. Interview. March 17, 2016.

For more on the ethics of bio-logging, see: Wilson, R. P. & McMahon, C. R. (2006) Measuring devices on wild animals: what constitutes acceptable practice? *Frontiers in Ecology and the Environment* 4 (3): 147–154.

A website called Movebank: Wikelski, Martin. Interview. December 16, 2015.

For more on Movebank, see: Kranstauber, B. et al. (2011) The Movebank data model for animal tracking. *Environmental Modeling and Software* 26: 834–35. Or go to: *movebank.org.*

To track progress of the ICARUS initiative visit: *icarusinitiative.org*

As much data as possible: Holland, Melinda. Interview. November 19, 2015.

CARTOGRAPHIC SOURCES

A wide range of sources were used for our maps. We abbreviated them throughout the book but include their full citations below. Many graphics also benefited from our own additions based on information provided by the researchers.

Terrain
GEBCO: General Bathymetric Chart of the Oceans
gebco.net

SRTM: Shuttle Radar Topography Mission, courtesy of NASA and downloaded from the OpenTopography Facility with support from the National Science Foundation under NSF Award Numbers 1226353 & 1225810

Roads, Rivers, Lakes, Ice, Urban Areas, Land Use
CLC: Corine Land Cover Classification 2012. Copernicus Land Monitoring Services
land.copernicus.eu/pan-european/corine-land-cover/clc-2012

GELU: A New Map of Global Ecological Land Units. Produced in collaboration with USGS and ESRI Inc.
aag.org/global_ecosystems

NE: Natural Earth
naturalearthdata.com

OSM: OpenStreetMap contributors CC-BY-SA *openstreetmap.org*

USGS: United States Geological Survey's "The National Map"
nationalmap.gov

Tree Cover
GLCF: Global Land Cover Facility
glcf.umd.edu/data/landsatTreecover

National Parks
WDPA: IUCN and UNEP-WCMC (2016), The World Database on Protected Areas
protectedplanet.net

Borders
GADM: GADM database of Global Administrative Areas
gadm.org

Coastline
GSHHG: A Global Self-consistent, Hierarchical, High-resolution Geography Database. *ngdc.noaa.gov/mgg/shorelines/gshhs.html*

Ocean Productivity and Currents
NPP: Net primary production Standard Products Oregon State University
science.oregonstate.edu/ocean.productivity

SODA: Carton, J. A. et al. (2000) A Simple Ocean Data Assimilation Analysis of the Global Upper Ocean 1950–95. Part II: Results. *Journal of Physical Oceanography* 30: 311–26. *atmos.umd.edu/~ocean*

Wind and Weather
NOAA: National Weather Service Enhanced Radar Images
radar.weather.gov

TCR: Twentieth Century Reanalysis (V2): Monthly Mean Pressure Level Data
esrl.noaa.gov/psd/data/gridded/data.20thC_ReanV2.pressure.mm.html

Satellite Imagery
LANDSAT: Courtesy of NASA
landsat.gsfc.nasa.gov

MODIS: Courtesy of NASA
worldview.earthdata.nasa.gov

All websites were live in August 2016.

ONE

You can hear them: Dillard, Annie. (1974) "Northing." *A Pilgrim at Tinker Creek.* New York: Harper's Magazine Press, 252.

The Elephant Who Texted for Help

Douglas-Hamilton quotes: Douglas-Hamilton, Iain. Interviews. March 16–17, 2016.

For more on Douglas-Hamilton's early radio tracking efforts, see: Douglas-Hamilton, I. & Douglas-Hamilton, O. (1975) "Radio-Elephants." *Among the Elephants.* London: William Collins Sons & Co. Ltd. 101–17.

The collars included: Douglas-Hamilton, Iain. (1998) "Tracking African Elephants with a Global Positioning System (GPS) Radio Collar." *Pachyderm* 25: 81–92.

It's revolutionary: Pope, Frank. Interview. March 16, 2016.

Nine elephants in southern Mali: Wall, J. et al. (2013) Characterizing properties and drivers of long distance movements by elephants (*Loxodonta africana*) in the Gourma, Mali. *Biological Conservation* 157: 60–68.

The trip to Samburu to check on Kulling was conducted on March 20–22, 2016.

Zebras

Bartlam-Brooks quotes and tracking study: Bartlam-Brooks, H. L. A. et al. (2011) Will reconnecting ecosystems allow long-distance mammal migrations to resume? A case study of a zebra (*Equus burchelli*) migration in Botswana. *Oryx* 45 (2): 210–216.

By comparing two years of tracks: Bartlam-Brooks, H. L. A. et al. (2013) In search of greener pastures—using satellite images to predict the effects of environmental change on zebra migration. *Journal of Geophysical Research: Biogeosciences* 188: 1–11.

Chobe River: Naidoo, R. et al. (2016) A newly discovered wildlife migration in Namibia and Botswana is the longest in Africa. *Oryx* 50 (1): 138–46.

Hyenas

Cozzi, G. et al. (2015) Effects of trophy hunting leftovers on the ranging behaviour of large carnivores: A case study on spotted hyenas. *PLoS ONE* 10 (3): e0121471.

Baboons

Strandburg-Peshkin, A. et al. (2015) Shared decision-making drives collective movement in wild baboons. *Science* 348: 1358–61.

In future studies: Farine, Damien. Interview. October 12, 2015.

All group members: "Baboon troop movements are 'democratic.'" University of Oxford press release. June 18, 2015. www.ox.ac.uk/news/2015-06-18-baboon-troop-movements-are-democratic

Orangutans

Wich, S. et al. (2016) A preliminary assessment of using conservation drones for Sumatran orang-utan (*Pongo abelii*) distribution and density. *Journal of Unmanned Vehicle Systems* 4: 45–51.

In twenty minutes: Wich, Serge. TEDxLiverpool: www.youtube.com/watch?v=GTsMi43Mugo

To see the drones, visit: conservationdrones.org

Jaguars

Tobler, Mathias. (2015) "Estimating jaguar densities and evaluating the impact of sustainable logging on the large mammal community of the Southwestern Amazon." Forest Stewardship Council report.

He began reviewing: Tobler, M. W. & Powell, G. V. N. (2013) Estimating jaguar densities with camera traps: Problems with current designs and recommendations for future studies. *Biological Conservation* 159: 109–18.

90 percent: Tobler, Mathias. Interview. February 1, 2016.

Mountain lions

Hollywood sign: Photograph by Steve Winter. "Cougars." *National Geographic,* December 2013.

Under a house: Groves, M. & Jennings, A. "P-22 vacates home, heads back to Griffith Park, wildlife officials say." *Los Angeles Times.* April 14, 2015.

Dismembered koala: Serna, J. & Branson-Potts, H. "Griffith Park mountain lion P-22 suspected of killing koala at L.A. Zoo." *Los Angeles Times.* March 10, 2016.

When people see him: Vickers, T. Winston. Interview. May 21, 2015.

In the late 1980s: Morrison, S. A. et al. (2009) Conserving Connectivity: Some Lessons from Mountain Lions in Southern California. *Conservation Biology* 23 (2); 275–85.

M56: Vickers, T. W. et al. (2015) Survival and Mortality of Pumas (*Puma concolor*) in a Fragmented, Urbanizing Landscape. *PLoS ONE* 10 (7): e0131490.

The DNA shows: Ernest, H. B. et al. (2014) Fractured Genetic Connectivity Threatens a Southern California Puma (*Puma concolor*) Population. *PLoS ONE* 9 (10): e107985.

M86 family tree: Vickers, T. Winston. Interview. August 24, 2015.

Fishers

LaPoint, S. et al. (2013) Animal behavior, cost-based corridor models, and real corridors. *Landscape Ecology* 28: 1615–30.

Two thousand coyotes: Dell'Amore, C. "Downtown Coyotes: Inside the Secret Lives of Chicago's Predator." *National Geographic,* November 21, 2014. news.nationalgeographic.com/news/2014/11/141121-coyotes-animals-science-chicago-cities-urban-nation

Leopards prowl downtown Mumbai: Conniff, Richard. "Learning to Live with Leopards." *National Geographic,* December 2015.

Wolf walked . . . Dutch village: Feltman, R. "For the first time in a century, a wolf was in the Netherlands." *The Washington Post.* March 12, 2015. *www.washingtonpost.com/news/ speaking-of-science/wp/2015/03/12/for-the-first-time-in-a-century-a-wolf-was-in-netherlands*

We went to that point: Kays, Roland. "Tracking Urban Fishers Through Forest and Culvert." Web blog post. *Scientist at Work.* The New York Times Company, February 9, 2011.

Getting out in the forest: Kays, Roland. "Following in the Footsteps of a Suburban Fisher." Web blog post. *Scientist at Work.* The New York Times Company, February 1, 2011.

Wolves

Chapron, G. et al. (2014) Recovery of large carnivores in Europe's modern human-dominated landscapes. *Science* 346: 1517–9.

Ražen, N. et al. (2016) Long-distance dispersal connects Dinaric-Balkan and Alpine grey wolf (*Canis lupus*) populations. *European Journal of Wildlife Research* 62: 137–42.

Potočnik quotes: Potočnik, Hubert. Interview. October 29, 2015.

Elk

Middleton, A. et al. (2013) Animal migration amid shifting patterns of phenology and predation: lessons from a Yellowstone elk herd. *Ecology* 94 (6): 1245–56.

Middleton quotes and collaring stories: Middleton, Arthur. Interview. August 27, 2015.

Four million people: National Park Service. *www.nps.gov/yell/planyourvisit/visitationstats.htm*

$138 million: "The Pulse of the Park." *National Geographic*, May 2016, supplement.

Pheasants

Norbu, N. et al. (2013) Partial altitudinal migration of a Himalayan forest pheasant. *PLoS ONE* 8 (4): e60979.

Tragopan mating dance: youtu.be/7I79rgG9bDk

I am afraid anything I can say: Smith, C. Barnby. (1912) The display of the Satyr Tragopan Pheasant, *Ceriornis satyra. Avicultural Magazine* 3 (6): 153–55.

Some go up: Wikelski, Martin. Interview. December 16, 2015.

Pythons

Pittman, S. et al. (2014) Homing of invasive Burmese pythons in South Florida: evidence for map and compass senses in snakes. *Biology Letters* 10: 20140040.

Python Challenge: pythonchallenge.org

Tens of thousands of pythons: Gade, M. & Puckett, C. "The Big Squeeze: Pythons and Mammals in Everglades National Park." *USGS.* February 6, 2012. *www2.usgs.gov/blogs/ features/usgs_top_story/the-big-squeeze-pythons-and-mammals-in-everglades-national-park*

For more on animals' use of magnetic fields, see: Lohman, K. J. et al. (2007) Magnetic maps in animals: nature's GPS. *Journal of Experimental Biology* 210: 3697–705.

Ants

Mersch, D. et al. (2013) Tracking individuals shows spatial fidelity is a key regulator of ant social organization. *Science* 340: 1090–1093.

Ant-inspired software: Miller, P. (2010) *The Smart Swarm.* New York: Avery. 20–26.

TWO

Consider the subtleness: Melville, Herman. (1922) *Moby-Dick; or, The Whale.* London: Constable & Co..

The Whales We Watch on Facebook

The trip to the Westman Islands was conducted on July 6–12, 2016.

Michael Bigg: en.wikipedia.org/wiki/Michael_Bigg

Earliest whale tracking devices: Burnett, D. G. (2013) *The Sounding of the Whale: Science and Cetaceans in the Twentieth Century.* Chicago: University of Chicago Press.

Townsend set about sourcing: Townsend, C. H. (1931) Where the Nineteenth Century Whaler Made His Catch. *New York Zoological Society Bulletin* xxxiv (6): 173–9.

More than 1,600 voyages: Townsend, C. H. (1935) The distribution of certain whales as shown by logbook records of American whaleships. *Zoologica* XIX (1): 8–18.

To see view the original Townsend maps and his data, visit: canada.wcs.org/wild-places/global-conservation/townsend-whaling-charts.aspx

Pequod route: Melville, H., Parker, H., & Hayford, H. (2002) *Moby Dick.* New York: Norton.

Paul Dudley White . . . part of a team: King, R. L., Jenks, J. L., White, P. D. (1953) The electrocardiogram of the beluga whale. *Circulation* 8: 387–93.

An expedition: White, P. D. W & Matthews S. W. "Hunting the Heartbeat of a Whale." *National Geographic*, July 1956.

The whales were singing: Payne, R. & McVay, S. (1971). Songs of humpback whales. *Science* 173 (3997): 585–97.

Nobody used it: Payne, R. *Among Whales.* New York: Pocket Books, 1995.

Largest one-time pressing: Burnett. (2013)

Johnson & Swift quotes: Interview. April 14, 2016.

DTAGs: Johnson, M. P. & Tyack, P. L. (2003) A digital acoustic recording tag for measuring the response of wild marine mammals to sound. *IEEE Journal of Oceanic Engineering* 28 (1): 3–12.

Sound exposure on beaked whales: Miller, P. J. O. et al. (2015) First indications that northern bottlenose whales are sensitive to behavioural disturbance from anthropogenic noise. *Royal Society Open Science* 2: 140484.

Northern right whales: Allen, Leslie. "Drifting in Static." *National Geographic*, January 2011, 28–30.

Caused a blue whale: Goldbogen, J. et al. (2013) Blue whales respond to simulated mid-frequency military sonar. *Proceedings of the Royal Society B* 280: 20130657.

For more on the Icelandic killer whales, see: Samarra, F. & Foote, A. (2015) Seasonal movements of killer whales between Iceland and Scotland. *Aquatic Biology* 24 (1): 75–9.

Samarra, F. (2015) Prey-induced behavioural plasticity of herring-eating killer whales. *Marine Biology* 162: 809–21.

To follow the Icelandic Orcas project, visit: www.facebook.com/icelandic.orcas

Humpback whales

Garrigue, C. et al. (2015) Satellite tracking reveals novel migratory patterns and the importance of seamounts for endangered South Pacific humpback whales. *Royal Society Open Science* 2: 150489.

IUCN Red List: Megaptera novaeangliae. www.iucnredlist.org/details/13006/0

Global Seamount Census: Wessel, P. et al. (2010) The Global Seamount Census. *Oceanography* 23 (1): 24–33.

Nuclear submarine: Drew, C. "Adrift 500 Feet Under the Sea, a Minute Was an Eternity." *The New York Times.* May 18, 2005. www.nytimes.com/2005/05/18/us/adrift-500-feet-under-the-sea-a-minute-was-an-eternity.html?_r=0

Sea turtles

My God, there's a lot of turtles: Hawkes, Lucy. Interview. March 3, 2016.

A loggerhead named Fisher: www.seaturtle.org/tracking/index.shtml?tag_id=49818a&full=1&lang=&dyn=1464532820

Ascension Island: Luschi, P. et al. (1998) The navigational feats of green sea turtles migrating from Ascension Island investigated by satellite telemetry. *Proceedings of the Royal Society B: Biological Sciences* 265 (1412): 2279–84.

Chagos Archipelago: Hays, G. C. et al. (2014) Use of long-distance migration patterns of an endangered species to inform conservation planning for the world's largest marine protected area. *Conservation Biology* 28 (6): 1636–44.

Cabo Verde: Hawkes, L. et al. (2006) Phenotypically linked dichotomy in sea turtle foraging requires multiple conservation approaches. *Current Biology* 16, 990–995.

Canary Islands: Varo-Cruz et al. (2016) New findings about the spatial and temporal use of the Eastern Atlantic Ocean by large juvenile loggerhead turtles. *Diversity and Distributions* 1–12.

Landscape of Fear

Hammerschlag, N. et al. (2015) Evaluating the landscape of fear between apex predatory sharks and mobile sea turtles across a large dynamic seascape. *Ecology* 96 (8): 2117–26.

Tiger sharks

Meyer, C. G. et al. (2010) A multiple instrument approach to quantifying the movement patterns and habitat use of tiger (*Galeocerdo cuvier*) and Galapagos sharks (*Carcharhinus galapagensis*) at French Frigate Shoals, Hawaii. *Marine Biology* 157: 1857–68.

Killed 4,668 sharks: Tester, A. L. (1960) Fatal Shark Attack, Oahu, Hawaii, December 13, 1958. *Pacific Science* 14 (2): 181–4.

Holland quotes and shark tales: Holland, Kim. Interview. November 24, 2015.

Three to four bites: dlnr.hawaii.gov/sharks/shark-incidents/incidents-list/

50 ocean drownings: Galanis, D. (2015) "Water Safety and Drownings in Hawaii." Presentation. Hawaii Department of Health. health.hawaii.gov/injuryprevention/files/2015/08/wsocon15a.pdf

Seals

Fedak, M. A. (2012) The impact of animal platforms on polar ocean observation. *Deep-Sea Research II* 88–9: 7–13.

Fedak quotes: Fedak, Mike. Interview. April 22, 2016.

Recalls unease from other researchers: Boehme, Lars. Interview. October 20, 2015.

First seal I introduce: Blight, Clinton. Interview. October 20, 2015.

MEOP: meop.net

Global Ocean: NOAA. oceanservice.noaa.gov/education/tutorial_currents

Sea otters

Tarjan, L. M. & Tinker, M. T. (2016) Permissible home range estimation (PHRE) in restricted habitats: A new algorithm and an evaluation for sea otters. *PLoS ONE* 11 (3): e0150547.

Tinker, M. T., Staedler, M. M., Tarjan, L. M., Bentall, G. B., Tomoleoni, J. A., and LaRoche, N. L. (2016) Geospatial data collected from tagged sea otters in central California, 1998–2012: U.S Geological Survey data release. doi:10.5066/F76H4FH8

Such a rare mammal: Anthony, H. E. (1928) *Field book of North American mammals.* New York: G. P. Putnam's Sons, 119.

Then in 1938: Sharpe, Howard G. Personal account. seaotters.org/pdfs/extinct.pdf

They are reliant: Tinker, M. Tim. Interview. March 2016.

Monterey Bay otter details: Staedler, M. Email. July 18, 2016.

Espinosa quotes: Espinosa, Sarah. Interview. September 30, 2015.

Ideal environment: Eby, Ron. Interview. September 30, 2015.

Elkhorn Slough otter details: Espinosa, S. Email. July 18, 2016.

For more on conserving sea otters in Monterey Bay, visit: www.montereybayaquarium.org/conservation-and-science/our-priorities/thriving-ocean-wildlife/southern-sea-otters

Crocodiles

Campbell, H. A. et al. (2013) Home range utilisation and long-range movement of estuarine crocodiles during the breeding and nesting season. *PLoS ONE* 8 (5): e62127.

Fewer than one person dies: crocodile-attack.info

I dread it every time: Franklin, Craig. Interview. March 17, 2016.

I can't deal with it: Ibid.

We tag pretty much: Dwyer, Ross. Interview. March 15, 2016.

Plankton

Ekvall, M. T. et al. (2013) Three-dimensional tracking of small aquatic organisms using fluorescent nanoparticles. *PLoS ONE* 8 (11): e78498.

Largest migration on Earth: van Haren, H. & Compton, T. J. (2013) Diel Vertical Migration in Deep Sea Plankton Is Finely Tuned to Latitudinal and Seasonal Day Length. *PLoS ONE* 8 (5): e64435.

To pinpoint cancer cells: McGinley, L. "Deadly and beautiful: The mesmerizing images of cancer research." *The Washington Post.* 11 July 2016. www.washingtonpost.com/national/health-science/deadly-and-beautiful-the-mesmerizing-images-of-cancer-research/2016/07/11/307edb24-43a3-11e6-8856-f26de2537a9d_story.html

Jellyfish: Hays, G. et al. (2012) High activity and Lévy searches: jellyfish can search the water column like fish. *Proceedings of the Royal Society B* 279: 465–73.

THREE

When the blackbird: Stevens, Wallace. "Thirteen Ways of Looking at a Blackbird." *Collected Poems by Wallace Stevens.* London: Faber and Faber Ltd.

Birdwatching Through a Wider Lens

It is one thing to study: Clarke, W. E. (1912) *Studies in Bird Migration*, vol. 2. London: Gurney and Jackson. 40.

Why do they leave: Ibid., vol. 1, 15.

It must be left: Ibid., 102.

Arthur Allen: Gallagher, T. (2015) "A Century of Bird Study." *Living Bird.* www.allaboutbirds.org/a-century-of-bird-study

The visit to the Cornell Lab of Ornithology was conducted on 7 April 2016.

Great Backyard Bird Count: gbbc.birdcount.org

eBird: ebird.org

For more on the academic motivations behind eBird, see: Sullivan, B. L. (2009) eBird: A citizen-based bird observation network in the biological sciences. *Biological Conservation* 142: 2282–92.

Wood, C. et al. (2011) eBird: Engaging birders in Science and Conservation. *PLoS Biology* 9 (12): e1001220.

For more on the science behind the eBird data models, see: Fink, D. et al. (2010) Spatiotemporal exploratory models for broad-scale survey data. *Ecological Applications* 20 (8): 2131–47.

Hochachka, W. M. et al. (2012) Data-intensive science applied to broad-scale citizen science. *Trends in Ecology and Evolution* 27 (2): 130–137

To download the Merlin Bird ID app, visit: merlin.allaboutbirds.org

Biggest Week in American Birding: biggestweekinamericanbirding.com

Bird highways: Kranstauber, B. et al. (2015) Global aerial flyways all efficient travelling. *Ecology Letters* 18 (12): 1338–45.

Radar stations: Leshem, Yossi. Interview and emails. March 23 – August 15, 2016.

For more detail on avian radar, see: Dinevich L. et al. (2004) Detecting birds and estimating their velocity vectors by means of MRL-meteorological radar. *Ring* 26 (2): 35–53.

Roughly 500 million: Uhlfelder, E. "Bloody Skies: The Fight to Reduce Deadly Bird-Plane Collisions." *National Geographic.* 8 November 2013. news.nationalgeographic.com/news/2013/10/131108-aircraft-bird-strikes-faa-radar-science

Three civilian airports: Rossen, J. and Davis, J. "Why don't more airports use radar to prevent dangerous bird strikes?" *Today.com.* February 29, 2015. www.today.com/money/why-dont-more-airports-use-radar-prevent-dangerous-bird-strikes-t4081

Terns

Egevang, C. et al. (2010) Tracking of Arctic terns (*Sterna paradisaea*) reveals longest animal migration. *PNAS* 107 (5): 2078–81.

Fijn, R. et al. (2013) Arctic Terns (*Sterna paradisaea*) from the Netherlands migrate record distances across three oceans to Wilkes Land, East Antarctica. *Ardea* 101: 3–12.

Penguins

Fretwell, P. et al. (2012) An emperor penguin population estimate: The first global, synoptic survey of a species from space. *PLoS ONE* 7 (4): e33751.

Between 270,000 and 350,000: del Hoyo, J., Eliot, A., Sargatal, J. (eds.) "Emperor penguin." *Handbook of the Birds of the World*, vol. 1. Barcelona: Lynx Edicions, 1992.

The great thing about emps: Fretwell, Peter. Interview. 14 October 2015.

For more on counting other animals from space, see: Fretwell, P. et al. (2014) Whales from space: Counting southern right whales by satellite. *PLoS ONE* 9 (2): e88655.

Stapleton, S. et al. (2014) Polar bears from space: Assessing satellite imagery as a tool to track Arctic wildlife. *PLoS ONE* 9 (7): e101513.

Yang, Z. et al. (2016) Spotting East African Mammals in Open Savannah from Space. *PLoS ONE* 9 (12): e115989.

Albatrosses

Croxall, J. et al. (2005) Global circumnavigations: Tracking year-round ranges of nonbreeding albatrosses. *Science* (307): 249–50.

Longline fishing boats: www.rspb.org.uk/ joinandhelp/donations/campaigns/albatross/ problem/threats.aspx

Geese

Hawkes, L. A. et al. (2012) The paradox of extreme high-altitude migration in bar-headed geese (Anser indicus). *Proceedings of the Royal Society B* rspb.2012.2114.

On an April night: Swan, L. W. (1961) The Ecology of the High Himalayas. *Scientific American* 205 (4): 68–78.

Geese tended to minimize: Hawkes, Lucy. Interview. March 3, 2016.

Gulls

Steinan, E. W. M. et al. (2016) GPS tracking data of Lesser Black-backed Gulls and Herring Gulls breeding at the southern North Sea coast. *ZooKeys* 555: 115–24.

To view more gull tracks and stories, visit: lifewatch.inbo.be/blog

Vultures

Williams, H. J. et al. (submitted). Identification of animal movement patterns using tri-axial magnetometry. *Under review at time of publication.*

Visualization is vital: Wilson, Rory. Interview. April 19, 2016.

Air is massively fickle: Shepard, Emily. Interview. March 17, 2016.

Snowy owls

Brinker, Weidensaul and McGann quotes and Project SNOWstorm details: Interview. Janaury 15, 2016.

To view more owl tracks and stories, visit: www.projectsnowstorm.org

For more on cellular tracking, visit: www.celltracktech.com

Storks

Flack, A. et al. (2016) Costs of migratory decisions: A comparison across eight white stork populations. *Science Advances* 2 (1): e1500931.

Aristotle: Birkhead, T., Wimpenny, J., Montgomerie, B. (2014) *Ten Thousand Birds: Ornithology Since Darwin.* Princeton: Princeton University Press.

Get up, fly to the dump: Flack, Andrea. Interview. December 16, 2016.

Prinzesschen: Berthold, P. et al. (2004) Long-term satellite tracking of white stork (*Ciconia ciconia*) migration: constancy versus variability. *Journal of Ornithology* 145: 356–9.

Headstone: Schmidt, O. "The Story of the Little Princess." *The Cape Bird Club.* *www.capebirdclub.org.za/articles-promerops%20au- gust%202007%20story%20little%20princess.html*

Fruit bats

Fahr, J. et al. (2015) Pronounced seasonal changes in the movement ecology of a highly gregarious central-place forager, the African straw-coloured fruit bat (*Eidolon helvum*). *PLoS ONE* (10): e0138985.

I am in the field: Dechmann, Dina. Email. March 3, 2016.

Imagine a fruit-eating bat: Ibid.

Oilbirds

Holland, R. et al. (2009) The secret life of oilbirds: New insights into the movement ecology of a unique avian frugivore. *PLoS ONE* 4 (12): e8264.

Where the light began to fail: Humboldt, Alexander von. (1814) Personal narrative of travels to the equinoctial regions of the New continent during the years 1799-1804. Available here: *archive.org/details/ personalnarrati00humbgoog*

A form of echolocation: Brinkløvv, S. et al. (2013). Echolocation in Oilbirds and swiftlets. *Frontiers in Physiology* 4 (123): 188–99.

Oilbirds fly out in the forest: Wikelski, Martin. Interview. December 16, 2015.

Warblers

Streby, H. M. et al. (2015) Tornadic storm avoidance behavior in breeding songbirds. *Current Biology* 25: 98–102.

All these things happen: Streby, Henry. Interview. April 8, 2016.

Songbirds

Farine, D. R. et al. (2014) Collective decision making and social interaction rules in mixed-species flocks of songbirds. *Animal Behaviour* 95: 173–82.

Wandered around Wytham Woods: Birkhead, T., Wimpenny, J., Montgomerie, B. (2014) *Ten Thousand Birds: Ornithology Since Darwin.* Princeton: Princeton University Press.

Bees

Hagen, M. et al. (2011) Space use of bumblebees (*Bombus* spp.) revealed by radio-tracking. *PLoS ONE* 6 (5): e19997.

Tiny vortices: Altshuler et al. (2005) Short-amplitude high-frequency wing strokes determine the aerodynamics of honeybee flight. *PNAS* 102 (50): 18213–8

Wright Brothers: Petersen, Robert. Interview. Dayton Aviation Heritage National Historical Park, Dayton, Ohio. June 30, 2014.

EPILOGUE

We shall not cease: Eliot, T. S. *Four Quartets.* London: Faber and Faber Ltd.

Look at the baiji: Johnson, Mark. Interview. April 14, 2016.

Alert your insurance company: www.insurethebox.com/telematics

Google's mapping app: en.wikipedia.org/wiki/Google_Traffic

Detect states of mind: Mehrota, A. et al. (2016) Towards multi-modal anticipatory monitoring of depressive states through the analysis of human-smartphone interaction. Proceedings of 1st Mental Health: Sensing and Intervention Workshop.

My own PhD research: Cheshire, J. A. & Longley, P. A. (2012) Identifying spatial concentrations of surnames. *International Journal of Geographical Information Science* 26 (2): 309–25.

Jack the Ripper: Le Comber S. C. & Stevenson M. D. (2012) From Jack the Ripper to epidemiology and ecology.

Trends Ecological Evolution 27 (6): 307–8.

Banksy: Hauge M.V. et al. (2016) Tagging Banksy: using geographic profiling to investigate a modern art mystery. *Journal of Spatial Science* 61 (1): 185–90.

Where a new school is most needed: Singleton, A.D. et al. (2011) Estimating secondary school catchment areas and the spatial equity of access. Computers, *Environment and Urban Systems* 35 (3): 241–9.

Interaction between Nature and Society: Hägerstrand, T. (1976) Geography and the study of interaction between nature and society. *Geoforum* 7: 329–34.

Barcoding Biodiveristy

Hebert, P. et al. (2003) Biological identifications through DNA barcodes. *Proceedings of the Royal Society B* 270 (1512): 313–21.

[ABOUT THE AUTHORS]

As a Senior Lecturer at University College London, James Cheshire (left) applies his cartographic and programming skills to the staggering amount of data that scientists are now collecting. Oliver Uberti is a former senior design editor for *National Geographic*, who has been sketching and admiring the natural world for as long as he can remember. Though he now lives in Los Angeles, Oliver designed this book while living in Ann Arbor, Michigan. James and Oliver's best-selling debut, *London: The Information Capital*, won the 2015 British Cartographic Society Award for cartographic excellence.

Barcoding Biodiversity

DNA is the blueprint that tells an organism to grow flippers or feathers. In 2000, Paul Hebert (University of Guelph) discovered that you can identify a species with one short segment of its DNA sequence, which he called a "DNA barcode." Here we show the animals in this book that have been barcoded, in order of appearance. For all our external differences, deep down, we're very much alike.

Giraffe
European badger
Painted lichen moth
African elephant
Burchelli's zebra
Spotted hyena
Olive baboon
Sumatran orangutan
Jaguar
Mountain lion
Fisher
Gray wolf
Elk
Satyr tragopan
Carpenter ant
Killer whale
Northern bottlenose whale
Humpback whale
Loggerhead sea turtle
Green sea turtle
Tiger shark
Bull shark
Hammerhead shark
Southern elephant seal
Weddell seal
Southern sea otter
Estuarine crocodile
Daphnia
Jellyfish
American robin
Indigo bunting
Arctic tern
Emperor penguin
Gray-headed albatross
Bar-headed goose
Lesser black-backed gull
Snowy owl
White stork
Straw-colored fruit bat
Golden-winged warbler
Great tit
Eurasian blue tit
Coal tit
Marsh tit
Eurasian nuthatch
Bumblebee (*B. hotorum*)
Bumblebee (*B. ruderatus*)
Bumblebee (*B. terrestris*)
Humans

DNA BASES ■ Adenine ■ Cytosine ■ Thymine ■ Guanine

A single strand of human DNA has 3 billion bases; the human barcode only requires 600.

SOURCE: SUJEEVAN RATNASINGHAM, UNIVERSITY OF GUELPH